Writers
Express

A Handbook for Young Writers, Thinkers, and Learners

Written and Compiled by
Dave Kemper, Ruth Nathan, Patrick Sebranek

Illustrated by
Chris Krenzke

Thoughtful Learning
www.thoughtfullearning.com/WritersExpress

Acknowledgments

We're grateful to many people who helped bring *Writers Express* to life. First, we must thank all the students who've contributed their writing and their ideas. We also thank authors and teachers who helped make *Writers Express* a reality.

Sandy Ashner	Gloria Nixon-John	Vicki Spandel
Nancy Bond	Susan Ohanian	Paula & Keith Stanovich
Roy Peter Clark	Anne-Marie Oomen	Peter Stillman
Toby Fulwiler	Marie Ponsot	Charles Temple
Will Hobbs	Peter and Connie Roop	Toni Walters
Stephen Krensky	Lorraine Sintetos	Allan Wolf

Another thank you goes to our team of educators, editors, and designers.

Steven J. Augustyn	Rob King	Janae Sebranek
Chris Erickson	Lois Krenzke	Lester Smith
Tim Kemper	Mark Lalumondier	

Writers Express Online

This book is just the beginning! Go to **thoughtfullearning.com/WritersExpress** for supplements to this book, additional resources, and more.

Sign up for our monthly newsletter at **thoughtfullearning.com/K12newsletter**.

ISBN (softcover) 978-1-941660-08-9

2 3 4 5 6 7 8 9 10 LSCC 25 24 23 22 21 20 19

ISBN (hardcover) 978-1-941660-09-6

2 3 4 5 6 7 8 9 10 LSCC 25 24 23 22 21 20 19

Printed in the U.S.A.

Express Yourself!

Writers Express is divided into four major sections . . .

1   **The Process of Writing** ■ Use this section to answer your questions about writing, from selecting a subject to proofreading a final draft.

2   **The Forms of Writing** ■ Use this section if you need help with an essay, a report, a story, a poem, or a response to a prompt.

3   **The Tools of Learning** ■ If your study, reading, or test-taking skills could use a little pumping up, turn to "The Tools of Learning."

4   **Proofreader's Guide** ■ Do you have a question about punctuation? Spelling? Capitalization? Here's where you find the answers.

Table of Contents

The Process of Writing

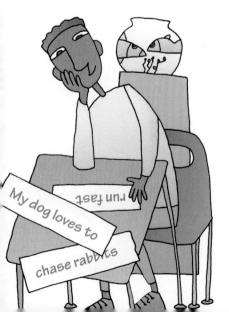

My dog loves to run fast

chase rabbits

The Forms of Writing

The Forms of Writing (cont.)

The Tools of Learning

Proofreader's Guide

Why Write?

One day last summer, my friend and I discovered a big old fishing boat that had washed up on the beach. We adopted the boat for the summer. We had a great time making up adventures about being shipwrecked on a deserted island, discovering a new country, and being ocean scientists.

As more friends joined us, we began sharing things we knew about boats and ships and the ocean. Then we decided to use our great adventure stories and write a play about them. We acted it out right in the boat for our families and friends. It turned out great! Everyone was amazed that we could write a play and act it out. So were we!

The Express Connection

This story is not unusual. Kids just like you have been writing and acting out plays for a long time. Writing is a great way to express what you feel or imagine and what you learn. That's why people write stories, essays, and reports, and that's why we've created *Writers Express* for you. We also hope it helps you become a better reader, thinker, speaker, and all-around student. Not bad for one little book!

2

Getting Started

A Basic Writing Guide

Your *Writers Express* handbook gives lots of good advice about writing. But there is only one way to learn how to write, and that is to do it—every day and everywhere you can. Your handbook gives you suggestions to get started, tips to keep going, and ideas for making your writing as good as it can be. Keep your handbook handy whenever you are writing.

This chapter has questions and answers about writing. The questions are the ones that many writers ask. The answers will help you find your way through the writing process from start to finish.

What's Ahead

- Questions and Answers About Writing
- Strong Writing Guide

Questions and Answers About Writing

1 Why is writing important?

Writing helps you think and learn. In fact, writing may be your most valuable learning tool. Each time you put words on paper, you are forming new ideas, making connections, and remembering information. Because of this, the writing you do in a learning log or journal is just as important as the writing you do for assignments.

2 How can I do my best writing for assignments?

Above all else, remember that writing is a process. If you develop your writing step by step, you have a good chance of doing your best work. But if you try to take shortcuts or do everything all at once, your writing will suffer.

3 What topic can I write about?

Try to write about a topic that really interests you and one that is worth learning about. But also remember that your topic must fit your assignment. Your assignment will identify a general subject area, and your job is to choose a specific topic related to it.

Gathering Ideas for Writing
Pages 36–37

Selecting a Topic
Pages 38–39

Using Writing Topics
Pages 40–41

A Closer Look at Freewriting
Page 42

4 How can I learn about a topic for my writing assignments?

You can collect information online, from your textbooks and other books, and in newspapers and magazines. You can also interview people (online or in person). Your teacher may have requirements for the number of different sources you should use.

Collecting Details
Page 43

Researching Your Topic
Page 44

Researching Online
Pages 299–304

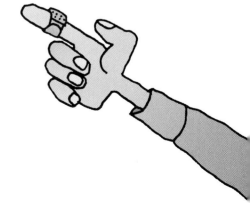

5 How do I know what to say about my topic?

You should choose a special part of the topic to emphasize or focus on. This will stop you from trying to say everything about the topic. Then form a writing plan by selecting and organizing the facts that support the focus.

6 How should I write my first draft?

Write the first draft freely, using your plan as a general guide. Your goal is to get your ideas on paper, so don't worry about getting everything exactly right.

7 How can I make my writing interesting?

Always keep your readers or audience in mind. Your writing should hold their interest and inform them about your topic. Since your classmates will be your main audience, write as if you were actually talking to them.

Qualities of Writing Pages 21–34	**Writing Terms and Techniques** Pages 99–108	**Tips for Stronger Writing** Pages 56–57	**Revising with Partners** Pages 58–60

8 Why do I have to write more than one draft?

No writers, not even your favorite authors, get everything right in just one draft. There will always be parts that need more detail or need to be clearer. Continue improving your writing until it is clear, complete, and interesting.

Revising Pages 54–60	**Revising Checklist** Page 55	**Qualities of Writing** Pages 21–34	**Publishing** Pages 67–73

When should I check for errors, and how should I go about it?

You're ready to check your writing for errors after you have made all of your revisions. First, grab your handbook and other editing tools. Then check for errors using an editing checklist as a guide. Also ask a classmate or teacher to edit your writing as well.

Editing
Pages 61–66

Using a Checklist
Page 66

Writing Basic Sentences
Pages 75–80

Common Editing Problems
Pages 64–65

10 How do I know if my final writing is strong?

If you can say *yes* to each of the following questions, you can feel good about your writing.

____ Do I follow the requirements for the assignment?
____ Does my topic interest me?
____ Have I learned a lot about the topic?
____ Have I created a writing plan, and do I follow it?
____ Is my writing clear and complete?
____ Is my final draft correct and neatly formatted?

Qualities of Writing Checklist
Page 33

Creating a Classroom Portfolio
Page 71

Understanding the Writing Process

You might wish that writing was like this: First, you plot out the assignment on your wrist pad like this:

Purpose: To report on the music performance at the nursing home

Audience: Students at Pierce Elementary School

Subject: The music performance

Type: Newspaper story

Then you key it in your new Superwriter app and relax while your story is being written. Just press a few buttons, and your writing comes out exactly the way you order it. Of course, this is only wishful thinking. To develop a piece of writing, you must do your own work and follow each step in the writing process.

What's Ahead

- Steps in the Writing Process
- A Closer Look at the Process

Steps in the Writing Process

- Prewriting
- Writing
- Revising
- Editing
- Publishing

■ **Prewriting** covers all the thinking and planning you do for a writing assignment. It includes thinking about the assignment, identifying a topic, collecting details, and creating a writing plan.

■ **Writing** the first draft means getting your ideas on paper. A first draft is your first look at your writing and your first chance to see how well things are coming together.

■ **Revising** refers to changing and improving your first draft. It's your opportunity to think about what you've written and then add, cut, or change it as needed. Your goal is to make all of your ideas clear and complete.

■ **Editing** is checking your revised writing line by line for errors. Also proofread for errors after writing the final copy of your writing.

■ **Publishing** refers to sharing the final copy of your writing. Publishing comes in many different forms depending on the purpose and audience for your writing.

Note During a writing assignment, you may repeat some of the steps. For example, after reviewing a first draft, you may collect more details for certain parts. The writing process almost always works this way, and a writer may go backward and forward any number of times before finishing an assignment. (See the graphic above.)

A Closer Look at the Process

These next two pages show what to do for each step in the writing process. If you follow the guidelines for each step, you should produce a strong piece of writing.

Prewriting

Study the Assignment ■ Be sure you know what is expected of you in terms of the Purpose, Audience, Subject, and Type of writing (**PAST**).

Pick a Specific Topic ■ Be sure to choose a topic that interests you and relates to the assignment.

Collect Details About Your Topic ■ First, gather your own thoughts; then collect details from other sources.

Find a Focus ■ Identify a main point about the topic to focus on. This will prevent you from trying to say too much about your topic.

Make a Plan ■ Select details that support your focus, and organize them into a list, outline, or graphic organizer.

Writing

Get Your Ideas on Paper ■ Use your plan as a general guide, but also be open to new ideas that pop up as you write.

Think of Your Audience ■ Write as if you were in a conversation with your readers.

Form a Complete Draft ■ Include a beginning, a middle, and an ending.

Revising

Review Your Writing ■ Read your first draft silently and out loud. Identify parts that need work.

Share Your Draft ■ Ask a classmate, family member, or teacher to review your first draft.

Follow a Checklist ■ Use a revising checklist to guide your work.

Make Changes ■ Add, cut, move, or rewrite parts as needed to make your writing clearer and more complete. Use these questions as a guide.

1. Does the writing follow the guidelines for the assignment?
2. Does the beginning identify the topic and the focus and get the reader's attention?
3. Do the details in the middle part support the focus? Are more details needed?
4. Does the ending restate the focus and make a final point?

Editing

Check for Accuracy ■ Correct any capitalization, punctuation, usage, grammar, and spelling errors.

Follow a Checklist ■ Use an editing checklist to guide your work.

Get Editing Help ■ Ask a classmate or your teacher to check your writing for errors, too.

Check for Style ■ Make sure you use interesting words and smooth sentences.

Write a Neat Final Copy ■ Be sure to format your writing correctly. Proofread your final copy for errors.

Publishing

Present Your Writing ■ Share your final copy with your class or with the appropriate audience.

Add It to Your Portfolio ■ Include your best work in your portfolio.

"The first draft is the down draft—you just get it down. The second draft is the up draft [revising]—you fix it up. The third draft is the dental draft [editing], when you check every tooth to see if it is healthy."

—Anne Lamott

One Writer's Process

Have you ever searched for wildlife? Some creatures are hard to find, so you need a plan to follow. You need a plan also when writing essays and reports. Luckily, the steps in the writing process serve as the perfect guide. If you follow these steps, you won't miss anything.

In this chapter, you will see how one student writer used the writing process to develop an essay for a project. For his school's learning fair, Gerald Lester created a display about protecting endangered species. He also wrote an essay to go along with the display. Gerald followed the writing process to complete his essay. Compare his writing to your own. You may find some strategies you'd like to try yourself.

What's Ahead

- Prewriting
- Writing the First Draft
- Revising
- Editing and Proofreading
- Publishing

Prewriting

Understand the Assignment ■ To get started, Gerald used the **PAST** strategy to name the main parts of his assignment. Doing this would help to keep him on track.

Purpose:	*To persuade*
Audience:	*Students in the school*
Subject:	*Protecting endangered species*
Type:	*Essay*

Select a Topic ■ Gerald had already created his display, so he knew he was going to write about protecting endangered species.

Write Freely ■ Gerald started by writing freely about his topic.

> I like watching nature shows about big animals like elephants, polar bears, and rhinos. Then one day in science, we started talking about endangered species, and I realized how serious the problem is for some species like rhinos and gorillas. That is when I decided to learn more about endangered species for the learning fair. . . .

Gather Details ■ Gerald learned a lot about endangered species. He created a cluster to show what he learned.

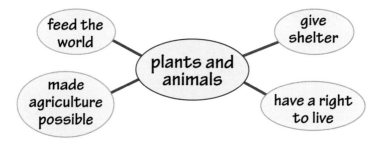

Learn More ■ Gerald also collected more information. Here are some of the details he learned from two other sources.

from <u>Living in the Environment</u>, pp. 195-197
  – species part of every ecosystem (wetlands, forests, plains, deltas)
  – 62% of cancer drugs come from plants
  – some people want to protect all species; other people want to be more selective

from "U.S. Fish & Wildlife Service" (Web site)
  – species have ecological, scientific, and economic value
  – need species to protect ecosystems
  – species help check the health of environment
  – wolves among first endangered species listed

Create a Focus ■ Next, Gerald wrote a sentence that focused on the opinion he would prove in his essay.

Protecting plants and animals benefits everyone.

Organize the Draft ■ Gerald then outlined the reasons and details that supported his opinion.

I. Plants and animals make life possible.
  A. They serve as resources for everyone.
  B. They contribute to the total ecosystem.
II. Many species have an economic value.
  A. The agriculture industry uses them.
  B. Plants and animals provide products for building and industry.
  C. They contribute to medical products.
  D. They create the wildlife tourism industry.
III. Protecting species makes us better stewards of the planet.
  A. They share the planet with us so they deserve to exist and be protected.
  B. The species alive today may save us in the future.

Writing the First Draft

Gerald used his outline as he wrote his first draft. He introduced the topic, stated his opinion, and gave reasons. Here is the beginning.

Saving the Species

The giant panda, black rhino, and Florida panther have something in common. Each of these great animals is dying off and it would be a tragedy to lose any one of them. It

Opinion Statement

would be a tragedy to loose any species. Protecting plants and animals benefits everyone.

First Reason

One benefit is that plants and animals makes life possible. Animals are the main food source for other animals. On another level, some species help protect us

Supporting Details

from disease-carrying pests, and others polinate our plants. The species also contribute to different ecosystems, including wetlands. When the species are allowed to work in their ecosystem, they keep things working like they should work and make the system healthy.

Second Reason

Many species have an important economic benefit. For instance, many plants and animals make agraculture possible. farmers grow crops and raze livestock to sell . . .

Revising

After reading over his first draft, Gerald tried to make his writing clearer and more complete. The notes are comments by a classmate.

Saving the Species

Spice up the first sentence.

What do

∧The giant panda, black rhino, and Florida panther have

~~something~~ in common. Each of these great animals is ~~dying~~

endangered   In fact,

∧~~off~~ and it would be a tragedy to lose any one of them. ∧It

would be a tragedy to loose any species Protecting plants

Transitions would help.

and animals benefits everyone.

The most important

∧~~One~~ benefit is that plants and animals ~~makes~~ life

Give another example.

possible. Animals are the main food source for other

and plants provide food, energy, and shelter

animals. On another level, some species help protect us

from disease-carrying pests, and others polinate our

plants. The species also contribute to different

, forests, plains, and deltas

Can you elaborate?

ecosystems, including wetlands. When the species are

it healthy.

allowed to work in their ecosystem, they keep ~~things~~

This sentence is repetitive.

~~working like they should work and make the system healthy.~~

also

Many species ∧have an important economic benefit. For

instance, many plants and animals make agraculture

possible. farmers grow crops and raze livestock to sell . . .

Editing and Proofreading

Next, Gerald and a partner checked his writing for errors. He also proofread his final copy. The notes show the changes he made.

Saving the Species

What do the giant panda, black rhino, and Florida

Question Mark and Comma
panther have in common? Each of these great animals is

endangered, and it would be a tragedy to lose any one of

Usage and Period
them. In fact, it would be a tragedy to ~~loose~~ *lose* any species.

Protecting plants and animals benefits everyone.

The most important benefit is that plants and animals

Agreement
~~makes~~ *make* life possible. Animals are the main food source for

Comma
other animals, and plants provide food, energy, and shelter.

On another level, some species help protect us from

Spelling
disease-carrying pests, and others ~~polinate~~ *pollinate* our plants. The

species also contribute to different ecosystems, including

wetlands, forests, plains, and deltas. When the species are

allowed to work in their ecosystem, they keep it healthy.

Many species also have an important economic benefit.

Spelling, Capital, and Usage
For instance, many plants and animals make ~~agraculture~~ *agriculture*

possible. ~~farmers~~ grow crops and ~~raze~~ *raise* livestock to sell . . .

Publishing

Gerald produced a neat final copy of his essay to include with his display for the learning fair. He made his essay clear and accurate and added headings.

Saving the Species

What do the giant panda, black rhino, and Florida panther have in common? Each of these great animals is endangered, and it would be a tragedy to lose any one of them. In fact, it would be a tragedy to lose any species. Protecting plants and animals benefits everyone.

Life-Giving Benefit

The most important benefit is that plants and animals make life possible. Animals are the main food source for other animals, and plants provide food, energy, and shelter. On another level, some species help protect us from disease-carrying pests, and others pollinate our plants. The species also contribute to different ecosystems, including wetlands, forests, plains, and deltas.

Economic Benefit

Many species also have an important economic benefit. For instance, many plants and animals make agriculture possible. Farmers grow crops and raise livestock to sell, and manufacturers build farm equipment to help farmers. Certain species contribute to other industries, too. For example, trees provide lumber for housing and furniture. Other species contribute to medical products. A United Nations study reports that 62 percent of all cancer drugs come from plant experiments. Still other species make wildlife tourism possible. Tourists spend millions of dollars to watch large animals in the wild.

Environmental Benefit

Finally, protecting other species makes us better stewards of the planet. This is a belief held by many people. They feel that since all living things share the planet, we should help all life continue. As biologist Michael Soulé states, "Other species have intrinsic value in themselves." Some people believe that we should choose which species to protect, because we can't save them all. But what if the next species we lose could cure cancer?

So we must protect the world's plants and animals. They give us life and keep the planet healthy. If we ignore them, we ignore the health of everyone and everything.

Qualities of Writing

Baseball pitchers concentrate on the speed, movement, and accuracy of their pitches. If they have all three elements working, they are tough to beat. Authors concentrate on the structure, development, and conventions in their writing. If they skillfully manage these qualities, they will write great essays, reports, and narratives.

You already know that the writing process helps you develop your writing step by step. The qualities of writing discussed in this chapter will help you form your ideas each step of the way.

What's Ahead

- Understanding Structure
- Developing Your Ideas
- Following the Conventions
- Using a Qualities Checklist

Understanding Structure

The dictionary defines structure as "something that has been built." A house needs a structure to hold up the walls and the roof. Writing also needs a structure to "hold up" the ideas.

Creating Three Main Parts

Writing is built part by part, starting with the beginning. It continues with the middle part and finishes with the ending. This is a basic rule of structure, no matter what kind of writing you are doing—a paragraph, an essay, or even a story. You must always include all three parts to form a complete piece of writing.

Beginning ■ The beginning of a paragraph is the topic sentence. This sentence names the topic and states what you plan to say about it.

The beginning paragraph of an essay includes a lead sentence that names the topic and gets the reader's interest. The other sentences build up to the focus or thesis statement, which tells what you plan to say about the topic. Here are four ways to write a lead sentence:

- Start with interesting details about the topic.
- Ask the reader a question.
- Begin with an important quotation.
- Share a brief story about the topic.

Middle ■ The middle sentences in a paragraph support the topic. These sentences may give facts, definitions, examples, and so on.

The middle paragraphs in an essay support the focus statement. The number of middle paragraphs depends on the number of main ideas and details you have to support the focus.

Ending ■ The ending sentence in a paragraph usually restates the topic. The ending paragraph in an essay should do two of these things:

- Remind the reader of the focus.
- Summarize your main ideas.
- Emphasize one key point.
- Give a final thought.

Honoring Great Americans

Beginning

What if you could choose three famous Americans to honor with a monument or statue? Would you choose more presidents or famous war generals? My choices would include three people who weren't involved in politics or war.

Focus Statement

Middle

First "Great American"

My first choice is Helen Keller. When Keller was only two, a serious illness left her deaf and blind. Later, a teacher named Anne Sullivan moved in with the Keller family and helped the girl learn to read and communicate. As an adult, Keller wrote and lectured about her life, and she became an inspiration to many people with handicaps.

Second "Great American"

Astronaut Neil Armstrong is my second choice. In 1969, he and Edwin E. Aldrin, Jr., landed the *Apollo 11 Lunar Module* on the moon. Then Armstrong stepped out of the module, becoming the first man to set foot on the moon. He stated these famous words: "That's one small step for a man, one giant leap for mankind" that will always be remembered.

Third "Great American"

Arthur Ashe is my final choice. He was the first African American to become the number one rated tennis player in the world. In his career, he won three Grand Slam tournaments. In the 1980s Ashe contracted AIDS from a blood transfusion. He spent the rest of his life educating people about AIDS and trying to defeat the illness.

Ending

Famous presidents and war leaders deserve to be honored, but so do other important people like Helen Keller, Neil Armstrong, and Arthur Ashe. Each of these people achieved great things and serves as an important role model.

Organizing Your Ideas

It is important to organize the information in your writing so it is easy to follow. You can organize details by time, by location, by cause and effect, and so on. Here are the main patterns of organization.

The Patterns of Organization

Time Order ■ When your purpose is to tell a story or show a process, use time order. (Time order is also called *chronological order.*) The transitions or linking words below are used with time order.

first	later	then	next	now
before	after	second	today	at the start
third	earlier	finally	when	soon

It takes patience to remove a tick. First, do not try to pull it off with force. If you do, part of the tick's head will break off and remain under the flesh, making you sick. Instead, cover the tick with rubbing alcohol or salad oil and wait until it relaxes its grip. Then carefully remove the tick with a tweezers. Finally, wash the affected area with soap and water.

Location ■ When your purpose is to describe something, you might organize your details by location—top to bottom, left to right, and so on. The transition words below are used to organize by location.

above	from	beneath	around
back	through	down	over
next to	behind	across	below

My grandmother's hair is always combed straight back and tied in a pony tail. Her blue eyes lie partly hidden beneath her dark eyebrows and behind her reading glasses. Her glasses perch on her thin, straight nose. I like her smile the best because it goes across her whole face.

Order of Importance ■ Reasons or qualities are often organized by their importance, starting or ending with the most important one.

also	first of all	most importantly
finally	in addition	for instance
for example	moreover	

> Mr. Brown has three great qualities. First of all, he is really organized. We always warm up, learn or practice a skill, and then play a team game. He always posts a schedule in the gym so we know just what to expect. In addition, he makes us do our best for every activity. He always encourages us to run harder and use all our muscles. Finally, Mr. Brown treats everyone fairly. It doesn't matter if you like gym or not. He is there to help.

Cause-Effect ■ Explaining the causes and effects of a topic is a common purpose in writing. To organize cause-effect writing, you might explain the causes first and then discuss the effects. These transitions are often used in cause-effect writing.

Causes:	the main reason is	since	the main cause is
	another reason	because	in fact
Effects:	the main effect is	as a result	
	then	therefore	

> There is less food for people in Africa today than there was 50 years ago. The main cause is the lack of rain in many areas. Some regions have gone years without enough rain. Another reason for the food shortage is the lack of planning by the governments. There are few storage areas for relief supplies or irrigation systems to use in dry areas. As a result, people have little chance to prepare for hard times. If these conditions do not improve, millions of people may starve.

Compare-Contrast ■ Comparing and contrasting two topics is another common purpose for writing. To organize a comparison-contrast essay, you might explain the similarities and differences. These transitions are often used in compare-contrast writing.

Comparing:	both	similarly	just as
	in comparison	in the same way	and
Contrasting:	although	despite	but
	in contrast	while	on the other hand

> Americans and Australians play a type of football. Both games involve running and tackling, and they both are played on grass fields. The field for American football is rectangular, but the Australian field is an oval shape. The object in both games is to score more points that the other team. American players score mostly by running and passing. In contrast, Australian football players score just by kicking. . . .

Using Different Structures

An essay may follow one main pattern of organization but also use a combination of mini patterns or structures within each paragraph. For example, here is one paragraph in an essay that compares two types of apples. One part of this paragraph uses comparison to describe an apple and another part explains the process of eating it.

> The Red Delicious is a beautiful apple. It is tall and very broad at the top. Then it gracefully slims down to a narrow bottom with nubs that curl under. If the Red Delicious were an athlete, it would probably be a tall, well-conditioned basketball player like LeBron James. The Red Delicious is great to eat, too. First, you take a big juicy bite that oozes with sweetness. The first bite is so enjoyable, that you want to keep going. After awhile, though, you realize how big this apple is because you start getting full. In fact, you have to be really hungry to eat a whole Red Delicious.

Developing Your Ideas

To do your best writing, you must learn as much as you can about your topic. Then you can develop ideas or "elaborate" on them with important information that holds your reader's interest. This section will help you better understand how to develop ideas with details.

Elaborating with Details

- **Facts** and **statistics** give specific information.

  The United Nations reports that 62% of all cancer drugs come from studying plants.

- **Examples** give a model or type of something.

  Animals and plants make life possible. Animals are food for many other animals, and plants are sources of food, energy, and shelter.

- **Explanations** make main ideas clearer.

  The different species are important to ecosystems like wetlands and forests. Species help to keep their ecosystems healthy.

- **Definitions** give the meanings of important terms.

  Endangered means "in danger of not surviving."

- **Reasons** answer the question "Why?"

  All plants and animals deserve our help. This is a belief held by many people. They feel that humans have created most of the problems many species face, so we should help them.

- **Reflections** show the writer's thoughts about an idea.

  The species alive today may help us in the future. Maybe the next species we lose holds a compound that could cure cancer.

- **Quotations and dialogue** give the exact words of the speakers.

  There has to be more than money involved when it comes to protecting animals and ecosystems. As environmentalist Aldo Leopold states, "A system of conservation based solely on economics is lopsided."

- **Anecdotes** are brief stories that help make a point.

  Once the warm weather comes, I hunt for grass snakes and toads under rocks along the river. I love studying amphibians, but I also know that many of them may soon disappear.

Combining Types of Details

When you write paragraphs and essays, you can use different combinations of details to develop an idea. Here are some combinations you might use in your writing.

Main Idea, Example, and Explanation

There are four main types of swimming strokes. The front crawl is the most common stroke. The swimmer starts face down, and he swings his arms forward one at a time, tilts his head to the side, and kicks his legs up and down.

Main Idea: *There are four main types of swimming strokes.*

Example: *The front crawl is the most common stroke.*

Explanation: *The swimmer starts face down, and he swings his arms forward one at a time, tilts his head to the side, and kicks his legs up and down.*

Main Idea, Reason, and Explanation

Trees may be the most important form of plant life on earth. One reason is that trees help clean the air. They absorb carbon dioxide and produce oxygen, which we need to live.

Main Idea: *Trees may be the most important form of plant life on earth.*

Reason: *One reason is that trees help clean the air.*

Explanation: *They absorb carbon dioxide and produce oxygen, which we need to live.*

Main Idea, Reasons, and Reflection

Kids need a safe place like our activity center to be together. At the center, we can get away from school and our little brothers and sisters for awhile and just be ourselves. I wonder what we would do without the center. Maybe we would hang out at the mall and get into trouble or just sit in front of the TV all day long.

Main Idea: *Kids need a safe place like our activity center to be together.*

Reason: *At the center, we can get away from school and our little brothers and sisters for awhile and just be ourselves.*

Reflection: *I wonder what we would do without the center. Maybe we would hang out at the mall and get into trouble or just sit in front of the TV all day long.*

Main Idea, Anecdote, and Reflection

My grandfather entertained me right in his backyard. I remember one day he placed two bowls with food and water on the railing of his porch. Right away, five or six sparrows started fluttering around the bowls. I loved watching them with my grandfather.

Main Idea: *My grandfather entertained me right in his backyard.*

Anecdote: *I remember one day he placed two bowls with food and water on the railing of his back porch. Right away, five or six sparrows started fluttering around the bowls.*

Reflection: *I loved watching them with my grandfather.*

Tip Using combinations like these helps you develop your ideas more clearly and completely.

Using the Best Words and Sentences

It's important to choose the best words and sentences to develop your ideas in all of your different types of writing. Follow these tips.

1 Use specific words.

Specific nouns, verbs, and modifiers give a reader a clear picture of what you are trying to say. This is especially important in essays and reports, or any time you are sharing information. (See page 104.)

General words: The falcon is a good hunter. When it goes after birds, it flies extremely fast.

Specific words: The Peregrine falcon is a fierce bird of prey. When it dives and attacks other birds, it can reach speeds of over 200 miles per hour.

2 Make helpful comparisons.

When you write essays and reports, you need to explain your ideas to make them clear. One of the most effective ways to make an idea clearer is to create a comparison using a metaphor or simile. (See pages 103 and 104.)

Metaphor: Your brain is a complex ecosystem where sensations, memories, emotions, desires, and dreams live.

Simile: Just as the eagle is sacred in Native American cultures, the dragon is sacred in ancient Chinese culture.

3 Write effective sentences.

For sentences to be effective, they need to have movement and rhythm. That means using sentences that vary in length and the way they begin.

The dragon combines the best traits of many animals. It has the horns of a stag, the ears of a bull, the eyes of a rabbit, the claws of a tiger, and the scales of a fish. In ancient Chinese culture, the dragon rules the sky and produces the rain. It is truly a magical creature.

4 Use language that matches your purpose and audience.

For many writing assignments, your purpose is to share information, and your audience is your classmates and teacher. For these assignments, use language that sounds important and interesting.

> Salt is a mineral that comes from rocks in the ocean. As the waves, tides, and currents beat on the rocks, salt goes into the water. The salt in the ocean is the same kind of salt that you put on your popcorn and French fries.

On the other hand, if your purpose is to share your personal thoughts and feelings or tell a story, your language might sound more like you are talking with your classmates and friends.

> When I moved to West Chester, I was really scared. I thought for sure I wouldn't have any friends, and I would hate school. But I was lucky. A girl named Josie, who is the same age as me, lived right next door. She became my friend right away and introduced me to all of her friends.

5 Use language that sounds sincere.

It is important to write about topics that you really care about and to use language that reveals this feeling.

> Frances Ann Slocum was a happy young girl living in Pennsylvania. Then in 1778, when she was just five, she was kidnapped by a hunting party. They carried her away into the forest, and she was lost to her Slocum relatives for 57 years. In 1835, Frances was discovered by a fur trader who was visiting an Indian tribe. He notified the Slocum family as soon as he could. This story is remarkable. But it is especially important to me because Frances is my great-great-great-great grandmother!

Pay attention to the words used by your favorite authors and by classmates whose writing you enjoy reading or listening to. Then try to use similar words in your own writing.

Following the Conventions

The conventions of writing are the rules for spelling, punctuation, capitalization, and grammar. These rules make your writing accurate and easy to follow. Notice the difference without rules:

With no rules: what is It like at the bottom of the Sea. cold dark Mysterious and exciting say oceanographer dan Anderson, Its a whole different world according to dr Anderson the best way. Too see the ocean be in a small submarine

With correct conventions: What is it like at the bottom of the sea? "Cold, dark, mysterious, and exciting," says oceanographer Dan Anderson. "It's a whole different world." According to Dr. Anderson, the best way to see the ocean is in a small submarine.

The chart that follows lists the parts of *Writers Express* that cover the conventions. Turn to these parts whenever you need help.

Using a Qualities Checklist

The following checklist covers the qualities of writing included in this chapter. Use this list to check the quality of your own writing.

Developing the Structure

___ Does my writing contain a beginning, a middle, and an ending?

___ Does my beginning include a strong lead sentence and name my focus or thesis?

___ Do my middle paragraphs support the focus?

___ Does my ending paragraph restate the focus and give an important final thought?

___ Does my writing follow one main pattern of organization, and do I use other patterns within the paragraphs?

Developing the Ideas

___ Do I include effective details to develop my topic?

___ Do I use combinations of details to fully explain certain ideas?

___ Do I use specific words to give the reader a clear picture?

___ Do I make helpful comparisons?

___ Do I vary the type of sentences I use?

___ Do my words and sentences match my purpose and audience?

___ Do I use language that sounds sincere and natural?

Checking for Conventions

___ Do I capitalize and punctuate my sentences correctly?

___ Do I follow the rules for grammar and usage?

___ Do I check for commonly misspelled words?

Using the Writing Process

Selecting and Collecting

When you spin a wheel, you have no idea where it will stop. That may be okay for a board game, but not when you have a writing assignment. To do your best writing, you must be in control right from the start.

Prewriting is the starting point for writing, and during this step, you have a number of important tasks to complete. As you begin, you must carefully review your assignment, select an interesting topic, and collect plenty of details about your topic. This chapter will help you complete all three of these tasks, plus introduce you to other valuable prewriting strategies.

What's Ahead

- Building a File of Writing Ideas
- Selecting a Topic
- Considering Writing Topics
- Collecting Details

Building a File of Writing Ideas

Most writers are interesting people. They know a lot about what's going on, and they try to save as many details from their experiences as they can. These ideas give them starting points for their writing. The activities below can help you save ideas just like your favorite authors do. Have fun!

Think and act like a writer . . .

Always keep your eyes and ears open to interesting sights and sounds. On the way to school, you might see two crazy squirrels dashing up and down a tree, as if they were running a shuttle race. In class, you might hear someone whisper, "What's the answer to number five?" Later at home, you might daydream about being famous someday. Without too much trouble, you could probably think of a story to write, using any one of these ideas.

 Tip Reserve a section in a notebook or journal where you can list some of the sights and sounds you collect each day.

Keep track of your experiences . . .

Start a "This Is My Life" list and keep adding to it throughout the school year. Here's what you might include:

- People I'll Never Forget
- Animals I'll Never Forget
- Important Places Near and Far
- Favorite Books and Movies
- Special Skills and Talents

- Unforgettable Moments
- Biggest Blunders
- Important Events
- Prized Possessions
- Wild Ideas
- Before and After School

Make new discoveries . . .

Get involved in as many different experiences as you can. Join teams and clubs, visit different places, and help people out. The more you do, the more you know.

Read a lot . . .

Read books, magazines, newspapers, and whatever else you like. Jot down any names, descriptions, or ideas that jump off the page as you read. These jottings may give you ideas for your own writing.

Write a lot . . .

Explore your thoughts and feelings in a personal journal or diary, and you will always have a good supply of writing ideas.

Draw a life map . . .

Start your life map with your birth and trace it right up to the present. Choose the experiences you want to picture along the way.

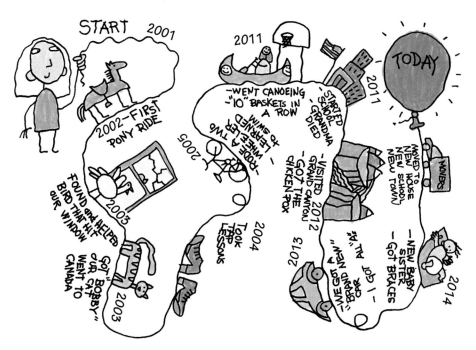

Selecting a Topic

Before you can begin your topic search, be sure you understand the assignment. The **PAST** strategy can help you do this. Each letter in **PAST** stands for one of the parts—**P** is for purpose, **A** is for audience, **S** is for subject, and **T** is for type.

Let's say your teacher gave you this assignment: *Write a paragraph about a favorite family story and be ready to share this paragraph with your classmates.* Here's how the **PAST** strategy can be used to understand each part of this assignment.

Purpose: Why am I writing? .... *to share*

Audience: Who are my readers? .... *my classmates*

Subject: What will I write about? .... *a favorite family story*

Type: What form will my writing take? .... *narrative paragraph*

Selecting Strategies

Once you understand the assignment, you need to select a specific subject. If you're lucky, you may think of a topic right away. If not, look through your file of writing ideas or your writing journal. Also check "Considering Writing Topics" on pages 40–41 for ideas. If you're still stuck, use one of the strategies that follow.

Freewriting ■ Write freely for 3 to 5 minutes. Do not stop to think during this time—just write. Begin freewriting with an idea related to your assignment. As you write, a number of subjects may come to mind. (See page 42 for ideas for freewriting.)

Listing ■ Freely list any ideas that pop into your head when you think of your assignment. You and a classmate can help each other think of possible subjects by brainstorming and listing together.

Clustering ■ Begin your cluster by writing an important word related to your assignment. Then list related words and ideas around it. Circle and connect the new words as shown in the model.

Sentence Completion ■ Complete a sentence starter in as many ways as you can. Make sure that your sentence starter relates to your assignment. Here are six samples:

I remember when . . .   I really get mad when . . .
One place I like . . .   I just learned . . .
I wonder how . . .   School is . . .

The Basics of Life Checklist ■ All of the things you need to survive fall into the categories listed below. Thinking about these categories can help you identify writing topics.

agriculture	education	food	love
animals	energy	freedom	machines
art/music	environment	friends	money
books	exercise	health	plants
clothing	faith	housing	technology
community	family	laws	work/play

Express Yourself Here's how you could use this checklist in a topic search about a favorite family story.
Category: *food*
Topic: *my first campfire meal*

Considering Writing Topics

The following topics are organized according to the four basic reasons to write. These ideas will be especially helpful when you need a topic for a specific kind of writing: arguments, explanations, narratives, or descriptions.

Persuasive Arguments

Arguing for or against homework, school rules, dress codes, lunch hour, cell phones, computer lab, Internet access, activity bus, standardized tests, school cliques, bullying, progress reports, bike paths, library books, store clerks, something that needs improving, something that's unfair, something everyone should see or do, something worth supporting.

Explanations

- **How to . . .** study for a test, bathe a dog, earn money, saddle a horse, perform a magic trick, do a back flip, complete a skateboard stunt, shoot a free throw, write a personal blog, teach something, build something, fix something, make something, grow something
- **The causes of . . .** animals becoming endangered, frostbite, hurricanes, headaches, dizziness, detentions, potholes, photosynthesis, rainbows, rust, shooting stars, shin splints, stage fright, stomach growls
- **Kinds of . . .** music, movies, commercials, clouds, cars, video games, bikes, cats, apples, spiders, laughter, swim strokes
- **The definition of . . .** friendship, fairness, teamwork, courage, love, loyalty, patience, creativity, problem solver, bullying

Personal Narratives

Getting lost, getting caught, getting stuck, making a big mistake, being surprised, making the news, learning to _____, winning, sledding or skiing, singing a solo, getting sick, taking charge, covering up, moving too fast, getting injured, making a discovery, receiving a gift, being different, visiting a relative, biking in the neighborhood, cooking, escaping, dealing with a brother or sister

Descriptions

- **People:** a relative, a teacher, a classmate, a neighbor, someone you admire, a first friend, a store clerk, a crossing guard, a character on a TV show, a character in a book, a singer, a star athlete, an inventor, a parent or grandparent

- **Places:** your room, an attic, the gym, a classroom, an ice rink, a swimming pool, the library, a yard, a river, a park, a hideout, the cafeteria, a favorite store, a doctor's office

- **Objects or things:** a poster, a stuffed animal, a computer game, a drawing, a junk drawer, a souvenir, a sandwich, a bike, a school bus, a gift, a jersey, a hat, a sweatshirt, a tree, a tree house

"I like to write about something I know a lot about. Then I learn even more about it."

—Kendrick Parks, student

A Closer Look at Freewriting

Freewriting can help you identify writing topics. Plus, freewriting can help you collect details and make it easier for you to express yourself on paper. Here is how freewriting works best:

Starting Out

- Write freely for at least 3 to 5 minutes. (Time yourself.)
- Begin writing about one idea—maybe the general subject for the writing assignment.
- Or you can begin with one of the topics on pages 40–41.
- Do not stop to make changes.
- Keep writing even when you can't think of anything. Write "I'm stuck" until another idea comes to mind.
- Write about a certain topic as long as you can before you go on to something else.

Following Up

- Review your writing and underline ideas that relate to your assignment or that you just like.
- Team up with a classmate and read each other's freewriting. Identify at least one idea that you like in your partner's writing.
- Consider using one of your favorite ideas as a topic for your assignment.
- Continue freewriting about ideas related to your assignment or ideas that simply interest you to see what you can discover.

 Tip If you freewrite two or three times a week, you should see an increase in the number of words that you can get on paper in the time you've set aside.

Collecting Details

If you already know a lot about a topic, you won't need to collect many additional details. On the other hand, for new topics, you may need to complete two or three collecting strategies. You can choose from the strategies listed below and on page 44.

Collecting Strategies

Additional Freewriting ▪ Write freely for at least 3 to 5 minutes about your topic. This writing will help you see how many details you already know.

Listing ▪ Make a list of ideas related to your topic. Keep listing as long as you can. (You can ask someone else to add to your list.)

5 W's and H of Writing ▪ Answer the 5 W's and H—*Who? What? When? Where? Why?* and *How?* to collect basic information and additional details about your topic.

Additional Clustering ▪ Write your specific topic in the middle of a piece of paper. Then cluster related words and ideas around it. (See page 39.)

Critical Thinking ▪ Think carefully about your topic by answering two or three of these questions.

- What do I see, hear, or feel about it? (*Describe it.*)
- What else is it like? What is it different from? (*Compare it.*)
- What can I do with it? How can I use it? (*Apply it.*)
- What parts does it have? How does it work? (*Break it down.*)
- What are its strengths and weaknesses? (*Evaluate it.*)

Creative Thinking ▪ Think creatively about your topic by answering a few offbeat questions about it. Here are some examples.

- What type of clothing is the person like?
- What does this place like to do?
- What movies is this experience like?

Research Your Subject

Sometimes you will need to gather facts from other resources. This is especially important for essays and reports.

Reading ■ Learn facts and details by reading about your subject in books, encyclopedias, and magazines.

Viewing and Listening ■ Watch TV programs, slide shows, and videos about your subject.

Online Researching ■ Explore the Internet for reliable, up-to-date information. (See pages 299–307.)

Interviewing ■ Ask an expert questions about your topic.

Discussing ■ Talk with classmates and other people about your topic.

Using a Gathering Grid ■ Use a gathering grid like the one below to keep track of all of your gathering notes. (See the finished gathering grid in "Writing a Classroom Report," page 257.)

	Sources of Information		
Subject			
Who . . . ?			
What . . . ?		Your Answers	
When . . . ?			
Where . . . ?			
Why . . . ?			

Questions About Your Topic (left axis label)

Focusing and Organizing

Before you take a trip, you need to plan. Where will you go? How will you get there? What will you do once you arrive? The same is true for writing. You need to plan out the route you are going to take once you have gathered plenty of details about your topic.

First you need to identify a focus for your writing. Then you need to decide which details to use and in which order. At that point, you will be ready to write. This chapter will help you with all your planning.

What's Ahead

■ Forming a Focus

■ Choosing a Pattern of Organization

■ Arranging Your Details

Forming a Focus

A focus helps you know what to say about your topic. For example, if you were writing a paragraph about meeting your half-brother for the first time, you could focus on how nervous you were.

> When I met my half-brother Jon for the first time *(topic)*,
> I was really nervous *(focus)*.

You can use this formula to form a focus for your writing:

> **Topic** (who or what you are writing about)
> + **Focus** (the part or feeling you want to highlight)
> ───
> = **Focus Statement**

Sample Focus Statements

Persuasive Writing

> Afternoon recess *(topic)* should be added to our school day *(focus)*.
>
> The bike path along Root River *(topic)* needs major changes *(focus)*.

Explanatory Writing

> There are four main types *(focus)* of swim strokes *(topic)*.
>
> An animal becomes endangered *(topic)* after meeting certain requirements. *(focus)*.

Narrative Writing

> Singing a solo in the Christmas program *(topic)* was the hardest thing I've ever done *(focus)*.
>
> My latest bike crash *(topic)* really embarrassed me *(focus)*.

 Tip Your focus statement becomes the topic sentence in a paragraph and the thesis statement in a formal essay.

Choosing a Pattern of Organization

Another part of planning is deciding how you will organize the details in your writing. Sometimes, a pattern of organization is built into the assignment. For example, if you are writing a narrative paragraph, you will organize your details by time (*first this happened, then this, . . .*).

Other times, your focus statement will help you decide how to best organize your details. Let's say this is your focus statement: *There are four main types of swimming strokes.* You might organize them from easiest to hardest. Each time you sit down to write, you need to think about the best pattern of organization to use.

Common Patterns of Organization

Patterns	Connecting Words
Time Order (chronological)	
when sharing a story or explaining a process	first, second, third, next
Order of Location (spatial)	
when describing people, places, and things	above, below, to the left, under, on, behind
Order by Examples	
when identifying examples or types	one, also, another example
Cause-Effect Order	
when explaining causes and effects	the main cause is, since, the main effect is, then
Comparison-Contrast	
when comparing or contrasting two topics	in comparison, both, in contrast, despite, but

Arranging Your Details

The final part of planning is arranging the details in the proper order for writing. This should be fairly easy once you have selected a pattern of organization for your details. Listing and outlining are two common ways to arrange your details before you begin to actually write.

Listing

Listing works well for paragraphs and other shorter forms of writing. Simply write down the details in the order that you want them to appear in your writing.

Focus Statement: **President James Garfield (topic) had some interesting talents (focus).**

- **excelled in Greek and Latin**
- **college president in his twenties**
- **famous general during the Civil War**
- **gave great sermons**
- **campaigned for U.S. president in English and German**

Your listing may also follow a more specific pattern of organization:

Focus Statement: **There are four main types of swimming strokes.**

Easiest   1. Crawl
          2. Backstroke
↓   3. Breaststroke
Hardest   4. Butterfly

Outlining

An outline works well for longer forms of writing like essays and reports. In an outline, ideas are listed from general to specific, with two or more ideas per level. If you have a I, you must have a II. If you have an A, you must have a B, and so on.

- A **topic outline** contains only words and phrases.
- A **sentence outline** contains complete sentences.

Sample Sentence Outline

Focus Statement: **Protecting endangered species (topic) benefits everyone (focus).**

I. Plants and animals support other life forms.
   A. They serve as resources for everything and everyone.
   B. They contribute to the total ecosystem.

II. Many species have an economic value.
   A. Plants and animals make the agriculture industry possible.
   B. They provide products for building and industry.
   C. They contribute to medical products.
   D. They create the wildlife tourism industry.

III. Plants and animals have a right to live.
   A. They share the planet with us, so they deserve to exist and be protected.
   B. The species alive today may save us in the future.

Note A topic outline would look the same except it would use phrases rather than sentences.

Using Graphic Organizers

You can also use any of the following graphic organizers to arrange your details for writing.

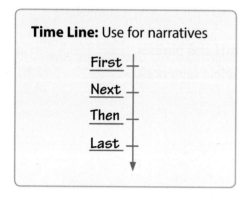

Time Line: Use for narratives

First
Next
Then
Last

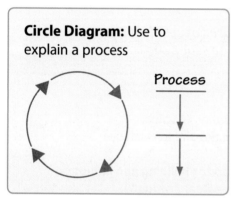

Circle Diagram: Use to explain a process

Process

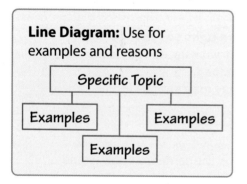

Line Diagram: Use for examples and reasons

Specific Topic

Examples   Examples

Examples

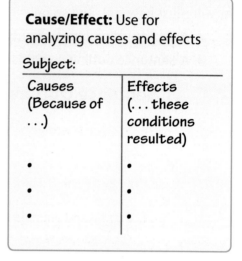

Cause/Effect: Use for analyzing causes and effects

Subject:

Causes (Because of . . .)	Effects (. . . these conditions resulted)
•	•
•	•
•	•

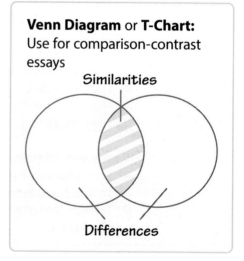

Venn Diagram or **T-Chart:** Use for comparison-contrast essays

Similarities

Differences

Writing and Revising

When you write a first draft, your goal is to get your ideas on paper. So you're not going to get everything just right, but this is okay. Just let the words flow as they come. A first draft does not have to be perfect because it is your first look at your writing.

During the revising step, you can improve upon the parts that need work. All writers, even your favorite authors, spend a lot of time revising their first drafts. It is important that you do the same in your own writing. This chapter provides tips for writing a first draft and some helpful strategies for revising it.

What's Ahead

- Writing a First Draft
- Revising the Writing
- Revising Checklist
- Making Your Writing Stronger
- Revising with Partners

Writing a First Draft

You're ready to write a first draft if you have selected an interesting topic, learned a lot about it, and decided on a focus. These tips will help.

- Write while your prewriting is fresh in your mind.
- Use your planning as a basic guide.
- Write as freely as you can, getting as much down as possible.
- Include a beginning, a middle, and an ending.
- Sound like you care about your topic.

Understanding the Three Parts

Remember that a complete first draft includes a beginning, a middle, and an ending. Here is a quick guide to these three parts. (See pages 22–23.)

Beginning

In a Paragraph ▪ A paragraph usually begins with the topic sentence. This sentence names the topic and focus of the paragraph. (The focus tells what you plan to say about the topic.)

The four main swimming strokes *(topic)* vary in important ways *(focus)*.

In an Essay ▪ The beginning paragraph in an essay has three important jobs. The lead or first sentence (1) identifies the topic and (2) hooks the reader. The next sentences build to the focus or thesis statement, which (3) gives the focus of the essay. Here are three ways to write a lead sentence:

- Start with interesting fact or quotation about the topic
- Ask the reader a question
- Share a brief story about the topic

> Sacagawea was a young woman who joined Lewis and Clark on their famous trip across the western frontier. She was a member of the Shoshone tribe. Her name means either "Bird Woman" or "Boat Launcher" in the Shoshone language. Sacagawea made many important contributions during this famous trip.

Middle

In a Paragraph ■ The middle sentences in a paragraph support the topic sentence with facts, examples, explanations, and so on.

In an Essay ■ The middle paragraphs in an essay support the focus statement with different types of details. The number of middle paragraphs depends on the number of main ideas you have to support the focus.

> Sacagawea and her fur-trapping husband met Lewis and Clark in the territory now called North Dakota. The explorers hired her husband to serve as an interpreter, and Sacagawea came along. As it turned out, she served as an interpreter, too. She also made the journey safe for the men as they traveled among other native tribes.
> Sacagawea also helped in other ways. Her brother was the chief of the Shoshones in the Rocky Mountains. Sacagawea asked her brother to help Lewis and Clark when they reached that point. He gave the explorers food and horses and had some of his braves lead the team over the mountains. Sacagawea was then able to lead them through the Rocky Mountains on the way back.

Ending

In a Paragraph ■ The closing sentence restates the topic sentence:

These are the four main strokes that swimmers learn.

In an Essay ■ The ending paragraph brings an essay to an effective close. The ending paragraph in an essay should do at least two of these things.

- ■ Revisit the focus.
- ■ Summarize main ideas.
- ■ Emphasize a point.
- ■ Give a final thought.

> Sacagawea was very valuable to Lewis and Clark. Her knowledge and experience came in handy at different points during the trip. In fact, without her help, the explorers may not have completed their exploration westward.

Revising the Writing

Revising is the step when you change and improve the first draft. Revising includes changes like these:

- adding details
- reordering sentences or paragraphs
- taking out information you do not need
- rewriting parts that are not clear
- adding graphics or illustrations

How to Get Started

When your first draft is done, you're ready to revise. Here are some ideas to get you off to a good start.

Take a Break ■ This step is easy! Put your first draft in a folder for a while. Later, when you read it again, changes will occur to you that you didn't think of before.

Read and Share ■ Read your rough draft aloud to yourself. Then read it to one of your classmates. Jot down any ideas or questions that come up during this sharing session. (Use the response sheet on page 60.)

What to Look For

Look for the Strong Parts ■ Always find one or two things you like in your draft. You may like a portion of dialogue or a certain descriptive sentence. Put a star next to these parts. It's good for the spirit.

Look for the Weak Parts ■ Also look for parts that need work. Important details may be missing, or your sentences may sound confusing. Or maybe too many of your sentences are the same length or start with the same word.

 Always use a revising checklist. (See the next page.) A checklist will remind you of the many possible ways you can revise and improve your writing.

Revising Checklist

Use this checklist each time you revise your writing. You can use it by yourself or with a classmate.

✓ **Does the writing follow an effective plan?**
___ Does the writing follow my list, outline, or graphic organizer?
___ Do I remember my audience?
___ Does the writing have a clear purpose (to explain, to describe, to persuade, to tell a story)?
___ Does the writing connect to the audience?

✓ **Is all the important information included?**
___ Does the topic sentence or thesis statement name the focus?
___ Do details help the reader understand the ideas or story?
___ Does the writing answer the reader's main questions?

✓ **Is the writing focused?**
___ Does the writing remain focused from start to finish?
___ Does the writing avoid repetition?
___ Does the writing avoid information not related to the subject?

✓ **Do all parts work well?**
___ Does the beginning get the reader's attention?
___ Are all ideas clearly worded?
___ Does the writing show, not just tell? (See page 56.)
___ Does the ending give the reader something to think about?

✓ **Do all parts appear in the best order?**
___ Do the most important points stand out?
___ Do details appear in the best possible order?

Making Your Writing Stronger

1 Show, don't tell.

When you are able to make readers feel, hear, smell, taste, or see things through your writing, you are "showing" rather than "telling."

- **Showing:** In *Charlotte's Web,* author E. B. White describes the barn where Wilbur the pig and his spider friend, Charlotte, live. White used showing details to place his readers right there with Charlotte and Wilbur:

   > It smelled of hay and it smelled of manure. It smelled of the perspiration of tired horses and the wonderful sweet breath of patient cows . . . And whenever the cat was given a fish head to eat, the barn would smell of fish.

- **Telling:** If the author had decided to tell, not show, his description might have sounded more like this:

   > The barn was full of interesting smells of many kinds. The smells came from all the animals and other things in the barn.

2 Connect your ideas.

Remember to use transitions to help readers follow the organization of your paragraphs and essays. (See pages 24–26 and 95.) See how the transitions make the passage below easier to follow. Each transition introduces an example.

   > Example transitions (in **black**): Veterinarian Louis J. Camuti made some strange house calls to treat cats. **One time**, he examined 27 cats in one house! **Another time**, he got a call from a lady who said her cat couldn't move. He knew the problem immediately. The cat was too fat. It weighed 28 pounds! **Then** there was the cat who liked to be vacuumed like a rug. It purred during the vacuuming.

Tip Be careful not to use too many transitions. Use just enough to tie things together and help the reader navigate your writing.

3 Put some power into the beginning, middle, and ending.

Your writing should be clear and complete from start to finish—from the beginning, through the middle, to the ending!

- **Beginning:** The beginning must get your reader's attention and also give a hint about what's coming.

    Sometimes, our bus looks like a garbage truck.

- **Middle**: The middle is your chance to put in the interesting details that answer a reader's questions. But be sure to stick to the point. All of the ideas in the middle (body) should support or explain your subject.

    How will we keep the buses clean?

    Who will help?

    When will we begin?

- **Ending:** Don't just end your paragraph or essay. Instead, leave your reader with an interesting thought or question to think about.

    I've seen too many gum wrappers, paper wads, and old tissues. I hope you have, too!

4 Add a snappy title.

A good title makes your reader curious about your subject. Compare these titles and ask yourself, "Which one grabs my attention?"

Facts on Ants	*or*	Big Brains in Tiny Bodies
Holiday Disaster	*or*	Cookies Can Be Dangerous
A Day I'll Remember	*or*	Swimming with Sharks!

Revising with Partners

It's important to give your classmates and family members a chance to react to your writing. They can help you decide what parts need to be revised. Writing partners can also help you find answers to questions like these:

- Have I included enough information?
- Will readers be able to follow my ideas?
- Will they have any questions?
- Does my writing hold their interest?

What Partners Do

A revising partner's main job is (1) to read or listen carefully, (2) to offer encouragement, and (3) to give advice. His or her responses may please you or surprise you. Either way, a partner can help you turn your first draft into a strong piece of writing. Helpful partners

- identify parts that they feel are strong,
- ask questions about unclear parts, and
- give honest answers to the writer's questions.

How to Help One Another

Partners can help throughout the writing process, but their advice is really important during revising. Partners should not correct the paper for you. Instead, they should offer advice. It is up to you, the writer, to decide what changes to make and how to make them.

Writing partners can also help you when you are ready to edit your writing. They may catch punctuation or grammar errors that you miss.

 **Note** Conference partners should praise a classmate when they like something in a piece of writing, but they should really mean it. Writing conferences should not be popularity contests.

How to Share Your Writing

During sharing time, classmates take turns reading their drafts aloud. Partners listen, and sometimes they take notes or use response sheets. (See page 60.)

Tips for the Writer

- Come prepared with a draft you want to revise.
- Tell your partner about your interest in the writing.
- Practice reading your draft out loud so that you can read it smoothly.
- Speak slowly and clearly. Don't rush.
- Ask questions like "Does my beginning get your attention?" "Does this title fit my story?"
- Listen to your partner's comments and suggestions. Don't take them personally. Your partner is just trying to help.

Tips for the Partner

- Listen carefully.
- Point out what you like about the writing.
- Ask about anything you do not understand, such as a word you don't know or a sentence that seems out of place.
- Be kind and polite. (Sharing makes some people nervous.)
- Make suggestions in a helpful way.
  Don't say, "Your writing is missing a lot of stuff."
  Do say, "I want to know more about that scary bear."

Express Yourself Compliments are great. However, specific compliments work best. "Good job, Scott!" makes Scott feel good. But it's more helpful to say, "That description of your dog Charlie bumping into the post was really cool!"

Sample Response Sheet

A partner can help a writer with revising by filling out a response sheet like this one.

Response Sheet

I noticed these strong parts in your writing . . .

I liked this part of your writing . . .

Here are ways to make your writing better . . .

Editing

Editing comes very near the end of the writing process. During this step, you check your writing line-by-line for punctuation, capitalization, spelling, and grammar. Editing becomes important after you have revised the contents of your writing. If you try to edit too early, you may not give proper attention to your ideas.

Being a careful editor shows that you value your writing and want it to be clear. For example, all of your sentences should read smoothly and be free of careless errors, and all of your words should be clear and correct. Student writer Catherine Ferrante understands the value of editing: "I think about what I write and put great care into picking the words I use." This chapter will help you put great care into your editing, too.

What's Ahead

- Editing Tips
- Making Changes
- Checking for Common Errors
- Editing and Proofreading Checklist

Editing Tips

Editing can't be done in a hurry. Instead, you need to take your time and check everything very carefully. Try to take a step-by-step approach using these tips as a guide.

Know Your Handbook ■ The "Proofreader's Guide" (the yellow pages) at the back of the handbook lists all the conventions or rules for good writing. (See pages 64–65 for a guide to common errors.) Also have a dictionary handy.

Edit on Clean Copy ■ Start with a clean copy of your revised writing, skipping every other line. (This will make it easier to edit.) If you are using a computer, print out a double-spaced copy of your revised writing, and do your editing on this copy.

Use a Checklist ■ Using an editing checklist will help you focus on one type of error at a time. Without a checklist, you may try to check too many things all at once. (See page 66.)

Double-Check Your Spelling ■ A spell checker may not catch everything, so carry out your own spell check, too. Start at the bottom of the page and work your way up one line at a time.

Enlist an Editing Partner ■ Have a trusted classmate or family member check your writing, too. They may find errors that you missed.

Tip The best advice for writers when they begin to edit their work is, "Make every word count!" That means making sure your words are clear, specific, and correct—and changing those that aren't.

Making Changes

The inside back cover of *Writers Express* has a list of common editing and proofreading marks. The sample below shows how you can use these marks when you do your editing.

	Tom Sawyer's adventurous spirit makes his life very
Capital Letter	exciting. One thing tom likes to do is prowl around town at
	night. One time, he sneaks out of his house at midnight
Period and Comma	and joins his friend Huckleberry Finn in the graveyard The
	boys see Injun Joe killing the town doctor and they are
Take Out	nearly caught themselves. Tom he also likes to read
	adventure stories and imagine himself as a daring
Spelling	adventurer adventurur At one point in the story he decides to run
	away and become a pirate. He convinces Huckleberry and
	another friend to join him. The newly formed band of
	pirates sets off to Jackson Island. Another one of Toms
	favorite adventures is looking for hidden treasures. Once,
	while searching an old, abandoned shack, Tom and Huck
Usage	belonging find a hidden treasure belong to Injun Joe.

Checking for Common Errors

Here are some common errors you should watch for when you edit.

1 Missing Comma in Compound Sentences

Be sure to place a comma before the coordinating conjunction (*and, but, or, nor, for, so, yet*) in compound sentences.

> Lake Superior is partly in Canada,and it is surrounded by forests and rocky cliffs.

2 Missing Commas in a Series

Use commas to separate three or more items in a series.

> Some of the best fish for food are cod,tuna,and sea bass.

3 Confusing *Its* and *It's*

Remember: *Its* shows possession and *it's* is a contraction for *it is*.

> its It's
> Our maple tree lost it's leaves so early. Its not even October yet.

4 Subject-Verb Agreement Errors

Make sure all of your subjects and verbs agree. A singular subject takes a singular verb, and a plural subject takes a plural verb.

> lives
> The president live in the White House.
> (*President* is a singular subject, and *lives* is a singular verb. They agree in number.)
> meet
> The senators meets in the Capitol.
> (*Senators* is a plural subject, and *meet* is a plural verb. They agree in number.)

5 Missing Commas After Introductory Phrases and Clauses

Check your commas and be sure to place a comma after phrases and clauses that introduce a sentence.

> During the 2013 season ⌃ the Seahawks had the best record in football.
>
> (A comma is placed after an introductory phrase.)
>
> When the season finally ended ⌃ the Seahawks were Super Bowl champs.
>
> (A comma is placed after an introductory clause.)

6 Writing Run-On Sentences

Use an end punctuation mark after a sentence, or connect two sentences with a comma and conjunction. Otherwise, your sentences will run together.

> Swimming the backstroke has one main challenge ⌇ you can't see where you are going.
>
> (A period is placed after each sentence.)
>
> , but
> Sarah is a really good swimmer ⌃ she wants to concentrate on diving.
>
> (A comma and the conjunction *but* connects two sentences.)

7 Using Double Subjects

A sentence is incorrect if it contains a double subject—a subject with a pronoun right after it.

> Gerald ~~he~~ takes piano lessons after school.
>
> (This sentence is correct because the pronoun right after the subject has been deleted.)

Editing and Proofreading Checklist

Use this checklist as a guide when you edit and proofread your writing.

✓ **Sentence Structure**

___ Are the sentences clear and complete?

___ Are the sentences easy to read?

✓ **Punctuation**

___ Does correct punctuation end each sentence?

___ Do commas appear before coordinating conjunctions (*and, but, or, nor, for so, yet*) in compound sentences?

___ Do commas punctuate a series (bears, tigers, and lions)?

___ Is dialogue correctly punctuated? (See page 144.)

✓ **Capitalization**

___ Does each sentence start with a capital letter?

___ Are the names of specific people, places, and things capitalized?

✓ **Grammar and Usage**

___ Do subjects and verbs agree in number? (See pages 79 and 467.)

___ Is the verb tense consistent?

___ Is usage correct (*to, too, two*)? (See pages 456–465.)

✓ **Spelling**

___ Is spelling correct? (See pages 452–455.)

Publishing

All of the work you do for a writing assignment—from prewriting to editing—leads to publishing. That's the goal of most pieces of writing you do. You want to share what you have written with others, whether it's your teacher and classmates or your family and friends.

Publishing comes in many forms. If you've written a story or poem, you might read it aloud to the class. If you've written a report, you might use it to teach the class about your topic. And if you've written an essay, you might place it in your portfolio to share later. In any case, this chapter will help you get your writing ready to publish and share with others.

What's Ahead

- Designing Your Writing
- Creating a Classroom Portfolio
- Publishing Ideas

Designing Your Writing

The most important thing to remember about writing is that content (what you say) and style (how you say it) count the most. But it's also true that any paper you share with others should look good and be easy to read. That's where "design" comes in. Before you hand in or publish any of your writing, consider the following tips for designing your paper.

Title and Headings

- Think up a catchy title, one that is just right for your topic.
- Use an easy-to-read font (type style) for the body and any headings.
- If your paper is long, consider using headings to make your writing clearer and easier to follow.

Margins and Spacing

- Double-space your writing and leave a one-inch margin on all four sides of your paper.
- Indent the first line of each paragraph.
- Leave one space at the end of each sentence (after the period, exclamation point, or question mark).
- Avoid putting a heading or one line of a paragraph at the bottom of a page.

Graphics

- Use a bulleted or numbered list if it makes information easier to read.
- Add a photo, illustration, or chart to add clarity and interest.
- Keep the graphics at a reasonable size: not too big or too small.

 Tip These guidelines are for your school writing—essays, reports, and other papers. For personal writing, you can be more creative and try other ways of designing your papers.

Effective Design in Action

The following student report illustrates effective design. See how each element adds something important to the appearance of the writing.

The title is 18-point and boldfaced.

The main text is 12-point type.

A helpful photo is added.

Margins are at least one inch all around.

Little Big Dog

Have you ever seen a dog with big, pointed ears and short legs? Was it so cute you just wanted to take it home? Chances are, you were looking at a Pembroke Welsh corgi. Let me introduce you to this special dog.

Physical Features

Welsh corgis were originally bred in Wales. Their average height is 10–12 inches, and an adult dog weighs approximately 25–30 pounds. The dog's small size means it doesn't take up much room as a pet.

Welsh corgis come in several colors: red, sable, fawn, black, and tan—and with or without white markings. Their coats are soft and thick and of medium length.

The headings are 14-point and boldfaced.

Special Traits

Since Welsh corgis are very intelligent, they are easy to train. One of the jobs they are good at is herding sheep and cattle. Welsh corgis are also loyal companions for people of all ages.

Welsh corgis are known for being bold but kind and alert. They are friendly to all and are especially good with children. Because of their herding instinct, young corgis might nip at a person's ankles until the dog has training. Dog owners sometimes enter corgis in dog shows.

Proper Care

A Welsh corgi needs proper care to lead a good life. Here are the main things you should do:

A bulleted list presents information in an effective way.

- Walk your dog using a leash.
- Give him toys and let him fetch and play tug-of-war.
- Feed him quality dog food.
- Brush him every day.
- Bathe him every three months.

Next time you see a dog that looks like a miniature German shepherd, look again. It may be a Pembroke Welsh corgi, with its full-sized body and half-sized legs. This dog is so special that Queen Elizabeth II has had more than 30 of them.

Creating a Classroom Portfolio

There are several different kinds of classroom portfolios. Two popular kinds are the *showcase portfolio* and the *growth portfolio.* Your teacher will tell you what kind to compile.

Showcase Portfolio

In a showcase portfolio, you show off your best work. Your best work may include writing that you like very much or writing that you've worked especially hard on. Your teacher will help you, but in the end, it's important that you decide which pieces are your best.

Growth Portfolio

If you've ever looked at a photo album, you know that people change over time. Writing is like that. It changes as the writer changes. A growth portfolio contains writing you have done throughout the year. It shows how your writing changes from September to December to May. By the time you get to May, you may look back at your September writing and say, "Wow! Did I write that? Can that really be mine?"

> "I used to think of writing as my most dreaded fear. Now it's what I look forward to. . . . When I look over my work, I feel honored that I wrote it."
>
> —Kristen Tomlinson, student

 An electronic portfolio is any type of portfolio available online. In addition to written work, it may contain graphics, video, and sound. An electronic portfolio provides classmates, friends, and family members instant access to your work.

Five Tips for a Super Portfolio

1 Date everything.

It's very important that you date everything, especially in a growth portfolio. Knowing when you wrote each piece will help you see how your writing has changed over time.

2 Keep your portfolio small, but not too small.

Adding a new sample of your writing every four to six weeks is usually about right for a growth portfolio. More samples than that can make your portfolio hard to manage, and fewer samples won't tell enough about you.

3 Attach a self-evaluation to every piece.

Besides telling what you like about the writing, mention one or two problems you had and how you solved them. Also give reasons for choosing each sample—it's fun for readers to know this information.

4 Write a letter of introduction.

Be sure to tell who you are and what kind of portfolio you've made. Suggest some things to look for, like interesting details, a strong voice, or your use of humor.

5 Keep on schedule.

Do not wait until the night before your portfolio is due to quickly write eight pieces and stick them in a folder. That would be like grabbing anything out of your closet to pack a suitcase. You won't like the result.

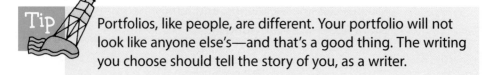

Tip Portfolios, like people, are different. Your portfolio will not look like anyone else's—and that's a good thing. The writing you choose should tell the story of you, as a writer.

Publishing Ideas

There are many different ways that you can publish your writing. The most basic form of publishing is sharing your writing in person with your classmates and teacher. This page lists other publishing ideas you can try.

(In Class)
- Perform your writing.
- Include it in the classroom blog.
- Display it in class.
- Share it with your writing group.
- Add it to a classroom collection.

(In School)
- Include it in the school's Web site.
- Submit it to the school newspaper.
- Perform your writing at an assembly.
- Post it in a hallway display case.
- Make copies for the library.

(In the Community)
- Submit it to the local newspaper.
- Enter it in a local writing contest.
- Submit it to a church or civic publication.
- Perform it for a community group.
- Make copies for waiting rooms.

(On Your Own)
- Include it in a family newsletter.
- Post it on a personal blog.
- Email it to relatives.
- Recite it in a Skype session.
- Submit it to an electronic publication.

Note Be sure to get an adult's approval before you try any of these ideas.

Learning Writing Skills

Writing Basic Sentences

A rope is an important tool for a cowhand, especially when it comes to catching and controlling livestock. In much the same way, a sentence is an important tool for you when it comes to controlling the ideas in your writing.

Your readers will have a hard time following your ideas if your sentences are out of control. If they can't follow your ideas, they'll stop reading. That's why it is so important to write sentences that are clear, complete, and correct. The guidelines in this chapter will help you write effective sentences.

What's Ahead

- Sentence Review
- Sentence Errors
- Sentence Agreement
- Sentence Problems

Sentence Review

A sentence is a group of words that expresses a complete thought. Your job as a writer is to write sentences that share interesting ideas in a clear, logical way. Start by thinking about the parts of a sentence.

The Basic Parts of a Sentence

Sentences have two basic parts—the <u>subject</u> and the <u>verb</u>.

Subject ■ The subject usually tells who or what is doing something.

<u>Mike</u> <u>invites</u> Venzel to his house.

Verb ■ The verb (also called the *predicate*) expresses action or links the subject to another part of the sentence.

<u>Mike</u> <u>invites</u> Venzel to his house. (action verb)

<u>They</u> <u>are</u> wild about adventure movies. (linking verb)

Additional Words ■ Most sentences also contain additional words that describe or complete the thought.

Mike invites Venzel to his house.

Compound Subjects and Verbs ■ A sentence may include more than one subject or more than one verb.

<u>Mike</u> and <u>Venzel</u> <u>watch</u> videos. (two subjects)

Sometimes the <u>DVD</u> <u>skips</u> and <u>ruins</u> the fun. (two verbs)

Compound Sentence ■ Two sentences may be connected with a conjunction (*and, but, or, nor, for, so, yet*).

Mike usually makes popcorn, and Venzel often provides peanuts.

Complex Sentence ■ An independent clause or complete sentence (in black) connects to one or more dependent clauses (in blue).

When the movie finishes, the boys talk about their favorite parts.

What Can Sentences Do?

Not all sentences function in the same way. Different types of sentences serve different purposes. Sentences do the following:

Make Statements

A statement gives information about a person, place, thing, or idea. It usually starts with a subject followed by a verb.

My **dog** **is chasing** his tail again.

Ask Questions

A question asks for information. It often starts with the verb and includes the subject later.

Do **you** **see** Spot?

Give Commands

A command tells people just what to do. It often starts with a verb and has an implied subject (You).

(You) **Stop** tapping your pencil.

Make Requests

A request gives directions or tells how to do something. It also starts with a verb and has an implied subject (You).

(You) **Try** adding some details to your story.

Express Emotions

An exclamation expresses strong emotion or surprise.

You're awesome!

You can find out more about sentences in the "Understanding Sentences" section.
(See pages 466–470.)

Sentence Errors

Sentence Fragment ■ A sentence fragment is a group of words that looks like a sentence but does not express a complete thought.

Incorrect:	Thinks water slides are cool. (The subject of the sentence is missing.)
Correct:	Martina thinks water slides are cool.
Incorrect:	Not my idea of fun. (The subject and verb are both missing.)
Correct:	Water slides are not my idea of fun.

Run-On Sentence ■ A run-on sentence happens when two sentences are joined without punctuation or a connecting word.

Incorrect:	The evening was warm it was time to catch fireflies. (Punctuation is needed.)
Correct:	The evening was warm. It was time to catch fireflies. (A period has been added, and a word has been capitalized.)
Correct:	The evening was warm, and it was time to catch fireflies. (A comma and the conjunction *and* have been added.)

Rambling Sentence ■ A rambling sentence occurs when you put too many short sentences together with the word *and*.

Incorrect:	I went skating down at the pond and three kids from my school were there and we fell again and again and again and we laughed so much our stomachs hurt! (Too many *and*'s are used.)
Correct:	I went skating down at the pond, and three kids from my school were there. We fell again and again and again. We laughed so much our stomachs hurt!

Sentence Agreement

Make sure that the subjects and verbs in your sentences agree with each other. If you use a singular subject, use a singular verb; if you use a plural subject, use a plural verb.

One Subject ■ Most basic sentences have one subject followed by the verb. When they are right next to each other, it is easy to check for subject-verb agreement.

> **Amy wants** to go bowling.
> (*Amy* and *wants* agree because they are both singular.)

> Her **parents want** to go bowling, too.
> (*Parents* and *want* agree because they are both plural.)

Compound Subjects Connected by "And" ■ If a sentence contains a compound subject connected by *and*, it needs a plural verb.

> **Harry** and **Emile spend** time playing basketball.

> **Sarah** and **Maria play**, too.

Compound Subjects Connected by "Or" ■ If a sentence contains a compound subject connected by *or*, the verb must agree with the subject nearer to it.

> Either the **cats** or the **dog pounces** on me each morning.
> (A singular verb, *pounces*, is needed because *dog* is singular.)

> **Anna** or her **brothers feed** the pets each evening.
> (A plural verb, *feed*, is needed because *brothers* is plural.)

 Tip
Sometimes the subject does not come before the verb. This happens in sentences beginning with the word *there*. (There **are** two **dogs**.) It also happens in questions. (**Is** this **dog** yours?)

Sentence Problems

Double Subjects ■ Do not use a pronoun immediately after the subject. The result is usually a double subject.

> **Incorrect:** Some cats **they** eat all the time.
> (The pronoun *they* should be omitted.)
> **Correct:** Some cats eat all the time.

Pronoun-Antecedent Agreement ■ Make sure the pronouns in your sentences agree with their antecedents. (Antecedents are the words replaced by the pronouns. See page 475.)

> **Incorrect:** If Carlos and his friends each eat three cheeseburgers, **he** will be overstuffed.
> (The pronoun *he* is singular. The antecedents—Carlo and his friends—are plural.)
> **Correct:** If Carlos and his friends each eat three cheeseburgers, **they** will be overstuffed.
> (Now the pronoun and its antecedents agree; they are plural.)

Double Negatives ■ Do not use two negative words (like *never* and *no*, or *not* and *no*) in the same sentence.

> **Incorrect:** Never give **no one** a note during class.
> **Correct:** Never give **anyone** a note during class.
>
> **Incorrect:** I didn't have **no** mistakes in my paragraph.
> **Correct:** I didn't have **any** mistakes in my paragraph.

Confusing "Of" for "Have" ■ Do not use *of* in a sentence when you really mean *have*. (When *have* is said quickly, it sometimes sounds like *of.*)

> **Incorrect:** We should **of** brought an umbrella.
> **Correct:** We should **have** brought an umbrella.

Combining Sentences

Sentence combining is making one smoother, more detailed sentence out of two or more shorter sentences. For instance, take a look at the following sentences:

My dog loves to run fast.

He loves to jump fences.

He loves to chase rabbits.

These sentences are okay, but all of these ideas can be combined into one smooth-reading sentence, which is even better.

My dog loves to run fast, jump fences, and chase rabbits.

The guidelines in this chapter will help you learn how to combine sentences, which will help you improve your writing style.

What's Ahead

- Combining with Key Words
- Combining with Phrases
- Combining with Longer Sentences

Combining with Key Words

Use a Key Word ■ Ideas included in short sentences can be combined by moving a key word from one sentence to the other.

> **Short Sentences:** Dakota's necklace sparkles. It is beaded.
> **Combined with an Adjective:**
> Dakota's **beaded** necklace sparkles.
>
> **Short Sentences:** I am going to a sleepover. I'm going tomorrow.
> **Combined with an Adverb:**
> **Tomorrow,** I am going to a sleepover.

Use a Series of Words or Phrases ■ Ideas included in short sentences can be combined into one sentence using a series of words or phrases.

> **Short Sentences:** The gym teacher is strict.
> The gym teacher is organized.
> The gym teacher is fair.
> **Combined with a Series of Words:**
> The gym teacher is **strict**, **organized**, and **fair**.

All of the words or phrases in a series should be *parallel*—stated in the same way. Otherwise, the sentence will be unbalanced.

Incorrect: His dog is friendly, playful, and he is pretty smart, too.
(The modifiers in this series are not parallel.)

Correct: His dog is friendly, playful, and smart.
(Now all the words in the series—*friendly, playful, smart*—are single-word adjectives. They are parallel.)

Combining with Phrases

Use Phrases ■ Ideas from two or more short sentences can often be combined into one sentence using phrases.

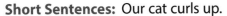

Short Sentences: Our cat curls up.
He curls up on top of my homework.

Combined with Prepositional Phrases:
Our cat curls up **on top of my homework**.

Short Sentences: Mrs. Jones makes the best cookies on the block.
Mrs. Jones is our next-door neighbor.

Combined with an Appositive Phrase:
Mrs. Keller, **our next-door neighbor**, makes the best cookies on the block.

Use Compound Subjects and/or Compound Verbs ■ A compound subject is two or more subjects connected by a conjunction. A compound verb is two or more verbs connected by a conjunction.

Short Sentences: Deena danced around the room.
Mary danced around the room, too.

Combined with a Compound Subject:
Deena and **Mary** danced around the room.

Short Sentences: Sherard skated around the pond.
He made a perfect figure eight.

Combined with a Compound Verb:
Sherard **skated** around the pond and **made** a perfect figure eight.

Combining with Longer Sentences

Use Compound Sentences ■ A compound sentence is made up of two or more simple sentences joined together. The conjunctions *and, but, or, nor, for, so,* and *yet* are used to connect the simple sentences. (Place a comma before the conjunction.)

> **Simple Sentences:** My puppy has hair hanging over her eyes.
> She looks just like a dust mop.
>
> **Combined with "And":**
> My puppy has hair hanging over her eyes, and she looks just like a dust mop.
>
> **Simple Sentences:** Our dog likes to eat shoes.
> He won't touch my brother's smelly slippers.
>
> **Combined with "But":**
> Our dog likes to eat shoes, but he won't touch my brother's smelly slippers.

Use Complex Sentences ■ A complex sentence is made up of two ideas connected by a subordinating conjunction (*because, when, since, after, before,* etc.) or by a relative pronoun (*who, whose, which,* or *that*).

> **Short Sentences:** My friend shares his lunch with me.
> He doesn't like what his dad packs.
>
> **Combined with "Because":**
> My friend shares his lunch with me because he doesn't like what his dad packs.
>
> **Short Sentences:** Very cold weather closed school for a day.
> The cold weather came down from Canada.
>
> **Combined with "Which":**
> Very cold weather, which came down from Canada, closed school for a day.

Writing Paragraphs

A paragraph is a group of sentences that describe or explain a topic or idea. Each sentence in a paragraph must give information about the topic. Also, the sentences must be in the right order so that your readers can understand and appreciate the information. A good paragraph presents a complete and interesting picture to the reader.

Learning to write clear, well-developed paragraphs will help you become an effective writer, whether you are writing a short essay or a full classroom report.

What's Ahead

- The Parts of a Paragraph
- Types of Paragraphs
- Writing a Paragraph
- Adding Details
- Putting Things in Order
- Transition Words
- Finding Paragraphs

The Parts of a Paragraph

A paragraph has three main parts. The *topic sentence* states the main idea. The sentences in the body of the paragraph are all connected to the main idea. The *ending sentence* sums up the main idea and brings the paragraph to a close.

Sample Paragraph

Topic Sentence

Trees may be the most important form of plant life on earth. First of all, trees add beauty to the landscape and give shelter to wildlife. They also provide wood, paper, food, medicines, and many other useful products.

Body Sentences

On top of that, tree roots prevent soil erosion and help store water. Though it is something you cannot see, the most important thing trees do is help clean the air. Trees absorb carbon dioxide and produce oxygen, and it's

Ending Sentence

oxygen that people need to breathe. People can thank trees for a lot more than shade!

A Closer Look at the Parts

The Topic Sentence

The *topic sentence* tells the reader what the paragraph is about. A good topic sentence does two things: (1) it names the topic, and (2) it gives the focus or main point.

Formula: An interesting topic
           + a specific focus or feeling
           _____
           = a good topic sentence

Topic Sentence:

Trees (an interesting topic) may be the most important form of plant life on earth (a specific focus).

The Body

The sentences in the *body* of the paragraph include the specific details the reader needs to understand the topic. The following sentences include plenty of specific details.

First of all, trees add beauty to the landscape and give shelter to wildlife. They also provide wood, paper, food, medicines, and many other useful products. On top of that, tree roots prevent soil erosion and help store water.

Organize your sentences in the best possible order. Three common ways to organize your sentences include *time order, order of location,* and *order of importance.* (See page 94.)

The Ending Sentence

The *ending sentence* comes at the very end and sums up the main point of the paragraph.

Ending Sentence:

People can thank trees for a lot more than shade!

Types of Paragraphs

There are four main types of paragraphs.

- To describe something, write a **descriptive** paragraph.
- To tell a story, write a **narrative** paragraph.
- To explain something, write an **explanatory** paragraph.
- To express your opinion, write a **persuasive** (argument) paragraph.

Sample Descriptive Paragraph

In a **descriptive** paragraph, you describe a person, a place, a thing, or an idea. When you write a descriptive paragraph, use words related to the five senses. Tell your audience about the sights, sounds, colors, smells, and textures related to the subject. This will help your readers feel as if they are right there with you.

The topic sentence sets the scene.

The details give sights and sounds about the topic.

A final thought brings the paragraph to an end.

> In the middle of Central Park, there's a tree that I love to visit. Whenever I ride my bike to the park, I can see that one tree towering above all the others. The tree's trunk is so wide I can't reach my arms around it! Its bark forms funny patterns as it crawls up the tree, and the tips of its branches reach for the sky. On a windy day, the leaves rustle, and small branches break off and fall to the ground. I often sit under this tree, watching the squirrels and listening to the birds. I love everything about this special tree.

Sample Narrative Paragraph

In a **narrative** paragraph, you share a personal experience. You try to pull your readers into the story and keep them wondering what will happen next. Be sure to include specific details to make your experience come to life.

The topic sentence identifies the experience.

Last Tuesday, I invited Danny, Julio, Renatta, and Mishiko to ride their bikes over to climb my favorite oak tree. We've all climbed the tree together before, but this time we decided to see who could climb the highest. Julio and Renatta climbed a little bit higher than usual, and I climbed almost to the end of one huge limb.

Specific details build suspense.

Mishiko climbed even higher than I did, but it was Danny who won our little contest. Unfortunately, I don't think he realized how high he had climbed—until he looked down. He froze. He clung to the limb he was on and was afraid to climb down. What if he had to stay up in the tree all night? Renatta took off on her bike to tell her mom. Her mom called the fire department, and before long, an engine—with sirens blasting—

The final sentence sums up the story.

arrived to rescue Danny. It was very exciting, but we also learned a lesson about climbing contests.

Note Be sure to include all the important details in your narrative paragraph. Answer the following questions: *Who? What? When? Where? Why? How?*

Sample Explanatory Paragraph

Your main purpose in an **explanatory** paragraph is to give information about a subject. You may give directions, present ideas, or explain how to do something. An explanatory paragraph often uses transition words such as *first, then, after,* and *finally.*

The topic sentence identifies the topic.

The details are listed in the order they happened.

The final sentence brings the explanation to an end.

Last summer, my friends and I put up a tree house in our back yard. Our first step was to agree on a design for the tree house. Then we made a list of materials we needed and located a store that sold building supplies. We took our list and the money we had saved and went shopping. We loaded everything into my dad's van and headed back. The first thing we had to do was build a frame for the floor of the house. (My mom helped with that.) Then we used a rope to raise all the wood up into the tree. Afterward, we carefully nailed the boards to the frame, and we soon had a floor. After that, we added walls and a roof. It took us all afternoon, but it was worth it. We now had a great place to hang out for the rest of the summer.

Tip Before you begin writing, it's helpful to list the facts or examples you are going to include in your paragraph. That way, you can put your supporting ideas into the best possible order before you begin.

Sample **Persuasive Paragraph**

In a persuasive or argument paragraph, you give your opinion about a topic and try to prove its value or worth. To do this, you need to give strong facts and examples that support your opinion. Otherwise, you won't be convincing.

The topic sentence states an opinion.

The body gives reasons.

The ending restates the opinion.

Kids need a place to call their own, and a tree house is the perfect place. A tree house gives my friends and me a chance to get away from the pressures of school, homework, and little brothers or sisters. We can just hang out and be ourselves. We can also decorate our tree house any way we want. A tree house is a good place for thinking, playing music, looking at the sky, or just being with friends. Sure, if we didn't have this kind of place, we'd find other ways to keep busy. We'd go to the mall, text our friends, play video games, or just watch TV. But doesn't a tree house sound like a better place for kids to spend their time?

Express Yourself Read your paragraph out loud so that you can listen for missing information. Also turn to page 397 in your handbook for more ideas about using facts and opinions in your writing.

Writing a Paragraph

Prewriting Planning Your Paragraph

■ As you start a paragraph assignment, ask yourself the **PAST** questions.

> **Purpose:** *Why am I writing—to explain, to describe, to persuade?*
> **Audience:** *Who will be reading my paragraph?*
> **Subject:** *Who or what will I write about?*
> **Type:** *What kind of paragraph will work best?*

■ After you answer these questions, start gathering details.

For a ...	you'll need ...
descriptive paragraph	details that tell how the topic looks, sounds, smells, feels, and tastes.
narrative paragraph	details about an experience: how it began, problems that came up, how it ended.
explanatory paragraph	details that give information or explain the subject you're writing about.
persuasive paragraph	facts, figures, and examples to back up your opinion.

Writing Developing a First Draft

Put your information in order. The topic sentence usually comes first. Next comes the body—the sentences that tell about the topic sentence. Your ending sentence should sum up the paragraph or remind the reader what it all means.

Revising and Editing Improving Your Paragraph

Read your paragraph as if you were reading it for the first time. Did you include enough details to support your topic sentence? Do your sentences read smoothly? Did you check for errors?

Adding Details

To bring your paragraph to life, you need to include facts, examples, and other specific details.

Personal Details

Many of the details you use in your paragraphs will be personal details—things you know from your own experience.

Details from Your Senses ■ These are things that you see, hear, smell, taste, and touch. Focus on senses when writing a descriptive paragraph.

On a windy day, the leaves rustle together, and small branches break off and fall to the ground.

Details from Your Memory ■ These details come from memories of things you've done and experienced. In descriptive and narrative writing, such details can bring the past to life. In an explanatory paragraph, they can help you explain how to do something.

Then we used a rope to raise all the wood up into the tree.

Details from Your Imagination ■ These details are things you hope for, wish for, and wonder about. Such details can make narrative paragraphs interesting and fun.

What if he had to stay up in the tree all night?

Details from Other Sources

When you write a paragraph, use what you already know about the subject. Then add details from other sources.

- **Ask someone you know** for the answers you need—teachers, parents, neighbors, friends.
- **Ask an expert.** For example, if you are writing about the flu, you could talk to a doctor or a nurse.
- **Study resources** such as newspapers, magazines, books, and reliable sites on the Internet.
- **Write, call, or email** companies or government offices.

Putting Things in Order

The sentences in the body of your paragraph must be organized so that readers can follow all of your ideas. Here are three ways to organize your sentences.

Time Order ■ It is easy to follow ideas when the facts are explained in the order in which they happened. Time order works well in a narrative or an explanatory paragraph. You may use words like *first, next,* and *finally.*

> The first thing we had to do was build a frame for the floor of the house. Then we used a rope to raise all the wood up into the tree. Afterward, we carefully nailed the boards to the frame, and soon we had a floor. After that . . .

Order of Location ■ When details are described in the order in which they are located, the description usually goes from left to right or from top to bottom. Order of location works well in a descriptive or an explanatory paragraph. Use words and phrases like *above, around,* and *up.*

> The tree's trunk is so wide I can't reach my arms around it! Its bark forms funny patterns as it crawls up the tree, and the tips of its branches reach for the sky. . . .

Order of Importance ■ News stories are often organized in the order of importance. They tell the most important news first. Persuasive or explanatory paragraphs are also organized in this way, with the most important detail coming first or last.

> Kids need a place to call their own, and a tree house is the perfect place. A tree house gives my friends and me a chance to get away from the pressures of school, homework, and little brothers and sisters. . . .

Transition Words

Words that can be used to show time:

about	before	later	soon	tomorrow
after	during	meanwhile	then	until
as soon as	finally	next	third	when
at	first	second	today	yesterday

Words that can be used to show location:

above	around	between	inside	outside
across	behind	by	into	over
against	below	down	near	throughout
along	beneath	in back of	off	to the right
among	beside	in front of	on top of	under

Words that can be used to compare things (show similarities):

as	in the same way	like	similarly
also	likewise	just as	while

Words that can be used to contrast things (show differences):

although	even though	on the other hand	still
but	however	otherwise	yet

Words that can be used to emphasize a point:

again	for this reason	in fact	so

Words that can be used to add information:

again	along with	besides	for instance
also	another	finally	next
and	as well	for example	

Words that can be used to conclude **or** summarize:

as a result	in conclusion	lastly
finally	in summary	therefore

Finding Paragraphs

You know how easy it is to go on and on when you have something important to say to one of your friends: "Guess what I did? . . ." Well, the same thing can happen when you are writing. You may start out writing a simple paragraph and end up filling a whole page or two with great ideas without any paragraph breaks.

Keeping Your Ideas Together

When your writing goes on and on, be sure to organize it into paragraphs before you share it. Otherwise, your readers may have trouble following your ideas. The guidelines that follow will help you find the paragraphs in your writing.

Label . . . Name . . . Find

To find the paragraphs in longer pieces of writing, keep repeating these three steps—*label, name, find*—until you come to the end of your work.

1. **Label** the first word in your paper with a paragraph sign (¶).

2. **Name** the first main idea in your writing.

3. **Find** the first sentence that is *not* about this idea.

1. **Label** that sentence (#3 above) with a paragraph sign (¶).

2. **Name** the main idea of this new paragraph.

3. **Find** the first sentence that is *not* about this idea.

 You'll want to repeat this process until you reach the end of your paper.

Sample Writing

Here is part of an autobiography by student writer Elizabeth Hartfield. As you can see, it is not divided into paragraphs.

My name is Elizabeth Frances Hartfield. I'm going to tell you about my life starting with the day something exciting and sad happened. What happened was that I moved from my home in Springfield to a house in West Chester. I was nervous and scared. I didn't think that I would make any friends, but I did. Since I moved to West Chester, I have gone to three different schools. The first one I went to was Saints Simon and Jude. I went there for first and second grade. I went to Sacred Heart Academy in Bryn Mawr for third grade, and now I go to Emerson Elementary. I am now in fourth grade. I like to draw a lot. On April 25, 1998, I won an award for a drawing I did of our dog, Reggie. My favorite activities besides art are reading and dancing. . . .

Following the Three-Step Process

Finding the paragraphs in this autobiography is easy if you follow the three-step process:

1. **Label** the first word with a paragraph sign.
   ¶ "My name is . . . "

2. **Name** the main idea in the first paragraph.
   Moved from my home in Springfield

3. **Find** the first sentence that is *not* about this idea.
   "Since I moved to West Chester, . . . "

---

1. **Label** that sentence with a paragraph sign.
2. **Name** the main idea of this paragraph.
3. **Find** the first sentence that is not about this idea.

Building Paragraphs and Essays

Sometimes not all of your ideas about a topic will fit in one paragraph. When this happens, you can write an essay. While a paragraph is made up of a series of sentences, an essay is made up of a series of paragraphs.

Both paragraphs and essays include three main parts, a beginning, a middle, and an ending. The graphic below shows how the parts fit together.

Three-Part Structure

	Paragraph	Essay
Beginning	Topic Sentence	Beginning Paragraph
Middle	Body Sentences	Body Paragraphs
Ending	Ending Sentence	Ending Paragraph

Note The beginning of a paragraph starts with a *topic sentence*. This sentence tells what the paragraph will be about. The beginning paragraph of an essay ends with a *focus* or *thesis statement*. This sentence tells what the essay will be about.

Understanding Writing Terms and Techniques

Style is personal. Let's say that you do a certain stunt that sends you and your skateboard skyward. That's part of your own special style. You may wear your hair short, or long, or half-and-half. That's your style, too. What's *in style* for you, depends on you.

As a developing writer, you have your own way of expressing thoughts and feelings. This is your writing style, and it will develop naturally as you continue to write. The suggestions in this chapter will also help you develop your style.

What's Ahead

- Developing a Sense of Style
- Using Writing Techniques
- Modeling the Masters
- Understanding Writing Terms

Developing a Sense of Style

Your writing style will grow strong and healthy if you follow this advice:

- **Practice often.**
  Keep a journal and write in it every day. This is one of the best ways to develop your writing style.

- **Try different forms.**
  Explore different forms of writing. Try poems and plays; write news stories and character sketches. Each form of writing can help you develop your style.

- **Write about ideas that are important to you.**
  If you write about topics that you care about, you will soon have a style of your own.

- **Use your voice.**
  Write with words you understand—words that sound like you.

- **Change writing that doesn't work.**
  If you don't feel good about your writing, fix it. Your handbook is full of ideas to help you do this.

- **Learn about the qualities of effective writing.**
  Qualities such as structure, ideas, and conventions ought to be part of your style, no matter what form your writing takes. (See pages 21–33.)

- **Use writing techniques.**
  The writing techniques listed on pages 101–104 can help you add color and variety to your style.

 Express Yourself Here's an activity to help you strengthen your writing style. List five sentences from your writing. Then try to make each sentence better by using a more lively verb or more specific noun.

Using Writing Techniques

Writing techniques can be used to add interest to your style. Try a technique or two each time you write.

Anecdote ■ An anecdote is a brief story used to make a point. Here's an anecdote student writer Charles Vodak included in one of his stories.

> To get me to keep my room clean, my mom always tells this story about her sister Ann. Ann was very messy. One day she was cleaning her closet, and she found some kittens in there. And guess what? She didn't even have a cat!

Try this: Use anecdotes in your writing when a little story can get your point across to your readers.

Colorful Adjectives ■ Colorful adjectives are lively words that describe nouns or pronouns.

> Mom made good spaghetti sauce. (bland adjective)
>
> Mom made delicious, spicy spaghetti sauce. (colorful adjectives)

Try this: If you're writing about food, think of words that make your mouth water when you say them.

Comparison ■ A comparison is a description of things that are similar. Comparisons can be used throughout a long piece of writing. (See pages 181–188. Also see *simile* and *metaphor.*)

> Those little butterflies look like flying flowers.

Try this: Use comparisons to make your writing clearer or more colorful. A well-written comparison paints a picture with words.

Details ■ Details are the specific facts, examples, and words used to support a main idea and add color to your writing.

> My cousin is nice. (few details)
>
> My cousin Lu loves to send notes to her classmates. (effective details)

Try this: When you are writing, use details that are specific and clear. Try to stay away from words like *good*, *is*, and *nice* because they are not specific and clear.

Dialogue ■ Dialogue is talking on paper.

> "Could you help me find the train station?" asked the traveler.
>
> "I'd be happy to," said the young man, "but I'm a lost traveler just like you."

Try this: Add dialogue to your stories and reports. (Dialogue in a report might be from an interview). It adds energy to your writing and makes your style memorable. (See page 144.)

Exaggeration ■ When you exaggerate in your writing, you create characters or scenes that stretch the truth a bit. (Use *exaggeration* in stories and fables, but not in essays or reports.)

> The giraffe peeked over the clouds and spotted the missing balloon.

Try this: Think of an animal and its characteristics. (The sample above uses a giraffe and its characteristic of being tall.) Then stretch or exaggerate these natural features, especially in tall tales or children's stories.

Idiom ■ An idiom is a word or phrase used in a way that is different from its usual or dictionary meaning.

> Maha and Jake ironed out their problems. (In this sentence, *ironed out* means "solved.")

Try this: Use idioms selectively to make your writing sound realistic. Idioms fit better in stories than in reports.

Metaphor ■ A metaphor is a figure of speech that compares two different things without using the word *like* or *as*.

> That sprinter in the red jersey is a real roadrunner.

Try this: Think of two things that have something in common, such as their color, size, shape, or behavior. Here are some examples: a sprinter and a roadrunner, blue eyes and the ocean, springtime air and a baby's breath.

Personification ■ Personification is a figure of speech in which an idea, object, or animal is given the characteristics of a person.

> The stubborn rock refused to move.

Try this: Use personification to add life to your writing. You have already used it if you've ever said, "The wind howled" or "My phone just told me its charge is running low."

Sensory Details ■ Sensory details are details that help a reader see, feel, smell, taste, or hear a subject.

> The black-eared kitten purred quietly as I cuddled her in my arms.

Try this: Use your senses to find words that will add sound, feeling, and color to your writing.

Simile ■ A simile is a figure of speech that compares two things using the word *like* or *as*.

> A cold lemonade is like a refreshing dip in a deep pool.

Try this: Use similes to add word pictures to your poems, stories, and descriptive writing.

Specific Nouns ■ A specific noun is a word that names a certain person, place, thing, or idea. In the chart below, **A** nouns are very general, **B** nouns are more specific, and **C** nouns are very specific.

	Person	Place	Thing	Idea
A	boy	outdoors	toy	celebration
B	cousin	park	puppet	holiday
C	Rich Jones	Yellowstone	Pinocchio	New Years

Try this: To make your writing as clear as possible, use very specific nouns whenever you can.

Vivid Verbs ■ A vivid verb is a powerful word that gives the reader a clear picture of the action.

> The children wiggled and bounced in their seats.

Modeling the Masters

Young artists can learn a lot about art by studying the work of famous painters. And you can learn a lot about writing by studying the work of your favorite authors. When you come across sentences that you especially like, try writing a sentence of your own following the author's pattern. This process is called "modeling."

Guidelines for Modeling

- Find a sentence (or short passage) that you especially like.
- Select a subject for your writing.
- Follow the author's pattern as you write about your own subject.
- Build your sentence one small section at a time.

One Writer's Experience

Cayla enjoys Roald Dahl's stories, so every once in a while she tries to write like him. Here is a sentence from Dahl's book *Danny the Champion of the World*:

> Grown-ups are complicated creatures, full of quirks and secrets.

Here is Cayla's sentence about her own subject, but modeled after Dahl's writing:

> Cats are peculiar pets, full of sleepiness and craziness.

Cayla might have written, "Some cats can be really nutty. They can be sleeping on the couch one minute and flying around the room the next minute." By modeling, she can use fewer words to share the same ideas in a powerful way. She has discovered how to model a master.

Remember, you "model" other authors to give you ideas for your own writing. Don't overdo it so that you end up with someone else's style.

Understanding Writing Terms

The following list of writing terms can be used whenever you want to talk about writing—yours or your classmates'.

Argument Writing: Writing that develops an opinion.

Arrangement: The way details are "arranged" or organized in writing. (See pages 24–26 and 94 for more information.)

Audience: People who read or hear what you have written.

Body: The main part of the writing that comes between the beginning and ending ideas. The body contains the specific details that support or develop the main idea. (Sometimes called the *middle*.)

Brainstorming: Freely sharing or listing ideas in groups in order to collect a variety of thoughts on a subject.

Cliché: A familiar word or phrase that has been used so much that it is no longer a good way of saying something. An example would be "as good as gold" or "as bright as the sun."

Composition: A piece of writing similar to an essay.

Description: Writing that helps a reader see a subject clearly with specific details and colorful modifiers.

Diction: The level or kind of language a writer decides to use. In a story about everyday life, a writer may use informal, ordinary language. In a business letter, a writer will probably use formal, proper language.

Editing: Checking a piece of writing to make sure it contains complete, smooth-reading sentences; strong, colorful words; and correct spelling, grammar, and punctuation.

Ending Sentence: The sentence that sums up the main point being made in a paragraph.

Explanatory Writing: Writing that explains, such as a report or research paper. (Sometimes called *expository* writing.)

Figure of Speech: A special way of describing a subject by comparing it to something else. (See *metaphor, personification,* and *simile* on pages 103–104.)

First Draft: The first attempt at writing about a topic.

Focus/Main Idea: The specific part of a topic a writer chooses to concentrate on. For example, a piece written about Abraham Lincoln could focus on his education.

Form: The shape of writing—a poem, an essay, a report, a play, and so on.

Freewriting: Writing quickly to discover new ideas.

Grammar: The rules and guidelines for correctly using language in your writing and speaking.

Journal: A daily record of thoughts, feelings, and ideas.

Modifier: A word or group of words that describes another word or idea.

Narration: Telling a story or recalling an experience.

Objective: Writing that includes facts but no opinions or personal feelings.

Parallelism: The repetition of words or phrases that are written in the same way: *Josie scratched her head, bit her nails, and shrugged her shoulders.*

Person: The angle or point of view from which a story is told.
> First person: *I; we*
> Second person: *you; you*
> Third person: *he, she, it; they*

Personal Narrative: Writing that tells a story about the writer's life.

Persuasion: Writing that is meant to change the way a reader thinks or acts.

Prewriting: Planning a writing project. *Selecting a subject* and *gathering details* are prewriting activities.

Process: A way of doing something that involves several steps. The writing process includes *prewriting, writing the first draft, revising, editing, proofreading,* and *publishing.*

Proofreading: Checking a final draft for spelling, grammar, usage, and punctuation errors.

Pun: A word or phrase used in a way that gives it a funny twist: That story about breeding rabbits is a real *hare raiser.*

Purpose: The main reason for writing about something.

Revising: Changing writing to make it clearer or more interesting. This is usually done by adding, cutting, or moving the ideas and details.

Sensory Words: Words that tell how something looks, feels, sounds, and so on.

Slang: Informal words and phrases used by friends when they talk to each other. "*Off the hook*" and "*photobomb*" are slang terms.

Style: The way a writer puts words, phrases, and sentences together.

Supporting Details: Specific details used to develop a topic or bring a story to life.

Theme: The central idea or message in a piece of writing.

Thesis Statement: The sentence that states the main idea or focus of an essay.

Topic: The specific subject of a piece of writing.

Topic Sentence: The sentence that contains the main idea or focus of a paragraph.

Transitions: Words that help tie ideas together in essays, paragraphs, and sentences. (See page 95.)

Voice: The way a writer expresses his or her ideas.

Understanding Text Structures

Imagine you are exploring the deep sea and discover a fish no one has ever seen! What do you do? You probably describe it. You maybe compare and contrast it to other fish. You might even tell the story of how you discovered this unknown fish!

In each case, you are writing for a different purpose. Each purpose has a *text structure* that can help you communicate your ideas. In this chapter, you will learn about many different text structures that you can use to get your point across.

What's Ahead

- Common Text Structures
  - Cue/Signal Words
  - Organizers
  - Examples

Common Text Structures

There is not one "official" list of text structures. There are, however, a few that are very common. Here are the ones used most often.

Sequence: Chronological Order

The chronological structure is organized from one point in time to another.

Cue/Signal Words: *not long after, first, then, next, finally, following, during, at last, until, since, when, after, before, as, now.* (Dates and times are also used.)

> Sometimes at the end of a rainstorm, you will see a rainbow. First the sun appears, and then its white light shines through the raindrops. When this happens, the water breaks the light apart, or refracts it, and that's when you see the colors of the light spectrum: red, orange, yellow, green, blue, indigo, and violet. This is what we call a rainbow.

First . . . _____

Then . . . _____

Next . . . _____

After . . . _____

At last . . . _____

Sequence: Process

The process structure is organized in a step-by-step sequence.

Cue/Signal Words: *before, after, next, when, as, until, first, following, then, at the same time, finally, during, at last*

> A car wheel is just a simple machine. First, an axle is connected to a pair of wheels. Then the car engine applies force to the axle. This causes the axle to rotate. As the axle rotates, it turns the wheels.

1. _____
2. _____
3. _____
4. _____
5. _____
6. _____

Cause and Effect

In this text structure, why something happens is the **cause**. What happens because of the cause is the **effect**.

Cue/Signal Words: *because, since, therefore, consequently, as a result, so that, accordingly, if . . . then, one reason for, for this reason*

> Our planet is pretty restless! Beneath the ground is a zone of very hot liquid called magma. Magma moves constantly, and this movement pushes and pulls the plates that our ground rests on. As a result, we experience earthquakes and volcanoes.

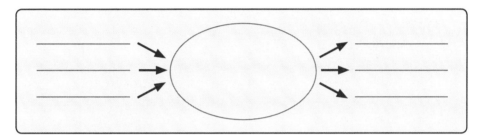

Problem/Solution

This text structure presents a problem and shows how it can be (or has been) solved.

Cue/Signal Words: *solve, problem, solution, effect, because, therefore, for this reason, consequently*

> Dr. Jan Grootenhuis is a wildlife veterinarian based in Kenya. He has been looking for practical solutions to the problem of Africa's vanishing wildlife. Recently, he has been working with the Maasai, an indigenous tribe. Slowly, the tribe has been converting some of its valuable grazing land into wildlife conservation areas.

Problem: _____

Causes of the Problem
- •
- •
- •

Possible Solutions
- •
- •
- •

Compare/Contrast

In this text structure, two ideas, events, or things are compared by showing how they are alike and different.

Cue/Signal Words: *compare, contrast, like, unlike, both, as well as, yet, in contrast, too, whereas, likewise, on the other hand, not only . . . but also, either . . . or*

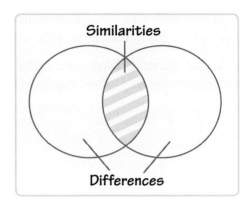

Hawks and owls are both raptors. They take their place at the top of the food chain. Owls, unlike hawks, are almost entirely nocturnal. This means that it's hard to observe them as they capture their prey. Hawks hunt during the day, so they are easier to observe. Because they sometimes hunt poultry and small game, both birds can cause trouble for farmers.

Question/Answer

In this text structure, a question (or a series of questions) is answered.

Cue/Signal Words: *question, answer, could be that, one may conclude, consider, perhaps, the best estimate, who, what, when, where, why, how, how many*

Q: _____
A: _____

Q: _____
A: _____

Q: _____
A: _____

Question: Tell me about yourself as a student.

Answer: I love to learn about things that interest me, so I'll climb any mountain to find out what I want to know.

Question: What are some of your interests?

Answer: Well, I am wild about music, so I am constantly . . .

Description

In a description, language is used to provide details and help readers form images so that they can understand how something looks, feels, sounds, tastes, or smells.

Cue/Signal Words: *for example, to illustrate, such as, to begin with, above, around, beside, atop, beneath*

> Different finger movements in a sock puppet show different emotions. For example, moving your fingers up and down expresses a yes. Opening thumb and fingers expresses shock. Clamping fingertips unevenly shows confusion or annoyance. . . .

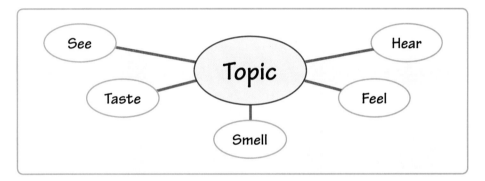

Categorical

In this text structure, ideas are arranged according to categories or types within a larger topic.

Cue/Signal Words: *category, types, an example of, many kinds of, parts, groups, characteristics*

> There are several types of skateboarding: street skating, vert skating, half pipe, and vert ramp. Street skating is skating on streets, curbs, and other places in cities and suburbs. Vert skating is skating on ramps and other vertical structures. Half pipe is skating on a . . .

Personal Writing

Writing in Journals

Your team won the soccer match during recess. You finally got all the words correct on your spelling test. Your best friend is coming over after school, and your dad is taking you to the movies. Days like this are so special that you want to remember each moment.

How can you be sure to remember every detail of your awesome day? Try writing about it.

After your wonderful day is over, pull out your personal journal. Write about what happened and how it made you feel. This is one of the best ways to capture your memories. You will then be able to read about your past experiences and feelings whenever you like.

What's Ahead

- Why Write in a Personal Journal?
- Kinds of Journals
- Sample Journal Entries

Why Write in a Personal Journal?

When you write in a journal, you can do any of these activities:

- Take notes about what you see and hear.
- Collect ideas for stories, poems, and reports.
- Practice writing by yourself.
- Deal with bad days.
- Remember good times.

Here's how to get started . . .

1. **Gather the right tools.**
   Grab a pen or pencil and a notebook, or use a computer.

2. **Find a special time and place to write.**
   Get up early and write while it is quiet in your house. Write at a regular time during school. Or find a cozy chair after supper, curl up, and write.

3. **Write every day.**
   Write freely about your thoughts and feelings as they come to mind. Don't worry about what you say or how you say it. Just keep writing for at least 5 to 10 minutes at a time.

4. **Write about what is important to you.**
   Write about something that is bothering you or something you want to remember. Write about what you did last weekend or something you saw. Write about one thing for a while and then go on to something else.

5. **Keep track of your writing.**
   Put the date on the top of the page each time you write. Read your journal now and then. Underline interesting ideas that you want to write more about sometime.

Note Writing in a journal is great practice. If the only writing you do is for assignments, you can't expect to write as well as students who regularly practice in their journals.

A Closer Look at Journal Writing

Journal writing gives you the chance to think. It lets you reflect on and learn from your experiences. When you do this, your writing becomes lively and interesting. It sounds like you.

Reflect

Explore your experiences by thinking and writing in any of the following ways:

Ask Questions ▪ What was special about this experience? How do I feel about it? Why do I feel this way? Then look for answers.

Wonder ▪ Think about what you learned from the experience. Compare it to other experiences. Do you wish you had done things differently? Predict what you might do in the future.

Express Yourself Read the sample journal entry on page 118. In this writing, a student reflects on something special that happens in her garden.

Keep Writing

Come back to your journal often to write and make more personal discoveries.

Write More ▪ Start a new journal entry. Write about something new, or pick up right where you left off in your last entry. When an idea surprises you, say more about it. When you are sure you've said all that you can, write a few more lines.

Make Connections ▪ Even if ideas seem really different, try to make connections between them. Make connections between your ideas and the news, movies, or songs.

Kinds of Journals

You can create all kinds of journals, from personal journals to special-events journals:

Personal Journal ■ A personal journal is a place for writing about your day and reflecting on what it means to you.

Dialogue Journal ■ In a dialogue journal, you and a friend, parent, or teacher write to each other about experiences, books, or other topics. (See the sample on page 119.)

Diary ■ In a diary, you write about personal things.

Learning Log ■ In a learning log, you write about subjects like math, science, and social studies. It helps you to understand the subjects better. (See pages 121–124.)

Response Journal ■ In a response journal, you explore your feelings about the stories and books that you read. (See the samples on page 120.)

Special-Event Journal ■ In a special-event journal, you write about big events—playing a sport, having a new family member, or working on a special project.

Sample **Personal Journal**

July 5

Today was so great! I saw a hummingbird in our garden! It was visiting the scarlet runner beans that we planted a few weeks ago. The vines are growing fast up the tepee poles that we tied together. This week, red flowers blossomed from the runner beans, and red attracts hummingbirds. I wonder why.

We were in the backyard, and I saw something moving by the flowers. It was a tiny hummingbird! It was so neat. In a second, it zoomed off. I hope it comes back.

Sample **Dialogue Journal**

In the dialogue journal below, a teacher and a student carry on a conversation about a book.

Dear José,

When I read your response to *It's Disgusting and We Ate It!*, I was flabbergasted myself. I had no idea that seaweed came in "snack" form or that it is in hot fudge! What a surprise. I enjoyed reading all the names of the types of seaweed, too. The funniest names were Cow Hair, Star Jelly, Sugar Wrack, and Sea Otter's Cabbage. Thanks for sharing!

Write back,

Ms. N.

P.S. Please give me more information on the book, so I can order it for our library.

Dear Ms. N.,

Yes, the seaweed names are funny. My favorite one is Sea Otter's Cabbage. What's yours? The author of this book is James Solheim, and the publisher is Simon and Schuster.

I also learned that millions of people like bird's nest soup. So my dad and I went to a local Chinese restaurant where the book said we could get some. We ordered it, and it was really great! Have you ever had bird's nest soup?

Please write back,

José

Response Journal

These two entries come from different parts of a response journal. The first entry is a response to fiction, and the second to nonfiction.

Rogues to Riches

March 24—This book is funny and strange. I like Rengie and Tooles, rogues who want to get rich. They start the book in prison, and they have a spitting contest to escape.

Rengie and Tooles pretend to be a couple of knights so that they can steal a treasure, but a cursed rose makes them have to actually become knights.

I'm only halfway through, but I like all the goofy jokes. Right now, they're back in prison. They've just convinced an orc guard to release them if they let him "come back at the end of the book." I wonder if he'll be back. . . .

Wonders of the Universe

July 22—I saw this show on the Science channel and loved it, so when I saw they had a book, I wanted to get it. It's great, with lots of pictures of planets, stars, and nebulas. But I think they wrote it for people in college.

Brian Cox is really good at explaining things, but some of the ideas are tough. Like, for example, that space-time is like a rubber sheet, and gravity is like wells in it. When I don't understand a part, I look up the show on YouTube and get the explanation that way. Is that cheating? I think it's just another way to figure out a good but tough book. I wish all good books had videos to go with them. . . .

Using Learning Logs

Have you ever written in a log? How about a learning log? A learning log is a place to write what you are thinking about a subject. You might write about a topic that your teacher talked about in class. Or you might ask questions about an idea you don't understand.

You can try many different learning-log activities. Any of them will help you learn. This chapter will introduce you to a number of them.

What's Ahead

- Keeping a Learning Log
- Learning-Log Activities
- Sample Learning Logs

Keeping a Learning Log

You can write about any of your subjects in a learning log. Here are just a few ideas:

- Write about the most important idea you learned from a reading assignment.
- Write about questions you have or things you want to know.
- Write about what you learned from a class project or experiment.
- Write about your feelings about something you just learned.

Making a Learning Log

1. **Divide a notebook into sections**—create one section for each subject you will write about.

2. **Plan a time to write in your learning log each day.** Write for a longer time about a subject that is difficult for you.

3. **Write freely and use your own words.** Start by writing the date. Then put all your thoughts down. Write without stopping for at least 3 to 5 minutes.

April 22, 2015

    I don't understand the rock cycle Mr. Ampe talked about today. All the rocks I've ever picked up are really hard. How do they turn into sand? And then back into rocks again? Mr. A. says erosion has something to do with it. That's a key word. We're supposed to read about the freeze/thaw cycle, too. That's another key word. The rock cycle is amazing, though. When I saw Big Thompson Canyon, I thought those rock walls would be there forever . . .

Learning-Log Activities

Here are many ideas for using a learning log. Try them all! Then choose the ones that work best for you.

First Thoughts

List your first impressions about something you are reading or studying. You can also make a list of key words that come to mind after a lesson. Key words help you focus on the most important ideas.

Stop 'n' Write

When you are studying something, stop and write about it. This helps you summarize along the way and keeps you on track.

Nutshelling

Do you know the phrase "in a nutshell"? It means "to say a lot in a few words." A nutshell is a kind of summary. Try it yourself. In one sentence, write the most important idea you heard in class or read in an assignment.

Unsent Letters

Pretend you are sending a letter to a friend, a relative, or an author. In your letter, tell what you have learned about a topic or an idea. Explaining will help you to understand the subject better.

Graphic Organizers

Use a graphic organizer to think about a lesson. A cluster or web works well for gathering facts. A 5-senses chart will help you describe a topic, and a Venn diagram lets you compare two things. (See pages 383–386.)

Drawing

Draw pictures to show what you have learned or are thinking about—anything from diagrams to maps to pictures.

Sample Math Log

May 7, 2015

Well, now we are into geometry. So far I think I get it.
These are key terms from class today.
- perimeter = the distance around the shape
- area = the amount of space inside the shape
- dimensions = the length of the sides of the shape

Here's how it works with a square.
- perimeter is
  3 cm x 4 sides = 12 cm
- area is ???
  (Find out how to figure this.)
- dimensions = All sides are
  3 cm long.

3 cm.

Area
???

3 cm.

Sample Science Log

March 12, 2015

Leaves have different shapes. Sometimes one stem
has many leaves, not just one. But the arrangement is
different for each plant.

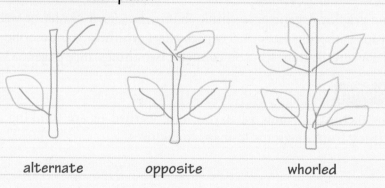

alternate   opposite   whorled

Writing Emails and Blogs

The word "email" is short for "electronic mail." In an email, you can write a letter to a friend or relative. You can also write to a classmate or a teacher about school work.

The word "blog" is short for "Web log." You can use a blog as an online journal. On a classroom blog, you can talk with classmates about topics, assignments, and projects.

This chapter gives tips and guidelines for communicating electronically.

What's Ahead

- Using Email
- Sample Email
- Using Blogs
- Sample Classroom Blog

Using Email

Whether you are writing a letter to a friend or sending a message about a school topic to a teacher, follow these steps to write and send an email.

1. Choose a topic.
- Think about who you are writing to and what you want to say.
- Make a list of the details you will include.

2. Fill in the email heading.
- Type in the email address of the person you are writing to.
- Include the topic of your message in the subject line.

3. Write the message.
- In the beginning, greet the reader and say why you're writing.
- In the middle, give all the details you want to share. If you need answers or want the person to write back, say so.
- In the ending, close with some polite words and your name.

4. Check your writing.

____ Is the reader's email address correct?
____ Does the beginning state the main point of the message?
____ Does the middle include all the details in the message?
____ Is the message easy to read—with short paragraphs, lists, and headings?
____ Are the spelling and punctuation correct?

5. Hit send.
- With a little luck, you'll get a reply.
- If you get no reply, try writing again.

Sample **Email**

This email was written by a student to his teacher. The message is easy to read, and the student checked it for errors before sending it. You can use this email as a model when you write your own.

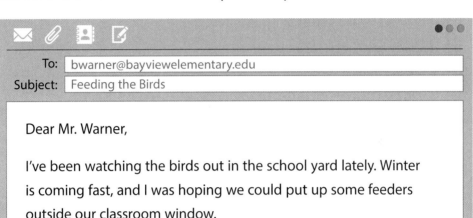

To: bwarner@bayviewelementary.edu

Subject: Feeding the Birds

Dear Mr. Warner,

I've been watching the birds out in the school yard lately. Winter is coming fast, and I was hoping we could put up some feeders outside our classroom window.

It looks like we have goldfinches, chickadees, juncos, and who knows what else flying around out there. Feeding them could be part of our science class, right? We could see the birds close-up and identify them.

Do you know where we can get the money to buy feeders and birdseed? I'd be happy to work on a fund-raiser for this project.

Thanks for reading my idea. Please let me know what you think of it tomorrow at school.

Thank you,

Reggie Baylor

Using Blogs

Blogs are like never-ending conversations. Someone posts a comment, someone else responds, and on and on it goes.

Think, Then Write

Here are some tips for blogging:

- Think about what you just read in a blog post.
- Do you have something to say about it? If you do, then write a response.
- Answer a question, share an opinion, or tell something you know. Use clear, polite words.
- Post your comment.
- Read what other people are saying.
- Write another comment if you have something else to say. Remember to be polite if you are commenting on what a classmate or a teacher said.

Use a Checklist

Review your comment before you post it to the blog. Ask yourself these checklist questions to help decide whether your comment is ready to post. (You can also use the "Editing and Proofreading Checklist" on page 66.)

___ Does my comment answer a question, share my opinion, or tell about something I know?
___ Is my comment friendly, informative, and polite?
___ Do I say everything I need to say?
___ Do I follow the rules for spelling, punctuation, and capitalization?
___ Do I have permission from my parent or teacher to share my blog post?

Sample **Classroom Blog**

The following classroom blog was set up by a teacher. It's a place for students to discuss the books they are reading.

● ● ●

The Wind in the Willows Discussion Group | View Topics |

Topic of Discussion: Posted on Monday, February 25

Who is your favorite character in *The Wind in the Willows?* Explain what you like about that character. How does the character relate to you?

| Add a Comment |

Comments:

Zack: I love Toad. He's so crazy. He is always trying something new and exciting. But he does learn how important friends are. I like to do exciting things with my friends.

Cody: My favorite is Ratty. That's because I love the water. Ratty teaches Mole all about boating. Boating is lots of fun!

Wilma: I like Mole best. He has a warm home, but he gets bored. He wants to see the world. I like my room at home, but I also want to travel the world.

Liz: I agree with Cody. My favorite character is Ratty because he reminds me of my older brother. Just like Ratty, my brother teaches me new things and takes me on adventures. Both Ratty and my brother are wise and caring, too.

LaTasha: Mole is my favorite character. He is a little shy, but that doesn't stop him from making new friends. I want to see new places and experience new things like Mole.

Cody: Liz has a cool reason for liking Ratty. I just realized that Ratty reminds me of my Uncle Jay. We do crazy stuff together, but he shows me how to do things safely. Ratty and Uncle Jay are alike in this way.

Narrative Writing

Writing Personal Narratives

Writing true stories about yourself is called autobiographical writing. It would be too much to write your whole life story, but you can write a short story or a personal narrative about a special time in your life.

You can think of the experiences in your life as different chapters. Any experience that has caused you to feel a strong emotion is a good subject for a personal narrative. It could be an unforgettable day, a special event, or an unusual coincidence. Whatever is memorable to you is a good topic.

What's Ahead

- Sample Personal Narrative
- Gathering Story Ideas
- Writing Personal Narratives
- Writing Family Stories

Personal Narrative

Here's a true story that Sandy Asher wrote about a special experience in her life. When it happened, she felt scared and sad—and then happy.

The Great Gerbil Escape

Beginning
The main characters and the problem are introduced.

When my daughter Emily was nine years old, she had a pair of gerbils named Farrah and Festus. One day, Festus escaped from our bathtub!

It sounds silly to have gerbils in your tub, but it's not. The sides are too high to jump over and too slick to climb. We plugged the drain. We put in toys and sunflower seeds. The gerbils could exercise and play safely.

But one day, I accidentally left a fuzzy blue bath mat over the edge of the tub. When Emily and I came back, Festus was gone. He'd grabbed the mat and climbed out!

Middle
The story is organized according to time (describing what happens first, second, third, and so on).

The only place he could have gone was down the heat vent in the wall. We knelt beside the vent. We could hear him! "Scritch-scratch. Scritch-scratch." We lowered a rope into the vent, but he didn't climb out. We stuffed in a towel, but he didn't climb that either.

And when we pulled the towel out, there was no more "Scritch-scratch." Oh, no! I thought. We've pushed him down the vent into the furnace. We've baked our gerbil!

Emily was heartbroken. I felt terrible. We put Farrah back in the cage and went downstairs. Then I noticed another heat vent in the hall, right below the one upstairs in the bathroom. And sure enough, we could hear Festus again: "Scritch-scratch. Scritch-scratch!"

Ending
A surprise rescue is described.

Finally, Emily remembered that gerbils love to explore boxes. We took all the tissues out of a small tissue box. Emily lowered the box into the vent as far as her arm could reach. Then Festus climbed aboard and rode to safety in his own private elevator. And that's how the Great Gerbil Escape became the Great Gerbil Rescue!

Gathering Story Ideas

You can start gathering ideas for personal narratives by writing in a daily journal or diary, or by making lists of personal experiences. A good way to find ideas is to answer the following types of questions:

1 Who are the important people in your life?

Family members? Friends? Classmates? Neighbors? Think about the times you've shared with each one. What do you remember best? What would you just as soon forget? (See page 136 for suggestions for family stories.)

2 Where have you been?

Every place you visit is an adventure, whether it's the doctor's office, the principal's office, or the county fair. Think of the biggest place you've been, and the smallest. Think of comfortable places, and places that cause you to squirm. Think of special meeting places from your past.

3 What do you like to do?

Do you enjoy drawing or cooking or caring for animals? Do you like to play basketball or just hang out? Do you like to talk on the phone or read at night when you're supposed to be asleep?

4 What do you not like to do?

Study? Clean your room? Baby-sit? Get up early? There are a lot of ways to answer this question, aren't there? And a lot of strong feelings are involved, too. Isn't it nice to know that even the worst times you can remember are at least good for story ideas?

If you don't know where you're going, you'll probably end up somewhere else.

Writing Personal Narratives

Now that you understand the "big picture" of how a personal narrative works, we need to look closely at each step in the process.

Prewriting Planning Your Story

Choose a Subject ■ First, be sure you understand the requirements of your assignment. Then choose a subject for a personal story. You want a memorable experience that happened over a short period of time.

 Tip Try completing this sentence starter: "I remember the time . . . " Continue listing until you find a subject.

Gather Your Thoughts ■ If the idea you choose is clear in your mind, begin writing. If you're missing some details, try clustering or listing for ideas. You should be able to answer the 5 W's—Who? What? When? Where? and Why?—before you write.

Writing Developing Your First Draft

Start at the Beginning ■ Put yourself at the beginning of your story ("There I stood" or "As I entered the room") and keep adding details as they come to mind.

Revising Improving Your Story

Review Your Work ■ Reading your first draft aloud allows you to "hear" your writing. Have you left out any important details? Are your details in the best order? Do you sound really interested in your subject? Make any necessary changes.

Editing and Proofreading Polishing Your Story

Check for Careless Errors ■ Make sure that your sentences are correct and read smoothly. Also make sure that your words are specific and correct. Then write a neat, final draft and proofread it. (You can use the checklist on page 66 to help with your editing and proofreading.)

Sample **Personal Narrative**

Jessica Gilbert recalls a motorcycle ride that taught her a lesson.

When I Got Burned on Dad's Motorcycle

Beginning
The scene is set right away.

As I was going outside, I was a little nervous because I was going to ride on my dad's motorcycle.

"Come on. Get up," said my dad cheerfully.

"Okay," I answered. But just as I was getting onto the seat, I burnt myself on one of the pipes!

"Ow!" I yelled as I started to cry.

"Are you all right?" asked my mom.

"No," I answered.

Middle
The story develops with dialogue.

"Come here," said my mom. "Let's take a look at that burn. It's not so bad, but I don't think you should go for a ride right now."

I felt glad that my mom had said that.

"Aw, come on. It won't hurt once we get going," said my dad.

Then he picked me up and set me on the seat of the motorcycle.

"Dad, I'm not sure I want to go!" I said.

"Nonsense. It'll be fun," said my dad. We took off.

I have to admit that during the ride, I started to laugh. My burn hardly hurt anymore. I wasn't nervous and I had a great ride.

Ending
The narrative ends on a positive note.

I'm really glad my dad convinced me to get on the motorcycle. If he hadn't, I probably never would have gotten on it again. From that day on, I knew I would never give up after I got hurt. I would just try again.

Writing Family Stories

Another kind of personal narrative you may want to write is a family story. Here are some starters to get you going.

Name Stories . . . Your Name ■ Write about how your first and middle names were chosen. If you don't know, go to the source. Ask a parent or guardian. There is a story behind every name. This one, the story of your name, may be the first in a whole collection of stories about your family.

. . . Other Family Names ■ Now check into other family names that interest you. Are there favorite first names or middle names in your family? How about nicknames? Last names? Tell these stories.

Birth Stories ■ Find out about the day you were born. Ask your parents. What was the weather like? What time of day did you arrive? What important events were going on in the world that day?

Holiday Stories ■ Write about the ways your family celebrates holidays— Thanksgiving, Christmas, Hanukkah, New Year's Day, Easter. Are there any special holidays that only your family celebrates?

Recipe Stories ■ Your family may have favorite recipes. Write about the times, places, and people who have shared these foods with you. You may want to write up some of the recipes, too.

Heirloom Stories ■ Many families have special pieces of furniture, jewelry, or photos that have been handed down from generation to generation. These objects are called *heirlooms*. What are the stories behind your family's heirlooms? Where did they come from? Why are they valuable to your family?

 Here are some topics to get you thinking about more family stories: spooky events, disasters, unusual relatives, rascals, pranks, and special sayings.

Writing Fantasies

Do you ever daydream? Have you ever had an imaginary friend? Have you ever made believe you could fly or invented your own private world? If so, you've used your imagination, which allows anything to happen—even impossible things.

Anytime you write stories, you use your imagination, but this is especially true when you write a fantasy. In this type of story, a spider can save a pig, or a young girl can race to the future. So let's begin by reading a fantasy story by a pair of student writers. Then learn how to write a fantasy of your own.

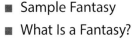

What's Ahead

- Sample Fantasy
- What Is a Fantasy?
- Writing a Fantasy

Fantasy

This fantasy tells of a heroic quest from an underground civilization into a forest maze to confront a dragon. With elves, kings, and mythical creatures, this story includes many common fantasy elements.

Into The Maze
Saul and Theo Weiss

Beginning

The setting, characters, and problem are introduced.

Just beneath the earth, in a world called Underville, there lived a community of elves called the Lombards. Their king, Brawnwin, seemed about to succumb to a rare disease when the most powerful of the King's subjects, Prius the Mage, called a meeting. At the meeting, Prius declared that six Lombards were needed to volunteer to go into the forest maze to retrieve one dragon's tooth from the Mighty Maze Dragon, Skull.

Middle

Dialogue is used to explain the problem.

"Why us and not you?" cried the Lombards. "You are a mage—a man of great learning and power!"

"And, why a tooth?" a man called out.

"My fellow Lombards," Prius said kindly, "had I trained a successor to my status as mage, I would have surely done the deed, but you cannot afford to lose me just yet. And the tooth I spoke of? I will tell you. A dragon's tooth is the last ingredient I need to make the potion that will heal our king, Brawnwin," answered Prius.

Six volunteers immediately stood up. The first to speak was Faith. "My friends and I are willing to retrieve a tooth from the Mighty Maze Dragon, Skull, but we will need some supplies."

The village elders gathered food, ropes, swords, and armor because, they agreed, the volunteers couldn't know what they would come upon nor how long the venture would take.

And so, the brave volunteers went forth into the forest maze in search of Skull. They weren't there long when they heard a mighty roar. Faith jumped back, as did the other five.

Right before their eyes stood Skull. But, surprisingly, Skull had tears in his eyes.

"Mighty dragon," Faith asked, "why are you crying?"

"I am crying," Skull said, "because you are the first living creatures I have seen in all my years in the maze. You are brave to come, if truth be told, to face the mage who has trapped me thus."

"Trapped you?" echoed the volunteers in unison. "What mage?"

"I am speaking of the one and only Mage of Antibion. All those living in your kingdom think a mage is a person of learning. That's true enough. But some mages learn and use what is mean and hateful. Such is the Mage of Antibion."

Faith spoke: "I have a grand solution, one that will help us both. You are in need of help to escape the maze, and we are in need of just one tooth—one tooth of yours."

With that, Skull began to gnaw on a nearby stone, with the hope of dislodging one mighty tooth. Slowly he worked at it, and while he did, the six brave volunteers began weaving a tree out of the rope the elders had gathered. Creatively, they spun a camouflage for Skull, and together they all headed back to Underville.

For a while everything seemed perfect. The spell worked. King Brawnwin survived. The Lombards rejoiced. Skull requested and received a name-change and was thereafter called Tearless Dragon of Underville— Tearless for short. Faith and her trusty volunteers brought Tearless into the fold, into the community of the Lombards.

But just when all seemed quiet, when Tearless was safe and free of worry, the Mage of Antibion returned under the cover of dusk. Coming in from the east and heading toward the setting sun, he stealthily flew through the undersky and called to the Lombards below: "I want my dragon back. I need him back!"

The characters discuss a plan to deal with their problem.

A twist in the plot leads toward a climax.

The Lombards looked up in sheer amazement, knowing what a mage could do. And, likewise, Prius, himself a mage, understood as well. Apprentice or not, Prius, was the one who had to act. And swiftly.

"I will take care of this," said Prius to the Lombards, as he flew to intercept the Mage of Antibion.

They were evenly matched, both outfitted with powerful wands, which they used like swords to ward off attacks and counter spells. The Mage of Antibion took the first initiative and cast a spell that would turn Prius into a cat. But mage that he was, Prius read the Mage of Antibion's mind and turned him into a mouse. The battle was now between Prius the Cat and Antibion the Mouse.

The battle might have ended right there, but just as Prius was about to capture Antibion, Antibion spoke: "Prius, before you eat me alive, you need to know that I have not always been mean and hateful. I am the victim of an enchantment put upon me thousands of years ago. The only way I could stay alive was to capture and keep a dragon within my reach. But if you will undo that enchantment, I will be free once again to be a kind and loving mage, one worthy of my title."

With that, Prius spoke in his usual kind manner: "Mage of Antibion, you have explained your situation, and in fairness, I must release you."

Both mages then turned themselves back into their original forms, and together they flew from the undersky back to Underville.

Once again, there was peace in the land. For the rest of time, Brawnwin ruled Underville with his usual compassion and fairness—always bolstered by his two loving subjects, Prius and the Mage of Antibion.

And, what about Tearless, you ask? Fear not. Tearless, Dragon of Underville, stands guard.

The climax features action, strategy, and dialogue.

Ending

The problem is resolved. Everyone is happy.

What Is a Fantasy?

A fantasy is a story in which something impossible is accepted as real. Our sample story features dragons, elves, wands, and a whole underground civilization.

Keep It Real ■ You might ask, "If it's impossible, how can I make my readers believe it?" Usually, readers are willing to pretend with the writer, as long as the characters' actions make sense within the story.

In our sample, the elves have a quest to undertake. Although their journey into the forest maze and their encounter with a dragon is entirely made up, it sounds believable. The elves' actions make sense because they are needed to solve the story's problem.

Gather Ideas ■ Ideas for fantasies can come from anywhere at any time. Most authors keep a notebook handy and write down ideas as they find them—a funny name, an unusual object, or a silly thought. Any one of these ideas can grow into a story in your imagination.

Ask "What If?" ■ Many fantasy stories explore "what if" questions. What if animals could talk? What if a rhinoceros wanted to become a tightrope walker? The author must then think about how this could work. What would happen first, second, and so on? How would other characters react? And before long a fantasy is born.

Once you have an idea, it's time to start writing. The next two pages show how to develop your fantasy idea step-by-step through the writing process.

Writing a Fantasy

Prewriting Planning Your Story

Invent Characters ■ Fantasy characters can be real people, talking animals, fire-belching dragons, or creatures you invent yourself. (Think of a main character and maybe one or two others.)

Express Yourself What are your characters' names? What do they look like? What do they like to do? What adventures have they had? Write about them and find out.

Create a Problem to Solve ■ Your main character may be searching for treasure, looking for the way back home, or trying to find the ingredients for a potion. The way your main character solves his or her problem is the plot, the main part of your story.

Find a Setting ■ Fantasy can take place anywhere, anytime—in your neighborhood or in a magical place. (Give sights, sounds, and smells so that your readers can see the setting in their minds.)

Writing Developing the First Draft

Get Started ■ Begin your story by introducing the main character or describing the setting. Or begin in the middle of the action—two characters arguing, a violent storm, a narrow escape. However you start, the beginning must lead to the story's main problem.

Keep It Going ■ As you continue, try to make the main character's life more and more difficult because of the problem. Include lots of dialogue and add complications. (See page 144.) This will keep your readers interested.

Stop When You Get to the End ■ When the problem is solved, you've reached the end of your story. Wrap things up as cleverly and quickly as you can. Sometimes writers go on and on and write too much.

Revising Improving Your Writing

Let It Sit ■ After you've written your story, let it sit for a while. Then, when you read it again, try pretending someone else wrote it, and see what you think.

Make It Believable ■ Remember that your story should be imaginary and believable. Ask, "Do my characters act in a way that fits the story? Do the actions make sense in the setting?"

Share Your First Draft ■ Listen carefully to the questions your friends ask after reading or listening to your story. One reader may be confused by something you have said. Another may think that part of your story is too unbelievable. Use their questions and comments to make your story better.

Tip If you don't like the ending, try removing the last sentence or paragraph. See if your story seems complete without it.

Editing and Proofreading Polishing Your Writing

Edit ■ After making the big changes, take a close look at the specific words and sentences in your story. Have you picked the best words to describe the setting, characters, and action? Are your sentences complete and clear? Have you checked for grammar, punctuation, capitalization, and spelling? (See page 66.)

Proofread ■ Compose a neat final copy of your fantasy. Then check it for errors before sharing it. (Use the editing and proofreading checklist on page 66 to be sure you've thought of everything.)

Express Yourself Writing and reading fantasies can be enjoyable. Here are some favorite authors of fantasy for young people: Joanna Cole, Roald Dahl, Kenneth Graham, Margaret Mahy, Cynthia Rylant, and C. S. Lewis.

Writing Dialogue

Dialogue is one of a story writer's most important tools. A well-written conversation between characters can draw readers directly into the action.

Without Dialogue

The Lombards wondered why the mage didn't go get the dragon and why he needed a tooth. Prius said he needed the tooth for a spell to save the king, and that he was the only one who could cast the spell, so they couldn't do without him.

With Dialogue

"Why us and not you?" cried the Lombards. "You are a mage—a man of great learning and power!"

"And why a tooth?" a man called out.

"My fellow Lombards," Prius said kindly, "had I trained a successor to my status as mage, I would have surely done the deed, but you cannot afford to lose me just yet. And the tooth I spoke of? I will tell you. A dragon's tooth is the last ingredient I need to make the potion that will heal our king, Brawnwin," answered Prius.

Punctuating Dialogue

Notice how the dialogue in the story "Into the Maze" is punctuated. The following rules make it clear who's talking, so readers don't get confused.

- The speaker's words are in quotation marks.
- The speaker's words are often identified by terms like *said* and *asked*.
- Each new speaker begins a new paragraph.
- Commas and periods after quoted material go inside the quotation marks.

Writing Realistic Stories

Amanda Lowe is 10 years old. She has three big brothers who love to tease her. Her wildly curling red hair matches her fiery temper. Amanda sounds like a real person, but she isn't. She is a character in Cassie Johnson's realistic story.

Realistic stories are part real and part made-up. They usually have characters, like Amanda, who remind you of people you know. These characters have realistic problems to solve. For example, Amanda has a problem with her brothers, which is a believable problem for a 10-year-old girl. Made-up details and events add suspense or humor to the story. This chapter will help you write strong realistic stories of your own.

What's Ahead

- Writing Realistic Stories
- Sample Realistic Story

Writing Realistic Stories

Before you can write your story, you need a main character who seems real, with a believable problem to solve.

Prewriting Planning Your Story

Create a Character ■ Choose three people you know and make a list or chart of their looks and habits. Pick details from each person's list to create a main character. The chart below is one way Cassie Johnson could have made up her character Amanda.

Name	Hair	Age	Wears	Mood	Likes	Dislikes
Su	straight black	10	glasses	stubborn	gum	swimming
Emma	short blond	9	jewelry	playful	sports	brothers
Katie	curly red	11	black shoes	fiery	TV	homework
Amanda	curly red	10	glasses	fiery	sports	brothers

Find a Real Problem ■ Your character needs a problem to solve. Think of problems that you and your friends know about—problems at school, with friends, with family, or in the neighborhood. List several problems for each category. Then decide which problem you want your character to solve.

> **School:** locker always jams, trouble with math class
> **Friends:** friend told my secret, friend embarrassed me
> **Family:** my brothers bug me, sister uses my skates
> **Neighborhood:** nowhere to ride my bike, lots of litter
>
> Amanda's Problem: My brothers bug me.

Create a Collection Sheet ■ A collection sheet like the one below can help you keep track of your planning ideas. You don't need to have all five story parts planned before writing your story. You may even want to make changes to the collection sheet as you write. Check your sheet after you complete your first draft, though, to see if you included your most important ideas.

Collection Sheet

Characters:
(List the main character first. How old are your characters, and what are their names? How do they look, speak, and act?)

Setting:
(Describe where and when your story takes place.)

Problem:
(What problem does the main character need to solve?)

Story Scenes:
(List some actions involving the main character. Also consider how he or she will solve the problem.)

Purpose:
(Will your story be serious, surprising, scary, funny, or sad? One specific feeling can guide your writing.)

Express Yourself Share your ideas with several classmates before writing your first draft. Ask them for their suggestions. Do the same thing after writing your first draft.

Writing **Developing the First Draft**

You can begin a story in many different ways. You can start out with a conversation, have a character doing something, or describe the setting. However you begin, make it realistic and interesting.

Start Your Story ■ Here are five ways to begin a story.

Begin with action or dialogue:
"Look what they did to my in-line skates!" Amanda shouted.

Ask a question:
How did I get stuck with three big brothers?

Describe the setting:
Our small white house on Evergreen Street looks completely normal from the outside.

Begin with background information:
My three brothers taught me how to shoot baskets. Now I'm a better shooter than they realize.

Have the main character introduce himself or herself:
I'm Amanda Lowe, little sister to Josh, Eric, and Matt.

Keep Your Story Going ■ Don't let your character solve the problem too easily. Try two or more actions before coming up with a final solution.

Solution 1: Throw a tantrum.

Solution 2: Talk to someone.

Solution 3: Make a plan to deal with the problem.

End Your Story ■ Give your story a realistic ending—your character may not be happy with his or her solution, someone else may have solved the problem, or the problem may still be there. However you end your story, make it believable.

Most people change as they deal with a problem, so you should show how your character changes by the end of the story.

Revising Improving Your Writing

Review Your Work ■ Review your first draft to be sure that the characters' words and actions make sense. Also check the length of your story—is it too short or too long? If some parts seem boring, change them or take them out. If something seems to happen too quickly, slow the pace of your story by adding to it.

Add Life to Your Story ■ If your story needs a little zip, try adding a few details, some dialogue, or more action.

- **Use specific details.** What interesting sights, sounds, smells, or feelings could you add?

- **Use interesting dialogue.** Dialogue shows how your characters feel. Where in the story could you have your characters talk to each other?

- **Use believable action.** There's nothing like a little action or suspense to keep a story exciting. What could you have your characters do?

Editing and Proofreading

Read Your Story ■ After making changes in your story, have a friend read it back to you. Is it smooth and clear from start to finish?

Check for Errors ■ Finally, check for spelling, punctuation, and grammar errors. Make a neat final copy of your story and proofread it before sharing it with your classmates. If you have time, divide the story into parts, illustrate the pages, and bind them into a book.

Tip   You can use the checklist on page 66 to make sure you've checked for every possible error.

Sample Realistic Story

You have seen how Cassie Johnson created parts of her story. Now read "Amanda Stands Tall" and see how all the parts fit together.

Amanda Stands Tall

Beginning
Amanda introduces herself and her problem.

I'm Amanda Lowe, little sister to Josh, Eric, and Matt. It's tough to have three big brothers. The day they took the rollers off my in-line skates to build their go-cart, I was steamed.

When I told my dad what happened, he grounded my brothers for two days. Then they didn't bug me for one whole week! That's when I found the rubber spiders in my shoes.

Middle
Amanda tries different solutions.

Well, I had to think of a way to stop their teasing once and for all. No one except my friend Anya knew how good I was at shooting baskets. So, I said, "Who wants to play a game of HORSE?"

"I do!" Josh, Eric, and Matt all yelled at once.

I said, "Okay, if I win, you have to stop teasing me forever."

The game started. Matt and Josh got out quickly. It was showdown time with Eric. The game was tied at HORS. I dribbled to the basket with my right hand, spun, and shot with my left hand. Eric was right-handed. I knew he'd have trouble. He drove to the basket, spun, and shot. The ball went in . . . and then spun out.

Ending
Amanda finally solves her problem.

"Yes!" I yelled. "I win. And if you back out of our deal, here's a surprise." Just then Anya came out of her hiding spot with the video camera. "If you guys give me any trouble, I'll show this video to the world!"

Writing Stories from History

Would you like to roam the Wild West? Would you like to meet Abraham Lincoln? Would you like to walk on the moon?

Well, by simply writing a historical story, you can do any of these things. A historical story is a time machine that takes you wherever you want to go. Some stories retell historical events the way they happened. Other stories ask *what if* and tell what could have happened. Whatever type of historical story you plan to write, this chapter will give you the tips you need to make it come alive!

What's Ahead

- Planning Your Story
- Writing Your First Draft
- Revising and Editing

Writing a Historical Story

Prewriting Planning Your Story

Get Historical ■ A historical story brings a time, a person, or an event to life. You may write about a real person . . . or create a character who takes part in a real event. Think of an interesting time in history and journey there in your mind. Who would you be? What would you be doing? Would you change history? As you consider these questions, ideas for your story may start to form.

List Ideas ■ Make a list of historical times, places, events, or people that come to mind. Here are some ideas:

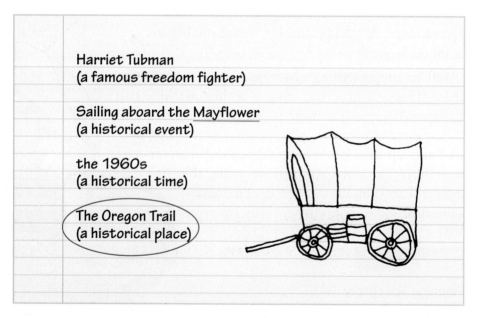

Harriet Tubman
(a famous freedom fighter)

Sailing aboard the Mayflower
(a historical event)

the 1960s
(a historical time)

The Oregon Trail
(a historical place)

Choose a Subject ■ Look over your list and circle the idea that interests you the most. This idea will be the starting point for your story. Write freely for 3–5 minutes about your subject. Write down everything you know about your subject. This will show you what already know and what you still need to find out.

Gather Facts ■ To begin your gathering, look in your history book to find facts about your subject. Then check other reference books, search the Internet, or watch a video. Ask your teacher or librarian for help. Carefully write down all the important facts and figures you discover.

The facts below were collected for a story about the Oregon Trail. Facts give you background information and interesting details you can use in your story. Remember, though, you don't need to use every fact in your story.

Facts About the Oregon Trail

- 400,000 people followed the trail from 1841 to 1869.

- It was hard to keep bugs and dirt out of food.

- Thousands of pioneers carved their names at Register Cliff.

- A family of four needed 1,000 pounds of food for the trip.

- The 2,000-mile trip took 4 to 6 months.

- Oxen pulled the wagons at about 2 miles per hour.

- Wagons carried supplies, so people walked, often without shoes.

- Because wagons started out overloaded, people left things along the trail.

- Wood was scarce, so buffalo chips were used as fuel.

- Wagons would go about 15 miles each day.

Identify Your Story Elements ■ After collecting a good number of facts, it's time to plan the basic elements of your story. You can begin by identifying the characters, the setting, and the action. A collection sheet like the one below can help you keep track of all these elements. Use your sheet as you write, but feel free to make changes as your story develops.

Collection Sheet

Characters:
(Decide how each character will look, speak, and act. Keep the time period of your story in mind at all times!)

Setting:
(Describe the time and place of your story. Keep the setting historically accurate.)

Main Action:
(What action or event will your character participate in? The details in this part may or may not be true, but they must be believable. The main action should include a problem to be solved.)

Story Scenes:
(What things will your character be doing in this story: eating, hunting, exploring?)

Purpose:
(Decide on a form—you may use the basic story form or try something different, like diary entries or a series of letters.)

Tip You could also collect information by answering these basic questions: Who? What? Where? When? Why? Why not? What if? How?

Writing Developing Your First Draft

Begin Your Story ■ Get your readers interested by introducing your characters and the historical event right away. Begin with dialogue, action, or a lively description. Here's how Rashon, a student writer, began his story:

> As the bright sun rose above the prairie, there were wagons everywhere. My hands shook as I helped Pa yoke the oxen. Ma packed away the last of the dishes, food, and supplies. Pa asked if everybody was ready. Just then we heard a gunshot. It was the signal to begin our journey.
>
> Pa cracked the reins, and the wagon lurched forward. Our 2,000-mile journey had begun.
>
> "Oregon, here we come!" I shouted and started walking.

Keep Your Story Going ■ Once you begin the main action, keep your characters moving forward with different actions and scenes. Add background facts where they fit. Here's a scene from the middle of Rashon's story:

> "Don't climb up so high, Jessie," Eliza warned.
> "I'm going to carve my name in Register Cliff," I replied.
> "Do it down here with all the other names," Eliza pleaded.
> "I could, but it wouldn't be as much fun," I told her.
> Just then a rock gave out beneath me. I began sliding. Eliza screamed. I grabbed a branch and hung on tight. I reached for another rock and pulled myself up on the cliff. I lay there for a minute and then stood up.
>
> When I looked back over the trail, I could see the Platte River below and majestic mountains stretching for miles in the distance. I took out my knife and carved my name in the sandstone cliff, higher than anyone else.

End Your Story ■ Don't drag your story out. End it soon after the main action is completed or the problem is addressed for good. Remember that not every story has to have a happy ending. Here's how Rashon ended his story:

> It was November. We had walked across the prairie and struggled over the mountains. Now we were finally in Oregon, but our journey wasn't over. We built a raft to float down the Columbia River to our new home. The river looked scary, but at least we didn't have to walk anymore. We all crowded onto the raft and huddled in the center.
>
> After we shoved off, the raft was soon crashing through whirlpools and rapids. White water swirled around us. Pa rested on his oars, and the swift currents carried us along. Finally, the roaring river slowed down, and our raft floated to a canoe landing. We had finally arrived at our new home.

Revising and Editing Improving Your Draft

Use a Checklist ■ Use the questions below as a guide for revising your story. (See page 66 for an editing and proofreading checklist.)

___ Is the story based on historical fact?
___ Do the characters' words and actions make sense for that historical time? (George Washington wouldn't look at a wristwatch and say, "Like, let's get to the mall, dudes.")
___ Does the story build interest? (The main character should complete some important action or solve a problem in the story.)
___ Does the story end in a logical, satisfying way?

Responding to Narrative Prompts

How do you know if you are doing a good job writing narratives? One way teachers test writing is by having you respond to a prompt. A prompt is a writing assignment that you do in a testing situation, so you need to do your best writing in a limited amount of time.

This chapter will lead you through the process of responding to a narrative writing prompt. The tips and pointers will help you do your best writing when you don't have lot of time to develop your ideas.

What's Ahead

- Writing a Narrative Response
- Sample Prompt and Response
- Responding Review

Writing a Narrative Response

When you are taking an important test, you may be asked to create a piece of narrative writing in a short period of time. The task begins with a narrative writing prompt. Make sure you analyze it closely before you begin planning your writing.

Prewriting Analyzing the Prompt

A prompt is a set of directions that tells you several different things. Most prompts will tell you what to write about, who your reader will be, and what the overall goal or purpose is. Therefore, you need to read the prompt very carefully to ensure that you follow all the directions.

You can use the **PAST** questions listed below to make sure you understand what is expected of you.

Purpose: *Why am I writing? What is my goal?* A narrative writing prompt will ask you to share a story, most likely from your own life.

Audience: *Who am I writing for?* Some prompts will identify a specific audience: "Pretend you are telling the story to an older relative." Other prompts do not indicate an audience, so you can just assume the testers or your teacher is the audience.

Subject: *What is the subject of my writing?* The prompt will name the general subject you should write about in your narrative. It may also ask you to include specific narrative elements, such as dialogue and specific details.

Type: *What type of writing should I do?* Most often the prompt will tell you what form of writing to create (a personal narrative, a realistic story, a fantasy, or some other form).

Sample Narrative Prompt

Everyone is scared of something, but certain experiences help us overcome our fears. Think about a moment in your life when you overcame a fear. Recreate the experience in a personal narrative. Organize your details in the order in which they happened (time order). Include action, dialogue, and your own thoughts and feelings. Show how you overcame your fear.

Purpose: Share a story from my life

Audience: General audience

Subject: A time when I overcame a fear

Type: Personal narrative

Sample Narrative Response

A Long Slide Down

Beginning
The first paragraph tells what the narrative will be about.

When Andre invited me to the water park, I wasn't sure I wanted to go. I was afraid of heights, and carnival rides made me dizzy.

"Water slides are different. They are smoother and so much fun!" said Andre.

Even though I thought I would hate it, I agreed to tag along.

Middle
Each middle paragraph gives details about the experience in time order.

We arrived at the park and headed straight for the wave pool. The wave pool is this giant swimming pool that creates waves, so it seems like you're in the ocean. This isn't so bad, I thought. At least we were not up too high. I dove into the waves and splashed around.

"Can we stay here all day?" I asked.

"No way. It's time to hit the slides," said Andre.

We left the wave pool, and Andre let me know

we were headed for "The Plunge." The next thing I knew, I was standing at stairs that led to the tallest water slide I had ever seen in my life.

"I'm just going to stay here," I told Andre. But he wouldn't go without me, so I had to follow him up the stairs.

Up and up we climbed. Finally, we reached a line of kids at the top. The wind blew hard and whistled like my dad. I kept telling myself not to look down. But when we reached the mouth of the slide, I made a huge mistake and looked down.

Andre must have seen my face go white, because he said I didn't look so good. "I'll go first, and you'll see it's safe," he said.

Before I knew it, Andre shot down the slide, and it was my turn. I wanted to turn around. That's when I realized that the fastest way to get to the ground was down the slide. So I sat down in the mouth of the slide and closed my eyes. The lifeguard gave me a push, and away I went.

I sped straight down, took one sharp turn, and splashed into a pool of water. When I floated to the top, I was smiling. "That was awesome!" I shouted. That's when I realized I loved water rides. To my surprise, heights didn't seem so scary anymore.

Dialogue helps the experience come alive.

The writer shares his thoughts during the experience.

Ending
The final paragraph shows how the experience ends and what the writer learns from it.

Prewriting Planning Your Response

Find a Specific Focus ■ Even though the prompt will tell you what the general subject is, you will still have to narrow your focus to one specific topic or event to write about. You can use this formula to find a specific focus to write about.

The Subject		**Your Specific Story**		**A Focused Subject**
A time when you overcame a fear	**+**	A trip to the water park with Andre	**=**	How a trip to a water park helped me overcome my fear of heights

Create a Quick Time Line ■ Once you decide on a focus, you need to think about and list (very quickly) the important things that happened during your story. Make sure the details are arranged in the order in which they happened.

> 1. Andre invites me to the water park.
> 2. We go to the wave pool.
> 3. He convinces me to go to The Plunge.
> 4. I get scared near the top.
> 5. I work up the courage to go down.
> 6. I slide down and learn it's not so scary.

Think About Your Time ■ You have only a certain amount of time to finish your writing, so watch the time closely. Sometimes your teacher will keep track of time for everyone, but not always. So keep track of time. Give yourself enough time to write about all the important parts of your experience.

Writing Developing Your Response

Once you've examined the prompt and created a brief time line, you should be ready to write.

Beginning ■ Introduce what the narrative will be about by starting right with the action.

Middle ■ Share events in time order. Refer to your time line as you write, but feel free to add other important details as you tell your story. Include the following elements:

- **Actions:** Show what people did during the experience. (Use active verbs.)

- **Dialogue:** Tell what people said during the experience. (Use quotation marks to indicate the speaker's words.)

- **Thoughts and feelings:** Give the inner thoughts and feelings you had while the event was happening.

Ending ■ The ending should describe how the experience concluded and what you learned from it.

Revising Improving Your Response

To create the best response, save time to check your work and change anything that isn't clear. Ask yourself these questions:

___ Does my beginning introduce what the narrative will be about?

___ Does the middle describe actions in time order?

___ Do I include enough details to recreate the experience?

___ Do I include dialogue and thought details?

___ Does the ending share what I learned?

Editing and Proofreading Polishing Your Response

Check for Careless Errors ■ Set aside a few minutes to look for errors such as missing words, run-on sentences, and incorrect punctuation.

Responding Review

This quick summary can help you respond to a narrative prompt.

1. **Analyze the prompt.** Use the **PAST** questions.

   > **Purpose:** *What is the purpose of my writing?*
   > **Audience:** *Who will I be writing to?*
   > **Subject:** *What is the prompt asking me to write about?*
   > **Type:** *What form will my writing take?*

2. **Plan your response.** Use the first 5 minutes for planning and the last 5 minutes for revising and editing. List your details and arrange them in time order.

3. **Begin well.** Try to start in the middle of the action. Don't do a lot of explaining.

4. **Describe the experience in the middle paragraphs.** Start each paragraph with the next part of the story according to time order. Include specific details, dialogue, and your thoughts and feelings.

5. **End in a meaningful way.** Tell how the story ended, and share something you learned from it.

6. **Revise your response using the PAST questions as a guide.** Make sure your writing is clear and complete.

7. **Edit your response.** Check for punctuation, capitalization, spelling, and grammar errors.

 Tip

Remember to have your characters talk to one another. Using dialogue will make your story more interesting and life-like.

Explanatory Writing

Writing Explanatory Essays

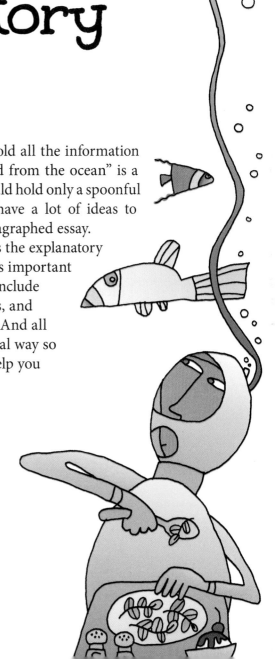

Sometimes one paragraph can't hold all the information you want to share. For example, "food from the ocean" is a very large topic, and one paragraph could hold only a spoonful of information about it. When you have a lot of ideas to present, you need to write a multi-paragraphed essay.

The most common type of essay is the explanatory essay. Like a classroom report, it shares important information about a subject. It might include facts, definitions, quotations, examples, and other information related to the topic. And all the information is organized in a logical way so it is easy to follow. This chapter will help you write an effective explanatory essay.

What's Ahead

- Sample Explanatory Essay
- Building an Essay
- Writing an Explanatory Essay
- Possible Writing Topics

Sample Explanatory Essay

The following explanatory essay was written by Keesha Brooks. She choose the ocean as her general subject, and then narrowed her topic to the ocean as a source of food for people around the globe. Notice how each new paragraph covers something different than the one before.

Still, all the paragraphs in Keesha's essay are about the ocean as a source of food. That makes her essay a good one for you to model when you write your own essay because all the information is unified.

Beginning

The focus statement (underlined) identifies the writing idea.

Middle

The first part is about the value of salt.

Food from the Ocean
by Keesha Brooks

When you look at a globe, you will see five different oceans: the Atlantic, the Pacific, the Indian, the Arctic, and the Southern. However, if you look closer, you will see that these oceans are connected. What we have on the Earth is actually one big ocean. This one big ocean provides salt and food for people all over the world.

First of all, salt is one of Earth's most important minerals. It comes from the rocks in the ocean and can be found nearly everywhere in the world. As the waves, tides, and currents beat on the rocks, salt is broken loose and dissolved into the water. The salt in the ocean is the same kind of salt you put on your popcorn and French fries. Salt is also used to preserve foods in places where there are no refrigerators.

Fish and shellfish are also important food sources.

In addition to salt, the ocean is home to countless fish and shellfish. Some of the most popular fish are cod, tuna, and sea bass. But you can find different kinds of fish in nearly every country in the world. The same thing is true for crustaceans and shellfish. Some parts of the world have lots of shrimp, while other parts have more lobster and crab. And oysters and clams can be found on the menu in nearly every country in the world.

A final source of food is a bit unusual.

Finally, did you know that you have probably eaten seaweed and didn't even know it? Seaweed can be found in certain kinds of ice cream and hot fudge. It helps to make them smooth and easy to eat. In some parts of the world, seaweed is eaten as a vegetable. It can be served with rice or in stir-fried foods.

Ending
The last paragraph ties everything together.

So even if you have never been to an ocean, the ocean has come to you. Maybe you tasted it on a bowl of popcorn, have eaten it as a fish dinner, or enjoyed it on top of a hot fudge sundae. The ocean is part of all of our lives in different ways. But most important of all, the ocean is a major source of food for the entire world.

Note Remember, the purpose of an explanatory essay is to inform your readers about a specific subject and to get them interested in it.

Building an Essay

The graphic shown below will give you a good picture of how the sample essay "Food from the Ocean" was built. Each paragraph introduces a new idea, but all of the ideas are about the same topic.

You'll also see that Keesha used transitions to link her main points together from one paragraph to the next: *First of all . . . In addition . . . Finally. . . .* When you link your paragraphs together in this way, readers can easily follow along—which makes your essay better.

Food from the Ocean

Beginning

This one big ocean provides salt and food for people all over the world.

Middle

First of all, salt is one of the Earth's most important minerals.

In addition to salt, the ocean is also home to countless fish and shellfish.

Finally, did you know that you have probably eaten seaweed and didn't even know it?

Ending

So even if you have never been to an ocean, the ocean has come to you.

Writing an Explanatory Essay

Now that you understand the "big picture" of how an essay works, you need to look more closely at each step in the process.

`Prewriting` **Planning Your Essay**

Subject ■ First, choose a general subject that interests you—let's say it's *the ocean*. You then need to narrow your subject to a more specific topic, such as *food from the ocean*.

Audience ■ You also need to ask yourself who will be reading your essay: your classmates, a friend online, your family, or someone else?

Voice ■ Next, think about your *voice*. In almost all cases, you will want to sound serious—but interesting. Your voice should match your subject and purpose (to explain).

`Prewriting` **Gathering Details**

Explore Your Topic ■ Begin gathering details by listing everything you already know about the subject. Then search books, magazine, and the Internet for additional details.

Focus Your Ideas ■ Examine all your details and decide which part of your topic you want to focus on. Then write a *focus statement* that tells exactly what you are going to be writing about. (This is sometimes called a *thesis statement*.)

Your focus statement should state the main point of your essay. You can use the following formula to write this statement:

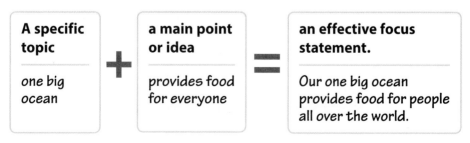

A specific topic		a main point or idea		an effective focus statement.
one big ocean	**+**	provides food for everyone	**=**	Our one big ocean provides food for people all over the world.

Prewriting Organizing Your Details

Make a List ■ Before you write your essay, identify the details that support your focus and put them in the right order. You can do so by making a numbered list.

1. There are five different oceans in the world.
2. It provides food for people all over the world.
3. The ocean is a source of salt, a valuable mineral.
4. The ocean is home to countless fish and shellfish.
5. Even seaweed is used to create foods.
6. The ocean is part of everyone's life.

Make an Outline ■ Your teacher may ask you to use an outline instead of a list. In that case, you need to decide which details will be going in the first paragraph, the second paragraph, and so on. See the sample below.

I. There are five different oceans in the world.
   A. All the oceans are connected.
   B. The ocean provides food for the world.
II. The ocean is a major source of salt.
   A. Salt is one of Earth's most important minerals.
   B. Salt is used to flavor and preserve foods.
III. The ocean is home to countless fish and shellfish.
   A. Popular fish are cod, tuna, and sea bass.
   B. There are lots of shrimp, lobster, and crab as well.
IV. Seaweed can also be used as food.
   A. Seaweed is used in certain kinds of ice cream
      and hot fudge.
   B. Seaweed can also be eaten as a vegetable.
V. The ocean touches everyone.
   A. It is part of all of our lives but in different ways.
   B. Most important of all, it is a major source of
      food for the world.

Writing Developing Your First Draft

After you have organized all your details, you're ready to write your essay. Use your list or outline and follow the suggestions below.

Beginning ■ Your first paragraph should say something interesting or surprising about your subject to get the readers involved. It should also include a focus statement that names the main idea of your essay.

Middle ■ The middle paragraphs should include lots of facts, figures, and examples that support your focus sentence. Each paragraph should develop a key supporting detail about the topic. Consider adding a drawing or photograph if that would make part of your explanation easier to follow.

Ending ■ The final paragraph should summarize the main points covered in the essay. It should also remind the readers of the importance of the topic and help them understand it better.

Revising and Editing Improving Your Essay

Answer the following questions to help you improve your first draft. (You can also use the checklist on page 66 to help you edit and proofread your essay.)

> ___ Does the beginning hook the reader?
> ___ Does the focus statement make the main idea clear?
> ___ Do details in the middle explain the focus statement?
> ___ Does the voice sound interested and knowledgeable?
> ___ Does the ending remind readers of the importance of the topic?

Publishing Sharing Your Essay

When you've finished all your revising and editing, write a final copy to share—one that looks good and is free of errors.

Possible Writing Topics

Explanatory writing gives information in an interesting way. You can write explanatory essays about all kinds of amazing things. Here are some ideas to get you going.

Animals ■ Write about your favorite type of pet. Write about the kind of wild animal you most admire. Explain how animals like horses and oxen work for people. Describe a favorite breed of dog. Explain how ants or bees work together.

Machines ■ Write about the different kinds of motorcycles. Explain how a steam locomotive works. Name and explain the parts of a light bulb. Explain how a simple machine like a lever or pulley works. Draw and describe how a catapult flings giant stones.

Games ■ Explain the rules of your favorite party game. Explain how to play different types of board games. Give specific strategies for beating someone in your favorite video game. Write about a game played by ancient Egyptians or Romans. Describe a jump-rope game.

Places ■ Name a country you would like to visit and explain why it is so interesting. Describe your favorite places in your town or city. Write about an important location in your school, such as the cafeteria, the music room, or the gymnasium.

Holidays ■ Describe the parts of a perfect birthday celebration. Explain a special festival in your town or city. Tell about the different types of things you see in a parade. Explain to a person from another country how we celebrate a specific holiday.

Note ▪ Think about anything you need to live—energy, friends, education, art, science, water, food, clothing . . . Each of these is a general subject that you can use as a starting point to find a specific topic to explain.

Writing Process Essays

A process is a series of steps for getting something done. Tying your shoes is an easy process. Baking a cake is a more challenging one.

What processes do you know well? Which of them could you explain to someone else?

When you write a process essay, you are explaining how to do something or how something works. Each paragraph in the essay focuses on a step in the process. The sentences in each paragraph follow time order, leading the reader through the process from start to finish.

The bottom line: Process writing is an important form of informational writing because it both explains and instructs.

What's Ahead

- Sample Process Essay
- Prewriting
- Writing the First Draft
- Revising to Elaborate
- Editing and Proofreading

Sample **Process Essay**

The following process essay was written by Gene Nelson. Gene chose food as his general subject, and then selected making a homemade pizza as his specific topic. Notice how each paragraph focuses on a step in the process. Also notice that the sentences in each paragraph follow time order, going from start to finish.

Beginning
The first paragraph introduces the topic (underlined).

Middle
Each middle paragraph covers a step in the process.

How to Make a Pizza

I'm not much for baking or cooking or anything like that. But I do have one thing I really like to make in the kitchen—and that's homemade pizza. So I'd like to explain to you how to make a pizza from scratch in less than an hour.

Before you begin, you will need to gather all of the ingredients. For most pizzas, that means you'll need ingredients for the crust, the sauce, and the toppings. If you look at your recipe, you'll see exactly what you need for the crust. The sauce can be any kind of tomato sauce you want, and the same thing is true for the toppings. You can use whatever toppings you want, from peppers to pineapple and anything in between.

The first thing you need to do is make is the crust. That means you have to add the ingredients—including warm water, yeast, and flour—in a bowl and mix them. Once everything is mixed together, you need to "knead" the dough. This means pulling and stretching it. Then form a firm ball and let it rest.

Specific examples and details are included in each paragraph.

Next, you need to put the crust on the pizza pan. Spread corn meal on the pan so that the crust doesn't stick. Once that's done, you're ready to stretch the dough out so that it covers the whole pan. Be sure to push it firmly into the edges so that it doesn't shrink when it's baked.

Then it's time to add the sauce and toppings. Spread the tomato sauce over the entire crust with a ladle. Next, sprinkle mozzarella cheese on top of the sauce and add whatever toppings you want. You can even add some of the toppings to half the pizza and different toppings to the other half.

The pizza is finally ready to put in the preheated oven. Make sure to turn the temperature to the correct setting, and set the timer to the time listed in the recipe (usually about 10 minutes). Check the pizza from time to time, but don't open the oven door unless you have to. When the pizza is golden brown, it is ready to take out of the oven.

Remove the pizza from the oven and prepare it for serving. Be sure to let it sit for a minute or two before you do anything. This allows everything to settle down into a solid pizza pie. Then slice the pizza with a pizza cutter and serve it.

Ending
The last paragraph sums up the process and gives you the result.

So there you have it: a homemade pizza in less than an hour. And if you followed the directions carefully, you will have a delicious pizza to enjoy. What could be better than that?

Writing a Process Essay

Prewriting *Selecting a Topic*

Most things don't happen all at once. They take time, and they usually follow certain steps from start to finish. Even something as simple as shooting a free throw.

1. Stand at the free-throw line.
2. Get the ball from the ref.
3. Dribble the ball, and take a deep breath.
4. Focus on the basket and shoot the ball.
5. If you make the first one, repeat the process.

Think of a process that you can do, or one that you can explain well. You might begin by making a list of all the possible topics. You can then take some time to think about each one and even make a quick list of what the process would be. That will make it easier to choose the best one.

 Tip

One way to find a topic is to use a list of verbs like the one below.

How to ... *fix* ... *clean* ... *build* ... *throw* ... *grow* ... *play* ... *make* ...

Then add whatever process comes to mind when you think of each verb.

How to make ... *a pizza* ... *a cake* ... *a necklace* ... *a music video* ... *a friend* ...

Prewriting *Gathering Details*

Begin gathering details by listing everything you already know about the topic. Then search books, magazines, and the Internet to fill in any gaps. Even if you think you know how to do something, you'll learn even more about the process by doing a little research. That will make your job easier and your essay more complete.

Prewriting *Organizing Your Details*

After you've chosen a topic and done a little research, you will want to make a list or a graphic organizer that covers each step in the process. Here's what a list and a time line for making a pizza might look like:

Numbered List

1. Check the recipe and gather all your ingredients.

2. Mix up the dough and roll out the crust.

3. Place the crust in the pizza pan.

4. Spread the tomato sauce over the crust and add the toppings.

5. Place the pizza in the oven and set the temperature.

6. Remove the pizza, slice, and serve.

Time Line

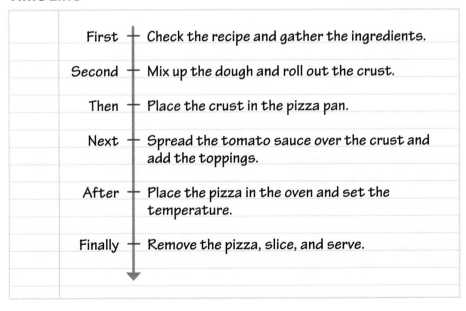

First — Check the recipe and gather the ingredients.

Second — Mix up the dough and roll out the crust.

Then — Place the crust in the pizza pan.

Next — Spread the tomato sauce over the crust and add the toppings.

After — Place the pizza in the oven and set the temperature.

Finally — Remove the pizza, slice, and serve.

Make an Outline

If your teacher asks you to do an outline instead of a list, you will need to decide which details are going to be in the first paragraph (I.), the second paragraph (II.), and so on. And remember, if you have an A, you should also have a B.

I. To start, gather all of the ingredients.
   A. Check the recipe for making the crust.
   B. Get tomato sauce and your favorite toppings.

II. The first thing you need to do is make the crust.
   A. Mix the flour and other ingredients together.
   B. "Knead" the dough until it's soft and stretchy.

III. Next, put the crust onto the pizza pan.
   A. Spread corn meal on the pan.
   B. Stretch the dough so that it covers the pan.

IV. Then it's time to add the toppings.
   A. Spread the tomato sauce over the entire crust.
   B. Sprinkle mozzarella cheese on top of the sauce.
   C. Add whatever toppings you like.

V. Place the pizza in the preheated oven.
   A. Make sure the temperature is at the correct setting.
   B. Set the timer and check the pizza as it bakes.

VI. Remove the pizza and prepare to serve it.
   A. Let it sit for a minute or two.
   B. Slice the pizza and serve it.

Note The outline shown above is a *sentence outline*. Your teacher may ask you to do a *topic outline*. That means instead of complete sentences you can use words or phrases to describe each step in the process.

Writing Developing the First Draft

Once you have organized your details, you are ready to write your first draft. Remember, it is just a "first" draft; you'll have a chance to revise it later.

Beginning ■ The first paragraph should introduce your topic and give the reader background information about it. You should also let your reader know the overall focus of the essay. Is the process easy, challenging, surprising, or something else?

Middle ■ In the middle paragraphs, you need to explain the steps in the process as clearly as you can. Add whatever details you need to make the process easy to follow and remember. (Consider adding a drawing or illustration if it would make the process clearer for the reader.)

Transitions

It's also important that your middle paragraphs are tied together effectively. That means using transition or linking words that make it clear to the reader where you are in the process. Here are some of the most common transitions used to show time or chronological order.

Time-Order Transitions		
first	continue by	before
next	afterward	when
then	last year	during
finally	a week later	after
to start	next month	
secondly	by the end	

Ending ■ Once you've explained all the steps in the process, it's time to bring your essay to a close. In the final paragraph, you should summarize the key steps in the process and let the reader know what the result of following these steps should be—what it will look, feel, taste, smell, or sound like.

Revising Elaborating Ideas

Once your first draft is finished, make sure that it is clear and complete. If you need more details, now is the time to add them. This is called *elaborating.* Consider using different kinds of details (facts, examples, explanations, etc.) to elaborate. Here is how Gene added an explanation in one paragraph to make a main point clearer.

Remove the pizza from the oven and prepare it for serving. This allows everything to settle down into a solid pizza pie. Be sure to let it sit for a minute or two before you do anything.∧

Then slice the pizza with a pizza cutter and serve it.

Revising and Editing Improving Your Essay

You can use the following questions as a general guide when you revise and edit your essay. (For a more detailed editing checklist, use the "Editing and Proofreading Checklist" on page 66.)

___ Do I introduce my topic and identify the focus of my essay?
___ Do I clearly explain each step in the process?
___ Does my voice sound confident and knowledgeable?
___ Do I bring everything to a logical conclusion in the final paragraph?
___ Have I checked for any missing words or confusing sentences?
___ Have I checked my essay for punctuation, grammar, and usage errors?

Publishing Sharing Your Essay

Once you have finished revising, editing, and proofreading your essay, you will want to make a final copy that is ready to share with others. Make sure that it is as error-free as possible and that any lists or illustrations are clear and in the right place.

Writing Comparison-Contrast Essays

When you are asked to write a comparison-contrast essay, you are being asked to explain how two topics (people, places, or things) are similar and how they are different. It's really very simple—and not so simple—at the same time.

When you consider the differences between two things— say two different sports—it may be quite clear how they are different. But when you look for similarities, it may not be as easy. Whatever the case, writing this type of essay requires special care because you are working with two topics. With the help of the guidelines in this chapter, you should be able to develop a strong comparison-contrast essay.

What's Ahead

- Sample Comparison-Contrast Essay
- Prewriting
- Writing the First Draft
- Revising
- Editing and Proofreading

Sample **The Comparison-Contrast Essay**

The following essay compares and contrasts two different types of bikes. The student knows quite a bit about both kinds and does a good job of pointing out their important similarities and differences.

Notice how the essay is organized: Each paragraph covers one of the differences between the bikes. This makes the essay easy to follow.

Tricks or Travel?

Beginning
The writer leads up to his focus statement (underlined).

Not all bikes are created equal. Some kids like BMX bikes best. Other kids prefer mountain bikes. It all depends on how you like to ride. <u>BMX bikes and mountain bikes are really different.</u>

The first major difference is the frame. BMX bikes have a short, light frame. This makes them easy to pick up and maneuver. It also allows them to get more air when riding off ramps. On the other hand, mountain bikes have a high, heavy frame. This makes them sturdy, even when riding over bumpy surfaces.

Middle
Each middle paragraph covers an important difference.

The bikes have different-sized wheels, too. BMX bikes have 20-inch wheels, which are short compared to most bike wheels. In contrast, mountain bikes have 26-inch wheels with thick tires. Bigger wheels give mountain bikes better balance than BMX bikes.

A final important difference is in the gears. BMX bikes typically have only one gear. They rely on momentum to gain speed. But mountain bikes have many different gears. Multiple gears allow mountain bikers to go up and down all sorts of surfaces more easily.

This paragraph explains the effects of the differences.

The contrasting frame, tires, and gears make for a different riding experience. Because they are short and light, BMX bikes are great for doing tricks and getting lots of air. The handlebars even spin all the way around. On the other hand, mountain bikes' heavy frames, big wheels, and many gears make them great for riding up and down hills and off the road.

Ending

The last paragraph connects the topics to the reader.

The bike type for you depends on how you like to ride. Do you like doing tricks? A BMX bike is built for you. Do you like traveling off road? A mountain bike is built for you. Try riding both types of bikes to experience the difference for yourself.

Writing a Comparison Essay

Prewriting Planning Your Essay

Most writing focuses on one topic, but comparison-contrast writing focuses on two topics. When you compare, you tell how the two topics are alike. When you contrast, you tell how the two topics are different. The topics you choose have to be similar to one another, but they also have to have some important differences in order to work for a comparison-contrast essay.

It's also important that you choose two topics that truly interest you. Consider people, places, things, animals, games, events, ideas—whatever comparison you think you and your reader would enjoy.

Sample Topics

Things: *A mountain bike and a BMX bike*
Events: *A tornado and a hurricane*
Games: *One video game and another video game*
Times: *One season of the year and another season*
People: *One soccer player and another player*
Animals: *One type of dog and another*

Prewriting *Choosing a Topic*

One way to choose a comparison-contrast topic is to use a simple chart like the one shown below. Draw as many lines or squares as you want and label each with people, places, things, animals, events, games, and so on. Then fill in the spaces with as many possible topics as you can think of.

People	Places	Things	Animals	Events

Prewriting Gathering and Organizing Details

Once you've chosen topics to write about, it's time to gather details about them. For this type of essay, it's a good idea to gather and organize your details at the same time. To do this, you can use one of two graphic organizers: a T-chart (see the sample below) or a Venn diagram (see page 385). Both organizers work well when you are gathering details about two subjects at the same time.

T-Chart

A T-chart is just what it sounds like—a chart that looks like a T.

1. List details about one of your subjects on the left side.

2. List details about the other subject on the right side.

3. Circle any important similarities.

4. Place check marks next to important differences.

Mountain Bike	BMX Bike
(Popular)	(Popular)
✓ High, heavy frame	✓ Low, light frame
✓ Hard to do tricks	✓ Easy to do tricks
Rides well on smooth surfaces	Rides well on smooth surfaces
✓ Rides well on bumpy surfaces	✓ Rides poorly on bumpy surface
✓ Thick tires with deep grooves	✓ Thin tires with smooth grooves
✓ Has gears	✓ Has no gears

Note As you list one detail on the left side, try to think of a similar (or different) detail to place on the right side. If there are no similarities, or no differences, you probably won't use that detail in your essay.

Writing Developing the First Draft

Beginning ■ With all beginnings, you need to introduce your topic and inform readers what you plan to focus on. You can also include a brief story about why this topic is important to you—if that would make the introduction more interesting.

Middle ■ In the middle part of a comparison-contrast essay, you must decide how to arrange your details so that they are easy to understand and interesting for the reader. There are three ways you can arrange your details in your middle paragraphs. Choose the arrangement that works best for your topic.

Arranging Your Details

1. You can explain all of your details about one of your subjects first, and then do the same with the other subject. In other words, you might write two or three paragraphs about one subject (Mountain bike) followed by two or three paragraphs about the other subject (BMX bike). This arrangement is called **subject-by-subject**.

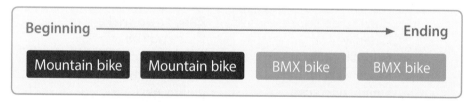

Beginning ———————————————→ Ending

Mountain bike Mountain bike BMX bike BMX bike

2. Or you can write about the similarities of both subjects before discussing the differences. In this case, you might have two or three paragraphs of similarities (between the two bikes) followed by two or three paragraphs of differences. This arrangement is called **similarities-and-differences**.

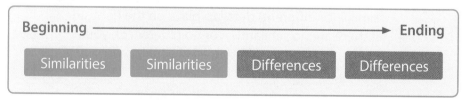

Beginning ———————————————→ Ending

Similarities Similarities Differences Differences

3. A third possibility is to write about one important detail for each subject before moving on to the next detail. In this arrangement, you would write one paragraph comparing and contrasting both subjects on the same detail (first, frames; then, wheels; and so on). This arrangement is called **point-by-point**.

Beginning ———————————————————→ Ending

| Frames | Wheels | Gears | Ride |

Using Transitions

It's also very important to tie your details (and your paragraphs) together as clearly and smoothly as possible. You can use the following transitions to do that.

Comparison and Contrast Transitions

Compare: *Both   Alike   Similar to   Like   Also*

Contrast: *Each   Different   However   Unlike   On the other hand*

Ending ■ You can end your essay by using one or more of the following strategies. The sample essay ends by connecting with readers and asking them which type of bike they might like to ride.

- ■ Restate your focus.
- ■ Offer a final comparison or contrast.
- ■ Connect with the reader.
- ■ Give a final summary or a closing thought.

Tip   It's important that you choose the best method of arranging your details. If one of the methods isn't working for you, try another one.

Revising Elaborating with Details

When you review your first draft, make sure that you have included enough detail to explain each topic equally. When he revised his essay, the writer added a detail about the mountain bike to make it equal to what he said about the BMX bike.

> BMX bikes have a short, light frame. This makes them easy
>
> to pick up and maneuver. It also allows them to get more air
>
> when riding off ramps. On the other hand, mountain bikes have
>
> a high, heavy frame. This makes them sturdy, even when riding
>
> over bumpy surfaces.

Revising Checking for Smoothness

The overall structure or flow of your essay is important. If things move along in a smooth, logical manner, the reader will be able to follow your ideas.

> ___ Do I introduce the topic and focus of my essay?
> ___ Do I tie my details (and paragraphs) together well using transitions and signal words?
> ___ Do I use different kinds of sentences to add variety and interest to my essay?
> ___ Does my voice sound confident and knowledgeable?
> ___ Do I end my essay with a summary or final thought?

Editing and Proofreading Polishing Your Essay

Once you have revised your essay, edit it for correctness. Also be sure to proofread your final copy. (You can use the "Editing and Proofreading Checklist" on page 66 for help.)

Responding to Explanatory Prompts

Many district and state tests ask you to respond to an explanatory writing prompt. An explanatory prompt asks you to write to explain or inform about a topic, and to do so in a limited amount of time. That can be challenging because you can't work like you normally do—spending as much time as you need from one step to another in the writing process.

This chapter gives you the tips and guidelines you need to form an effective response to an explanatory prompt.

What's Ahead

- Writing to an Explanatory Prompt
- Sample Explanatory Prompt
- Responding Review

Writing to an Explanatory Prompt

Responding to a prompt is different from other writing assignments because you don't have a lot of time to complete your work. So you have to know what you're doing and get right to work. To get started, you need to study the prompt.

Prewriting Analyzing the Prompt

A prompt gives you the basic directions for your writing. Most prompts—but not all—will tell you what to write about, who your reader will be, and what the overall goal or purpose is. Read the prompt very carefully to identify the parts of your writing task. You can also use the **PAST** questions listed below to identify these parts:

Purpose: *Why am I writing?* What is my goal? When you respond to an explanatory prompt, your goal is to explain or inform. Look for clues or key words (*compare, define, demonstrate*). These words can help you know how to develop your writing.

Audience: *Who will be reading my writing?* Look closely at the prompt to see who the reader will be (parent, classmate, principal). If the prompt doesn't say, the audience is probably the tester or your teacher.

Subject: *What am I supposed to write about?* The prompt will name a general subject, but you will need to identify a specific topic related to the subject.

Type: *What type or form of writing should you create (letter, essay, blog post)?* Make sure to organize your writing according to the form.

Sample Explanatory Prompt

In an essay, explain to new students how certain things are done at your school (fire drills, recess, clubs or sports teams, the lunchroom, the library). Choose three things you think any new student should know and explain how each one works.

Purpose: To explain

Audience: New students

Subject: Three things at school

Type: Essay

Sample Explanatory Response

Beginning
The first paragraph introduces the topic and focus (underlined).

Middle
Each middle paragraph explains a new thing every new student should know.

I am a student at Mitchell School, and I have been attending it since kindergarten. If you are a new student at our school, you will have a lot to learn. You will catch on to most things within a week or two, but there are three things you really need to know about our school.

First of all, you should know about recess because that's one of the great things about our school. Depending upon the weather, you will have two or three choices. You can choose to go to the library to look for books, but you have to stay there until recess is over. You can also go to the small gym where Mr. Phelps will have two or three activities to choose from. And, if the weather is good, you can go outside and use the playground equipment or play games with classmates.

Another thing you should know right away is how to manage the lunchroom. If you bring your

Transition words are used to tie everything together.

lunch, it's pretty simple. Just follow the crowd and pick out a place to sit down. If you are having hot lunch, you need to buy your ticket on Monday for the whole week. You can't buy a ticket for just one day—unless you forget to bring your lunch. And then you have to go to the principal's office to buy a ticket for that day. You can get in line with everyone else and grab a tray. Then just watch what everyone else is doing, and you'll be fine.

One more thing you will want to know is what clubs and sports we have at our school and how you can join them. Each club or sport meets after school, so you need to ask your teacher (or a classmate) where and when the one you're interested in meets. Most clubs have their first meeting in the library, and most sports meet for the first time in the small gym. Then they'll tell you where to meet after that.

Ending
The closing paragraph recaps the topic and shares a final point.

So those are three tips for you to start with. There's a lot more to know about our school, and you'll figure out most of those things on your own. Don't worry if you get a little confused. There's always someone around you can ask—especially your teacher. People here at Mitchell are very helpful.

Prewriting Planning Your Response

Find a Specific Focus ■ Even though the prompt may tell you what the general subject is, you may still have to narrow it down to a specific topic and focus. You can use this formula to find a specific focus:

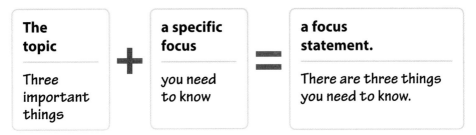

The topic	**a specific focus**	**a focus statement.**
Three important things	you need to know	There are three things you need to know.

List Your Details ■ Once you have a specific topic and focus, you need to list (very quickly) all of the things you may want to include in your response. (You don't have to write about every detail in your list.)

> • Which sports and clubs you can join.
> • Where to go and what to do during recess.
> • How the lunchroom routine works.

Arrange Your Details ■ Next, you need to choose the details you think will be the best to write about and arrange them in the best possible order.

> 1. First, you need to know where to go during our morning recess.
> 2. Then, you'll want to know how things work in the lunchroom.
> 3. Last, there are a number of clubs and sports teams you can join.

Think About the Time ■ You have only a certain amount of time to finish your writing, so watch the time closely. Sometimes your teacher will keep track of time for everyone, but not always. So pay attention!

Writing Developing Your Response

Once you've examined the prompt and made a brief list, you should be ready to write. Remember to stick to your plan as much as possible.

Beginning ■ In the beginning, you should tell the reader what you will be writing about—your topic and focus.

Middle ■ The middle part of your response should include the key points you want to make (*The things every new student should know,* for example). Try to put each of your main points in separate paragraphs. That way you can support each point one at a time and keep all the important details together.

Ending ■ In the final paragraph, you need to tie everything together and remind the reader why your topic is important.

Revising Improving Your Response

Remember that responding to a prompt is a way of measuring your writing skills, so you'll want to do your very best. This means you need to save some time to check everything over and change anything that isn't clear. Ask yourself these questions when you revise:

___ Does the beginning clearly state my topic and focus?
___ Does the middle explain the key points to support my focus?
___ Do I include enough details to make my points clear and interesting?
___ Does the ending offer a final, helpful thought to the reader?

Editing and Proofreading Polishing Your Response

Check for Careless Errors ■ Try to set aside some time to read through your response one last time—and to look for careless errors such as missing words, run-on sentences, and incorrect punctuation.

Responding Review

This quick summary can help you respond to an explanatory prompt.

1. **Analyze the prompt.** Use the **PAST** questions.

> **Purpose:** *What is the purpose of my writing?*
> **Audience:** *Who will read my writing?*
> **Subject:** *What is the prompt asking me to write about?*
> **Type:** *What form will my writing take?*

2. **Plan your response.** Use the first 5 minutes for planning and the last 5 minutes for revising and editing. List your details and arrange them quickly.

3. **Begin well.** Grab your reader's attention. Write sentences that lead to a focus statement that names your topic and specific focus.

4. **Support your ideas in middle paragraphs.** Start each paragraph with a main point. Support each point with steps or examples.

5. **End in a meaningful way.** State a final important idea. Remind the reader why your writing is important.

6. **Revise using the PAST questions.** Make sure your writing is clear and complete.

7. **Edit your response.** Check for punctuation, spelling, and grammar errors.

 Tip If time permits, read through your response one last time to make sure everything is good to go.

Persuasive Writing (Argument Writing)

Writing Persuasive Essays

Everyone has opinions, and most people like to share them. Let's say that you think your school's winter vacation should be longer, and you want to share this opinion with your parents and school principal. To persuade them, you will need very good reasons. A good reason might be that students learn more if they have two weeks off in January. A less convincing reason might be that students want more time to relax.

One way to share an opinion is to write a persuasive essay. Your goal is to convince someone to agree with you. To do this, you need to support your opinion with strong facts and details. Read the sample essay on the next page to see how it's done. Then follow the guidelines to write effective persuasive essays of your own.

What's Ahead

- Sample Persuasive Essay
- Writing a Persuasive Essay
- Ideas for Persuasive Writing

Sample Persuasive Essay

It is Marah Mehta's opinion that manatees need to be saved. She supports her opinion with valuable information about the problem.

Beginning
The writer introduces her topic and states her opinion (underlined).

Middle
The middle paragraphs tell why manatees are important, why they are in decline, and what we can do to help.

Ending
The writer restates her opinion.

Help Save Our Manatees

Manatees are giant marine mammals that live in the rivers that flow into the ocean. There are only about 2,000 of these lovable animals still around. The manatees are in danger and need to be saved.

Manatees are important to both boaters and fishers. They help clear rivers by eating water plants. A 1,000 pound manatee can eat 150 pounds of river-clogging weeds in one day! They also provide recreation to millions of people who just enjoy watching them in Florida's coastal waterways.

Unfortunately, people are the cause of more than two-thirds of all manatee deaths. The most common cause is when boats accidentally hit them. Manatees also die from swallowing fishhooks, old fishing line, and garbage that litters the waterways.

People are part of the problem, and people can be part of the solution, too. People can start by not littering the waterways. They can also make sure none of their fishing gear ends up in the water. They can obey all boating rules, especially in manatee areas. And, finally, people can send emails to lawmakers asking for their help to save manatees.

If we all do our part, we can save the manatees, and these rare and beautiful animals will be around for many years to come. It's worth the effort.

Writing a Persuasive Essay

The sample essay about saving the manatees is a good model of persuasive writing. Here are writing guidelines for you to follow as you create your own essay.

Prewriting Planning Your Essay

Choose a Topic ■ Select a topic that you feel strongly about. It is much easier to develop a strong opinion when you write about something that you really believe in.

Topic: Focus on a specific topic, one that's not too general. For example, it would be easier to write about a topic like "Clean up Rainbow Beach" than it would be to write about "Clean up our oceans."

Audience: Think about your audience. Choose a topic that will be important to them. For example, "Save our swimming pool" might be more interesting to your classmates than "Save our town hall."

Voice: When writing a persuasive essay, be sure that you sound sincere and knowledgeable. You need to assure your reader that you know what you're talking about and that you really do care.

Think of an Argument ■ Whatever your topic is, it should have two sides. There is little point arguing for something everyone already agrees with.

The same topic for an explanatory (informative) essay could be changed into a persuasive essay.

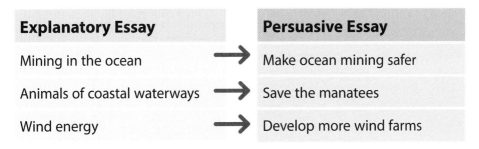

Explanatory Essay		Persuasive Essay
Mining in the ocean	→	Make ocean mining safer
Animals of coastal waterways	→	Save the manatees
Wind energy	→	Develop more wind farms

Prewriting *Gathering and Organizing Details*

List Details ■ Start with details you already know about the topic. Then collect any additional information you may need.

Manatees are	– weed eaters that help unclog rivers – gentle creatures – endangered animals
Problems are	– injuries by boats – deaths by litter consumption
People can	– stop littering – stop speeding in boats – write letters to lawmakers

Outline ■ You can also outline the information that you want to use to support your opinion. (You do not have to outline your beginning and ending paragraphs.)

Opinion: **Manatees should be saved.**

I. Manatees are worthwhile creatures.
 A. They help keep rivers clean.
 B. They eat 150 pounds of weeds each day.
 C. They give people pleasure.

II. People destroy manatees.
 A. They kill two-thirds of the manatees.
 B. They hit them with boats.
 C. They litter the waterways.

III. We can save the manatees.
 A. We can stop littering.
 B. We can obey boating speed limits.
 C. We can write our lawmakers.

Writing Developing the First Draft

Your persuasive essay may be a few paragraphs or many, but that will depend upon how much support you have to offer. Write your essay following your outline and the guidelines below.

Beginning ■ The first paragraph should introduce your topic and clearly state your opinion about it.

Middle ■ In the middle paragraphs, you need to support your opinion. Each main supporting idea and its supporting details go into a separate paragraph. So if you have two main ideas, the middle of your essay will most likely have two paragraphs.

Ending ■ The last paragraph should restate your opinion and tell your readers what action they might take or how they should feel.

Revising Improving Your Writing

Review your first draft using the following questions as a guide. Then ask someone else to review your essay.

___ Does my beginning paragraph introduce my topic and clearly state my opinion?

___ Do my middle paragraphs support my opinion?

___ Does each main idea have its own paragraph?

___ Does the ending restate my opinion?

___ Do I give my readers an action they can take?

___ Does the title help identify my essay's subject?

Editing and Proofreading Polishing Your Essay

Check for Careless Errors ■ Once you've made the necessary changes and improvements in your first draft, it's time to edit it. That means checking it for spelling, grammar, and punctuation errors. (See page 66 for a helpful checklist.) Then make a final copy and proofread your essay before sharing it.

Ideas for Persuasive Essays

Persuasive writing is about stating an opinion and supporting it with strong reasons. You can write persuasively about all kinds of important issues. Here are some starters to get you going.

Problems and Solutions ■ Write about a problem that needs to be solved in your town or your school. Explain a bad habit. Point out something that isn't fair or just. Name something that is wrong with the world and show how you would make it right.

Campaigns ■ Write an essay that gets people excited about a fund-raiser for an important cause. Help a friend run for office in your school. Explain a campaign to help a local charity. Ask readers to join an organization in your community.

Entertainment ■ Rate a movie and tell why you gave it the rating you did. List the three best songs you've ever heard and give reasons they are so good. Argue who is the best pop singer right now. Evaluate a new video game and tell why it is good or not so good.

Possibilities ■ Explain how a vacant lot in your neighborhood should be developed. Tell what mascot you think your school should have and why. Describe what types of fashion people should wear in the future. Give your vision for a city of tomorrow and show how it is better than cities of today.

Politics ■ Write about a candidate that you support and tell why. Name a law that you don't support and tell why it is not fair or right. Describe a law that should exist and convince readers to help make it happen.

The best persuasive writing presents a thoughtful argument. In other words, it is based on facts and details that can be checked for accuracy. It is not based on just the writer's strong feelings.

Writing Persuasive Letters

You can think of words and sentences as the main tools that you use in writing. When you form persuasive writing, you must use these tools in a special way. That is, you must convince readers that one of your opinions is worthy of their support.

What opinions do you have about your school or neighborhood? You can write about them in a persuasive letter. In the model persuasive letter in this chapter, a student shares his opinion with his principal. After reading this model, you will learn how to write a persuasive letter of your own.

What's Ahead

- Parts of a Business Letter
- Sample Persuasive Letter
- Writing a Persuasive Letter

Parts of a Business Letter

Heading
The heading includes the sender's address and the date. Begin an inch from the top of the page at the left margin.

Inside Address
The inside address includes the name and address of the person or organization you are writing to. Place it at the left margin, four to seven spaces below the heading. If the person has a special title, such as *park ranger*, include it after his or her name. (Use a comma first.)

Mr. Martin Jones, Principal

Salutation
The salutation (greeting) should begin on the second line below the inside address. Place a colon at the end of the salutation.

■ If you know the person's name, write it:

Dear Principal Jones:

■ If you don't know the name, use clear, fair language:

Dear Principal: Dear Sir or Madam:

Dear Mitchell School: Greetings:

Body
The body is the main part of the letter. Begin this part two lines below the salutation. Do not indent. Double-space between paragraphs.

Closing
Write the closing at the left margin, two lines below the body. Use *Sincerely* for a business letter closing. Always place a comma after the closing.

Signature
End your letter by writing your signature beneath the closing. If you are using a computer, skip four lines and type your full name. Then write your signature above it.

Sample **Persuasive Letter**

Writing a persuasive letter is very much like writing a persuasive essay. But it follows the business-letter format. Here is one student's persuasive letter.

1
123 Middle Road
Dearborn, IL 60540
April 15, 2015

2
Mr. Martin Jones, Principal
Mitchell Elementary School
Dearborn, IL 60540

3
Dear Principal Jones:

4
I am a student in fifth grade here at Mitchell School. As you know, last year we started a food bank at the school. Every Saturday morning, we take turns packing bags and boxes and handing out food in our school cafeteria. Everyone agrees that it's a great idea, and it has already helped many kids and their families. But we're running out of ideas for raising money to buy the food we need.

Beginning
The writer explains the reasons for the letter.

We have already tried bake sales and candy bar sales, and they've worked pretty well. But people aren't buying as much as they did at first, and everyone is getting tired of trying to sell the same thing day after day. So I think it's time to find other ways to raise money.

One idea I had was that our school could adopt a mascot. Right now, we don't have one, and I think

Middle

The middle paragraphs give background information and offer a new idea.

having a mascot would be great. It could raise school spirit, and it would be a good way to raise the money we need. Everyone likes to wear cool-looking clothes, so we could sell T-shirts and sweatshirts with our mascot's picture on them.

We could even have a contest to pick the best mascot, which would get everyone excited about the idea. Once we choose a mascot, we could ask students to design ideas to use on the shirts. We could sell them at school, in local stores, and even online.

I've talked to my cousins who go to Bedford Middle School, and they sell hundreds of school sweatshirts and T-shirts every year. They use the money to help pay for their class trip, but we could use it for the food bank.

Ending

The writer offers a next step.

I think this idea would work really well at Mitchell. If you agree, I would like to talk to you and some of the teachers about it. Would you please let me know what you think? We all want to keep the food bank open, and this is the best way I can think of to raise the money we need.

5 Sincerely,

6 *Densel Clemens*

Densel Clemens

Writing a Persuasive Letter

Planning Your Letter

Select a Topic ■ When you decide to write a persuasive letter, you will probably have a topic or issue in mind. It will most likely be an issue that you have a strong opinion about.

> **Topic:** If you need to choose a topic, you will want to focus on a specific issue or problem—one that is important to you and those around you.
> - We need to find more ways to raise money for the school food bank.
> - Our school should allow us to take more field trips.
> - We should choose a mascot for our school.

> **Audience:** Once you've chosen a specific problem or issue to write about, you need to decide who will read your letter. You need to choose a person or group who can help solve the problem.
> - The school principal or school board
> - A teacher or member of the community
> - A parent or a parent group

> **Argument:** All issues or problems have two sides. Otherwise, there would be no argument. You need to think about the arguments, opinions, and reasons on both sides of the issue. That way your opinion will be an "informed" opinion, and it will be more likely to convince people.
> - Consider all the reasons your opinion is the right one.
> - Consider some of the reasons people would disagree with you.
> - Choose the reasons and details that together make up the best argument.

Prewriting Gathering and Organizing Details

List Your Details ■ List all of the details you think you might want to use in your letter. (You don't have to use all of the details in your list.)

- Having a mascot would raise school spirit.
- We would have cool T-shirts and sweatshirts to wear.
- It would help raise funds for the food bank.
- We wouldn't have to sell candy bars anymore.

Writing Developing the First Draft

Beginning ■ Introduce the topic in the first part of the letter and then let the reader know why you're writing. You can do this by telling a story, asking a question, or sharing background information.

Middle ■ The middle part of your letter should summarize the issue or problem and offer solutions. Each paragraph in your letter should cover one part of the problem, one of the solutions, or one of the benefits. Use transition words to tie your paragraphs together.

Ending ■ At the end of your letter, you will want to repeat your main point and tell your reader what he or she can do to help.

Revising and Editing Improving Your Writing

When you've finished your first draft, revise it using the following questions. (Use the checklist on page 66 to help you edit your letter.)

____ Does my beginning clearly introduce the topic?
____ Does the middle of my letter explain the problem or situation and include solutions?
____ Does my letter move smoothly from start to finish?
____ Does my voice sound polite and sincere?
____ Do I follow the business-letter format?
____ Does my ending offer next steps?

Writing Problem- Solution Essays

One of easiest things for people to do is to complain about a problem. And one of the most difficult things is to try to solve it.

Writing about problems and solutions is a form of persuasive writing. You identify a real problem, one that you and your readers care about. Then you offer a solution—or several possible solutions— to the problem.

This chapter contains a problem-solution essay and guidelines to help you write an essay of your own. Who knows? Maybe you'll find a real solution to a real problem.

What's Ahead

- Sample Problem-Solution Essay
- Prewriting
- Writing the First Draft
- Revising and Editing

Problem-Solution Essay

The following essay examines a school-related problem: the condition of a school's gym. The writer identifies three areas or parts of the gym that are especially in need of attention. The writer uses specific details to explain each of these areas and offers solutions to fix each one.

We Need to Fix Our Gym

Beginning

The details in the beginning paragraph lead up to the problem (underlined).

Over the summer, our school was cleaned up to make it ready for the start of the new school year in August. Most of the rooms were repainted, and a new mural now decorates part of the main hall. Almost everything looked good when we walked in for the first day of school. Sadly, the old gym is still in poor condition and needs a face-lift.

First of all, the old gym is dark and dreary. This is because the windows are very small, so little sunlight gets in. The ceiling lights are not bright enough, either. It would be a great improvement if the small windows could be replaced with larger ones or if the lights could be changed. A new coat of lighter paint to cover up the old green paint would help, too.

Middle

Each middle paragraph describes a problem area and offers a solution.

Next, the bleachers in the gym are in poor shape. Some of the boards are cracked, which makes them hard to sit on for very long. It is also embarrassing when parents or kids from other schools come to watch a game in our gym. Someone needs to repair the broken bleachers and give them all a fresh coat of paint.

Lastly, the gym always seems stuffy. This is understandable because the gym is old, but sometimes it actually smells during gym class. The air almost seems unhealthy. It might help to add ceiling fans or improve the ventilation system. Either change would get the air moving. In addition, new windows could be opened in good weather.

Parkview students deserve a nice space for gym class. Other parts of our school are clean and ready to go, but this cannot be said about the gym. Not all of my suggestions would have to be done right away, and we could have fund-raisers to earn money for the work. Students and parents could also volunteer to help with the project. The bottom line is that the gym is old, and it's time to fix it up.

Transitions like *first of all, next,* and *lastly* **link the middle paragraphs.**

Ending
The writer restates the problem and discusses her solutions.

Note This problem-solution essay gives strong solutions for each problem area. Each solution is equal in value. In other problem-solution essays, the writer may mention a few possible solutions, but then focus on the best solution to a problem. The approach all depends on the problem that the writer is writing about.

Writing a Problem-Solution Essay

Planning Your Essay

Choose a Topic ■ For your essay, select a topic that you have strong feelings about. If your readers know you really care about your topic, they are more likely to pay careful attention to your ideas.

To begin your topic search, list possible problems related to your school or community. Here is the start of a list identifying school-related problems. Review your list, and select one problem to be the topic of your essay.

> School problems
> • **too much homework**
> • **not enough field trips**
> • **the condition of the gym**
> • **no afternoon recess**

Gathering Details

Use a Graphic Organizer ■ The next step is to collect details about your topic. You need to think about the causes of the problem and possible solutions. Here is how the writer of the sample essay used a graphic organizer to collect details about her problem.

> Problem: The poor condition of the gym
>
> Causes of the Problem
> • The gym is dark and dreary.
> • The bleachers are in poor shape.
> • The gym is always stuffy.
>
> Possible Solutions
> • Replace the small windows with larger ones.
> • Change the lights.
> • Repair and paint the bleachers.
> • Add ceiling fans.
> • Improve the ventilation system.

Prewriting *Organizing Your Ideas*

After collecting your details, you should organize all of your ideas in the order that you want them to appear in your essay. You can form a topic or sentence outline to do this. (See page 49.)

Another way is to create an organized list to arrange your ideas for writing, just as the writer of the sample essay did. Her list combines the causes of the problem and possible solutions. (The solutions are in *italics*.) Each cause became a separate paragraph in her essay.

Organized List

Problem: The poor condition of the gym

Cause 1: The gym is dark and dreary.
- windows too small
- ceiling lights not bright enough
- old green paint dull
- *install larger windows and stronger lights*
- *repaint gym to be brighter*

Cause 2: The bleachers are in poor shape.
- some boards cracked
- uncomfortable and embarrassing
- *repair and repaint bleachers*

Cause 3: The gym is stuffy.
- sometimes smells in the gym
- air unhealthy
- *add ceiling fans, improve ventilation*

Other Forms of Organization

You could also organize your ideas in the following way:

- Summarize the problem.
- Name possible solutions.
- Explain the best solution.

Writing Developing the First Draft

When you write your essay, use your outline or organized list as a general guide.

Beginning ■ The beginning part of your essay is very important. You need to get the reader's attention, introduce your topic, and state the problem. Therefore, you need to be clear and clever at the same time.

Middle ■ The middle part of your essay is where the real works gets done. You need to break down the problem into its causes and effects and provide specific solutions to fix the problem.

As you move from one paragraph to the next, use transition words to help your reader follow along. Here are some common ones.

First of all	Next	The best solution
In addition	Lastly	The final thing

Ending ■ In a problem-solution essay, the ending is very important. You need to summarize your solution to the problem and add some final thoughts. You might also say how readers can get involved.

Revising and Editing Improving Your Writing

Once you've finished the first draft, make sure that it is complete, clear, and well organized. The following questions should help you revise your writing. (Use the checklist on page 66 to help you edit it.)

____ Did I choose a problem that my readers really care about?
____ Did I state the problem clearly in my beginning paragraph?
____ Did I describe each cause of the problem in detail?
____ Did I use a strong but sincere voice?
____ Did I offer reasonable solutions to the problem?
____ Did I end by summarizing the solutions and offering some final thoughts?
____ Did I suggest what the readers can do to help?

Responding to Persuasive Prompts

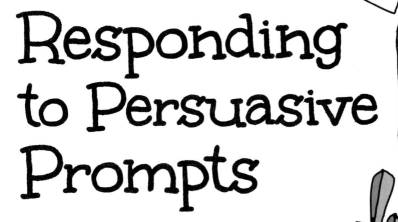

On some tests, you'll be asked to present an opinion and support it in writing. You might focus on a problem on the bus, or one in the lunchroom. Whatever your topic, you'll need to write persuasively about it in a short amount of time.

This chapter shows you how to write in response to a persuasive prompt. You'll learn how to analyze the prompt, take quick notes, and get writing.

What's Ahead

- Writing to a Persuasive Prompt
- Sample Prompt and Response
- Responding Review

Writing to a Persuasive Prompt

Many schools today use writing tests or prompts to measure the progress you're making. You'll find persuasive, explanatory, and narrative prompts. The first step is to analyze the writing prompt.

Prewriting Analyzing the Prompt

A prompt is a set of directions that tell you what to write. It's very important that you read the directions carefully and consider the purpose of the writing, your audience, the subject you will write about, and the type of writing you need to do. To do this, you can use the **PAST** questions:

Purpose: Why am I writing? What is my goal? A persuasive prompt asks you to state an opinion and support it using evidence. Your goal is to convince readers to agree with your opinion.

Audience: Who will read my writing? Some prompts tell you who your audience is: "Write to convince your classmates about the type of classroom pet you should adopt." If the prompt does not clearly identify an audience, you can assume that the tester or your teacher is the audience.

Subject: What should I write about? The prompt will give you a general subject area, but you will need to narrow your focus to a specific topic. Make sure you choose a persuasive topic that you feel strongly about.

Type: What type or form of writing should I create? The prompt will usually indicate the form your response should take (essay, letter, blog post). Organize your response to match the form.

Sample **Persuasive Prompt**

The school board is considering purchasing iPads for every student at your school, but they aren't sure it would be worth the money. In a letter, try to convince your reader that this is a good idea and would be a great investment of money.

Purpose: To persuade the board to buy the iPads

Audience: Teacher, principal, or school board

Subject: Buying iPads for each student

Type: A persuasive letter

Sample **Response**

Beginning
The first paragraph clearly states the writer's opinion.

Middle
Each middle paragraph states and explains a reason.

Dear School Board Members,

I'm a student at Wiseman Elementary School, and I know that you are thinking about buying iPads for all of our students. I think it's a great idea, and I have a number of reasons to back up my opinion. I hope you'll read my letter and agree that it's a good idea, too.

First of all, iPads make things easier to learn. You can see what you are trying to learn, not just hear the teacher talk about it. IPads can also be used to bring the Internet into our classrooms. All students would be able to go to the Internet right at their desks. They could use the iPads to learn things that they could share with the rest of the class.

Secondly, using iPads every day will make every student better at using computers, and that's something everyone needs to be able to do. Having iPads will make doing writing assignments and homework much easier and quicker, and students will be able to use the extra time to learn even more.

Finally, and most importantly, iPads will actually save money. According to our teacher, Mrs. Meade, nearly all textbooks are now available in an ebook form, and ebooks are a lot cheaper than printed textbooks. Also, if we replace textbooks with ebooks, students won't have to lug such heavy backpacks around all the time. As long as a student has an iPad, he or she will have every book for every class.

I'm sure there are even more good reasons to buy iPads for every student, but at least I've given you a few. I really hope you decide to buy the iPads. It would change the lives of the students at Wiseman, and it would save money in the long run. What could be better than that?

Sincerely,

Trevon Hughes

Notice how this student sounds serious and polite, which is the appropriate voice to use in persuasive writing like this.

Prewriting Planning Your Response

State Your Opinion ■ Once you carefully analyze the prompt, you need to form a personal opinion. You can do this by using the following formula:

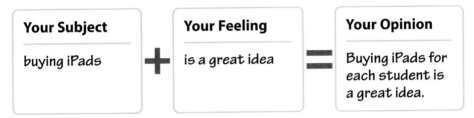

Your Subject		Your Feeling		Your Opinion
buying iPads	**+**	is a great idea	**=**	Buying iPads for each student is a great idea.

List Your Details ■ Next, you need to list the reasons you plan to use to support your opinion.

> • Using iPads would improve students' computer skills.
> • Having iPads would make things easier to learn.
> • Textbooks would always be up to date.
> • Students would be interested in learning.
> • Buying iPads would save money on textbooks.

Arrange Your Details ■ Look at your list and decide which reasons you are going to use and what order you are going to put them in. Sometimes it's a good idea to use your best reason first; other times, it's better to wait and use your best reason last. You have to decide.

> 1. Having iPads would make things easier to learn.
> 2. Using iPads would improve students' computer skills.
> 3. Buying iPads would save money on textbooks.

Think About the Time ■ Before you begin writing, think once again about how much time you have to complete your writing and plan accordingly. You want to make sure that you get all of your points down before time runs out.

Writing Creating Your Response

Once you've decided which reasons you are going to use (and in what order), you can begin writing.

Beginning ■ No matter what form of writing you are going to use (letter, essay, or another), you will want to state your opinion very near the beginning. You might begin with a few thoughts about the topic, and then clearly state your opinion.

Middle ■ Your reasons belong in the middle of your response. If you have two reasons, you will have two middle paragraphs. If you have three reasons, you will have three middle paragraphs. (Be sure to connect your paragraphs with transition words.) Follow your list as you write, but be ready to add details if you think of some good ones.

Ending ■ The last part of your response should bring everything together. You can remind your readers what your opinion is and encourage them to agree with you. You can also tell them what they can do to help.

Revising Improving Your Response

As soon as you finish, review your writing and ask yourself the following questions.

___ Does the beginning clearly state my opinion?
___ Do the middle paragraphs support my opinion?
___ Do I use transitions to tie my ideas together?
___ Does the ending repeat my opinion and leave the readers something to think about?

Editing and Proofreading Polishing Your Response

Check for Careless Errors ■ If you have time, go back and look for missing words, run-on sentences, and incorrect punctuation. You want to make your response as clear and correct as possible.

Responding Review

This quick summary can help you respond to a persuasive prompt.

1. **Analyze the prompt.** Use the **PAST** questions.

   > **Purpose:** What is the purpose of my writing?
   > **Audience:** Who will be reading my writing?
   > **Subject:** What should I write about?
   > **Type:** What form will my writing take?

2. **Outline your response.** Write down the main idea of your answer and list your supporting points. Keep your purpose in mind and choose a pattern of organization. (See pages 24–26 and 47.)

3. **Write your beginning paragraph.** Start with a few general comments about the topic and then state your opinion.

4. **Add your middle paragraphs.** Write a topic or controlling sentence that includes one of your reasons. Then add specific details that support it.

5. **Write your ending paragraph.** End your response by restating your main point and leaving the reader with a final thought.

6. **Revise using the PAST questions.** Use these questions to make sure you've answered the prompt accurately.

7. **Edit your response.** Check for punctuation, spelling, and grammar errors.

Writing About Literature

Writing Book Reviews

The students at Rancho Elementary often write book reviews. They pin them on bulletin boards, post them on their classroom blog, and sometimes include them in their classroom newsletter. Why? Because their classmates enjoy reading the reviews. A book review can help them decide which book they want to read next!

In a book review, you tell what a book is about. You share what you like about the book and explain its overall theme or message. In this chapter, you'll learn how to plan and write a review of a book you have read—one you'll be proud to share with your classmates.

What's Ahead

- Sample Nonfiction Book Review
- Sample Fiction Book Review
- Writing Guidelines
- Sample Book Review Brochure

Sample Nonfiction Book Review

In the following model, Maria Rodriguez reviews the nonfiction book *Shipwreck at the Bottom of the World*. The review gives just enough information to help the reader decide whether or not to read the book. If the review would tell too much, a reader may decide that he or she already knows enough about the book.

Beginning

The first paragraph introduces the book and gets the reader's interest.

Middle

The middle paragraphs answer three key questions about the book.

Shipwreck at the Bottom of the World

Shipwreck at the Bottom of the World is an exciting nonfiction book by Jennifer Armstrong. Just imagine heading to Antarctica to be the first person to cross the entire continent—only you never get there—and you almost die!

What is the book about?

In 1914, 28 explorers set out from London on the River Thames. Sir Ernest Shackleton and his crew sail to South Georgia Island where the captain hears a warning. The winter ice pack around Antarctica isn't melting like it should. Maybe the trip is doomed.

Shackleton sails on anyway, and the worst possible thing happens. They get stuck in the ice where the temperature can drop to minus 100° Fahrenheit! The ship, according to one crewman, is stuck "like an almond in the middle of a chocolate bar."

What do I like about the book?

Specific details from the book are included.

I loved all the photos in this book. They made me feel like I was right there with the explorers. I kept reading page after page to find out what the crew did to survive. One example is that Ernest Shackleton sailed 800 miles in a 20-foot boat to look for help. Most of the time, I couldn't believe what they were going through.

What is the book's theme?

This is a book about bravery. Both Shackleton and his entire crew were courageous. Their story shows how important it is to work together as a team during hard times. It also shows what a difference a good leader can make. The book is great from beginning to end. And it made me think, "How would I have handled such a tough time?"

Ending
The last paragraph answers a final question.

Why would others like it?

Reading this book is a true adventure. Don't miss it, especially if you like true stories about real explorers!

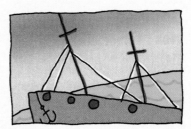

Sample **Fiction Book Review**

In the following model, Luke Bromwell reviews a mystery titled *The Real Thief.* Luke's review shows that he has thought very carefully about this exciting book. And he says just enough to help the readers decide for themselves if they want to read the book.

Beginning
The first paragraph introduces the book and gets the reader's interest.

Middle
The middle paragraphs answer three questions about the book.

The Real Thief

One day, sometime during the Middle Ages, valuable jewels disappear from the Royal Treasury. Rubies, gold ducats, and the world-famous Kalikak diamond are missing! And so begins an exciting mystery by William Steig, *The Real Thief.*

What is the book about?

Everyone thinks Gawain robbed the treasury. Who else could it be? Other than King Basil, only Chief Guard Gawain holds keys to the vault. And even though Gawain is innocent and has always been loyal to the king, the townspeople find him guilty. Gawain escapes and runs away to live by himself. Then something surprising begins to happen. Will Gawain ever come back? How does he feel now about the townspeople?

What do I like about the book?

I loved reading this mystery. I kept wondering what would happen next. It was interesting, too, to watch how the characters acted. Questions kept popping up. Why would the king think his most loyal friend would steal from him? How does Gawain feel about the king's betrayal? Why was the trial so exciting and thrilling to the townspeople?

What is the book's theme or message?

This book is all about loyalty, honor, and forgiveness. It really made me think: What do I do when I think someone has been falsely accused? Would I do the right thing?

Ending

The last paragraph answers a final question.

Why would others like it?

In this book, poor Gawain is suspected, taken to court, and found guilty. Things do not look good for him. How will anything turn out right? If you want to find out how things turn out, you'll have to read this book. If you like a good mystery or a suspense-filled story, this is the book for you.

Note When you write your book review, you do not have to include the four questions, as Luke's review does. That's your choice. But, whether you list them or not, you will want to answer each of them somewhere in your review.

Writing Guidelines

Prewriting Planning Your Book Review

Choose a Topic ■ First, choose a book you want to review. You can read a mystery, an adventure story, a book about your favorite sports figure, or even a book of poems. Pick a book that you enjoyed and want to share with others.

Gather Your Thoughts ■ Next, answer four basic questions about the book: *What is the book about? What do I like about the book? What is the book's theme or message? Why would others like it?* (See the next page for more information.)

Writing Developing Your First Draft

Share Your Thoughts ■ **(1)** In the first paragraph of your book review, give the book's title, the author's name, and a general idea of the subject of the book. **(2)** Then, in separate paragraphs, answer the first three questions: What is the book is about? What do I like about the book? What is the book's theme or message? **(3)** In the last paragraph, answer the final question: Why would others like it?

Revising Improving Your Book Review

Make It Clear ■ Check your first draft for ideas. **(1)** Did you introduce the book? **(2)** Did you answer the four basic questions about it? **(3)** Did you end with an invitation to read the book? **(4)** Overall, did you share enough details about the book, without giving the whole story away?

Editing and Proofreading Polishing Your Review

Check It Over ■ Correct any errors in capitalization, punctuation, and spelling. Remember that book titles must be underlined or italicized. Then write a neat final draft and proofread it line by line. (See page 66 for an editing checklist to use as a guide.)

Collection Sheet

The ideas below will help you answer the basic questions about either a fiction book or a nonfiction book. The last question will help you invite others to read the book.

1 What is the book about?

Fiction: What happens in the story? A good book review should highlight a few events rather than tell the whole story.

Nonfiction: What is the basic subject of this book? Generally, what happens? Is there one part that seems really important?

2 What do I like about the book?

Fiction: Does the book start in an exciting or interesting way? Does it contain a lot of action or suspense? Do I admire the character's actions? Is the character like me?

Nonfiction: Does the book contain interesting and easy-to-follow information? Does the book include some useful diagrams or colorful illustrations?

3 What is the book's theme/message?

Fiction: What message about life is the author sharing? Here is an example: *It's not always easy to stand up for what is right.* Themes about ambition, courage, jealousy, good vs. evil, and happiness are common. What details or events in the story help show the theme?

Nonfiction: Why did the author write this book? What basic information or message does the author share?

4 Why would others like it?

What is special about the book? What interest area does it cover?

Sample Book Review Brochure

Another way to write a book review is to make a brochure. Book review brochures use words and pictures to invite others to read the book.

On the Cover
Invite others to read the book. (Draw pictures or find photos related to the subject.)

Inside the Brochure
Use details about the story to persuade others to read the book.

Shipwreck at the Bottom of the World

Jennifer Armstrong, Author

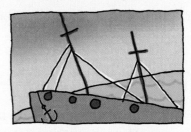

Read This Amazing Adventure Story!

A Book Filled with Danger

- The crew is trapped in their ship for seven months! The ship gets crushed.
- The crew escapes from sea lions and moving ice floes.
- To get help, Captain Shackleton sets sail in a 20-foot boat.

I highly recommend this book for both kids and adults.

An Icy Setting

- The trip starts in 1914 and ends in 1916.
- The explorers face many dangers crossing the icy Antarctic.

Brave Characters

- The brave captain keeps everyone calm.
- The crewmen and a stowaway are rough, wild men, but they are brave.
- You can learn about bravery from this crew.

Writing About Literature

Writing about a book, a short story, a poem, or a play makes you think very carefully about its ideas. Writing also lets you share your thoughts about what you have learned. When you write about literature, you answer important questions like these: *How does this piece of writing make me feel? What do I see? What do I hear? What does it mean?*

Writing about literature begins with careful reading. You must read the piece closely, think about it, and jot down your ideas. Only then will you discover what you want to say. Afterward, you will share your thoughts in a paragraph or an essay.

What's Ahead

- Sample Essay About Literature
- Writing a Literature Essay

Sample **Essay About Literature**

In the following model, student Gina Farthing writes about a poem. (See page 288.) She shares her opinion about the poem's meaning. She also includes specific details from the poem to support her ideas.

Beginning
The student gives her opinion about what the poem means.

Middle
She shares details to support her opinion.

Ending
A final idea makes the reader think.

Friendship Dance

"The Alley Dog" is a serious poem by Anne-Marie Oomen, and I believe it's all about friendship. Making a friend is like a dance. I don't mean an actual dance, but the kind you do with your parents when you want something. You take one step at a time. You hope they'll finally see things your way.

The child in the poem wants the dog as a friend. The first step is feeding him: "So I toss him my bread and butter." The hungry dog rushes to get the food, but he's careful: "he gobbles his treat, watching me." He doesn't trust anyone yet.

The child takes another step: "I climb down the fire escape and wait." She doesn't rush, and neither does the dog. Slowly, the dog "belly-scrapes down our alleyway and stops near me, but not to bite." Still, they wait, and then "He eases up close, curls next to me." Finally, the child and the dog sit together. And they watch the "sun push the alley bricks into shadow. No tricks. Real cool. Friends rule."

The poet uses vivid verbs—*toss, stutter, wait, ease*. They're like the steps in the friendship dance: We try. We wait. We hope. We wait. We find a friend.

Writing a Literature Essay

Here is a sample assignment for writing about literature: *Write an essay reflecting on a story or a poem you have recently read. In your essay, (1) give your opinion about what the writing means, or (2) explain something you find special about the writing.*

Use the **PAST** strategy to help you understand the assignment better.

> **Purpose:** To give an opinion, or to explain
>
> **Audience:** My teacher and classmates
>
> **Subject:** A story or poem
>
> **Type:** An essay

Prewriting Planning Your Essay

Find a Topic ■ To start, choose a story or poem that interests you.

Reread the piece. If it is short, reread all of it; if it is long, reread the section you feel strongest about. As you read, make observations and take notes. Answer questions like these: *What is awesome about this story or poem? What makes me smile? What is really interesting?*

Collect Details ■ Make a cluster or list ideas from the story or poem. Write down whatever interests you—favorite characters, special words, images, surprises. Then study your observations. They will lead you to your own idea for the writing.

Sample **Cluster**

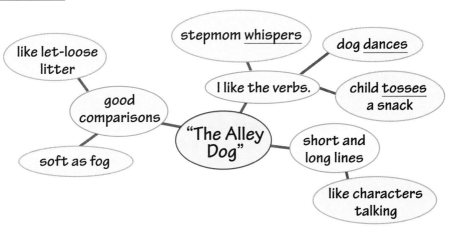

Possible writing idea from the cluster: Explanatory essay

I feel like I am right there in this poem. Maybe the poet's great verbs, the different line lengths, and cool comparisons make that happen.

Sample | List

- The stepmom doesn't want the child to go near the stray. "Do not touch that strange dog!"
- But the child throws the dog some of her own bread and butter, and "he dances."
- The child reaches out to the dog, like she knows how it feels to need a friend.
- It takes time for the dog to trust her . . . "he gobbles his treat, watching me."
- The dog finally comes closer. "Slow as a car in a backed up street, he belly-scrapes down our alleyway."
- And then the friends sit close. "No tricks. Real cool. Friends rule."

Possible writing idea from the list: Persuasive essay

To me, this poem is all about making a new friend. You're careful, at first, just like the child and the dog are.

Write Your Main Idea ■ After clustering or listing your observations, choose a writing idea. This will be the main idea of your essay. Refine it by asking these questions: *Is this what I want to say? Can I say it better?* Then rewrite your idea until you are satisfied with it.

Original Idea	To me, this poem is all about making a new friend. . . . You're careful, at first.
First Revised Idea	This poem shows how making friends takes time. It's like getting parents to agree to something.
Second Revised Idea	I believe this poem is all about friendship. Making a friend is like a dance—the kind you do with your parents when you want something.

Writing Developing the First Draft

Beginning ■ In the first paragraph, do two things:

- ■ Name the title and author of the story or poem.
- ■ Share your main idea—your opinion or explanation.

> "The Alley Dog" is a serious poem by Anne-Marie Oomen, and I believe it's all about friendship. . . .

Middle ■ In the middle paragraphs, support your main idea. Use the details you collected (cluster, list). Look over the text again to find even more information.

- ■ Include the best details to explain your main idea.
- ■ Include exact words (quotations) to make your point.

> The child in the poem wants the dog as a friend. The first step is feeding him: "So I toss him my bread and butter." The hungry dog rushes to get the food, but he's careful . . .
>
> The child takes another step: "I climb down the fire escape and wait." She doesn't rush, and neither does the dog. Slowly, the dog "belly-scrapes down our alleyway and stops near me . . . "

Ending ■ In the last paragraph, make a final comment about the writing. Here are some ideas:

- ■ Repeat your main idea.
- ■ Tell how a character has changed.
- ■ Include an idea that makes the reader think.

> The poet uses vivid verbs—*toss, stutter, wait, ease.* They're like the steps in the friendship dance: We try. We wait. We hope. We wait. We find a friend.

Revising Improving Your Writing

Review your first draft by asking the following questions. Then make any needed changes.

___ Does my essay have a beginning, a middle, and an ending?

___ Does the first paragraph include the title and author? Does it give my main idea?

___ Do the middle paragraphs include details from the piece of writing?

___ Does the last paragraph repeat the main idea and end the essay effectively?

Editing and Proofreading Checking for Errors

Then check your revised writing for spelling, grammar, and punctuation errors. (See the "Editing and Proofreading Checklist" on page 66.)

Publishing Sharing Your Work

When you've finished editing and proofreading your essay, make a neat final copy to share. You might share it by reading it aloud to the class, posting it on the classroom blog, or pinning it to the bulletin board. Your teacher may have suggestions as well.

If you use quotations in your essay, make sure you work them in smoothly and punctuate them correctly.

Responding to Literature Prompts

On some tests, you'll be asked to read a story or poem and respond to a prompt about your reading. You'll need to use your best reading skills as well as your best writing skills to form a strong response. And you will have to do this within a limited amount of time. Don't worry. This chapter has specific strategies to help you succeed.

The first step is to understand the writing prompt. You can use the **PAST** questions for that job. Then you need to read the literature and take notes. Afterward, you'll write a paragraph or an essay about the story or poem, using evidence from the literature.

What's Ahead

- Writing to a Literature Prompt
- Sample Literature Prompt and Response
- Responding Review

Writing to a Literature Prompt

Responding to a prompt is different from other writing assignments because you don't have a lot of time to complete your work. So you must know what you are doing and get right to work. The first thing you need to do is study the prompt.

Prewriting **Analyzing the Prompt**

A literature prompt is a set of directions for writing. Think of the prompt as your target. You need to look closely at it and focus on it in order to hit the target. You can use the **PAST** questions listed below to make sure you fully understand a literature prompt.

Purpose: *Why am I writing? What is my goal?*
The prompt for a story will tell you to summarize the plot, explain a theme, describe a character, or do some other task. The prompt for a poem will ask you to analyze meaning, rhyme, rhythm, figures of speech, or some other part of the poem.

Audience: *Who will read the writing?*
Some prompts will name a specific audience: "Explain the story to someone who has never read it" or "Review the story for readers of your class blog." Other prompts do not indicate an audience, so you can just assume the testers or your teacher is the audience.

Subject: *What literature am I writing about?*
The prompt will name the literature and often who wrote it. The prompt might also point you to specific types of details or themes to use from the literature.

Type: *What type of writing should I do?*
Most often the prompt will tell you what form of writing to create (a review, an essay, a blog post, or some other form).

Sample **Literature Prompt**

In an essay, identify the theme, or central message, in Sandy Asher's story "The Truth About Rowf." Explain how the main character, plot, and setting support this theme.

Purpose: To identify and explain the theme

Audience: Testers or teacher

Subject: "The Truth About Rowf"

Type: Response to literature

Sample **Literature Response**

Beginning
The writer names the literature and author and gives a quick summary.

Middle
The writer first identifies a theme.

The next paragraphs explain how the character, plot, and setting support the theme.

"The Truth About Rowf" by Sandy Asher is about a girl who wishes she could control her mouth. When the local bully threatens her friends during a rummage sale, Jessica learns to control what she says.

This story's theme is about learning how to use your judgment when you speak to other people and to control what you say. Jessica learns that sometimes it's good to hold back the truth, especially when holding back is the kinder or smarter thing to do.

Sandy Asher develops this theme through her main character. The main character, Jessica Gentry, is a smart and kind kid. But she can't control her mouth. "I know these things too late," she says, "after my mouth opens and truth pops out." But because she is both smart and kind, she is able to change. This is important to the theme because the theme is about learning how to control what you say.

The plot of the story also supports the theme. At the beginning, Jessica is way too honest as she tells the story about calling her neighbor's soup "stinky." In a later part, she doesn't hold back again, but this time it's because she truly wants to be honest. Finally, in one last episode, Jessica learns that holding back can be a good thing, when she doesn't tell Rags, the neighborhood bully, that Rowf is harmless. These episodes allow us to see Jessica change from a girl who says everything to a girl who can think before she speaks.

Lastly, the setting is also pretty important to the theme. The story takes place in front of an apartment building where the three friends hold a rummage sale to earn money. This means that Jessica will have a chance to learn how to think before she speaks, because rummage sales are open to everyone. Even the neighborhood bully can go to a rummage sale.

In conclusion, Sandy Asher's main character, plot, and setting work together very well and help to support her theme. It's a very simple—and very important—theme: "Think before you speak."

The writer includes specific details from the book.

Ending
The final paragraph summarizes the response.

Note You can read the short story "The Truth About Rowf," on pages 313–316.

Prewriting Reading the Literature

Read Closely ■ As you read, think about the parts of the story: the characters, setting, conflict, episodes, climax, and resolution.

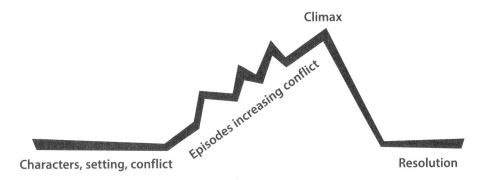

Climax

Episodes increasing conflict

Characters, setting, conflict

Resolution

Summarize the Plot ■ Write one or two sentences to capture the overall plot of the story.

> Jessica Gentry, a girl who wishes she could control her mouth, holds a rummage sale with two good buddies. During the sale, Jessica learns to control what she says by not telling a local bully that her dog Rowf is harmless.

Suggest a Theme ■ Ask yourself what the story is about. How did the protagonist change, or what lesson did the protagonist learn?

> This story is about learning how to use your judgment when you speak to other people and learning how to control what you say. Jessica learns that sometimes it's smart to hold back the truth.

Jot Down Other Ideas ■ You may feel ready to start writing. If not, jot down ideas about the main character, plot, and setting that will help you form your response.

Writing Developing Your Response

Reread the prompt just to be sure you follow what you are asked to do. Begin by naming the literature and its author. Then lead to your focus statement. Add quotations from the story to help develop your ideas. Conclude by summarizing your major points.

Revising Improving Your Response

Responding to a prompt is a way of measuring your writing skills, so you'll want to do your very best. That means you'll need to save at least five minutes to check everything over and change anything that isn't clear or appropriate.

So, after you've finished writing, go back to the prompt. Ask yourself the **PAST** questions again. Make sure you have done everything you were supposed to do:

I'm supposed to

✓ 1. summarize the plot
✓ 2. suggest a theme
✓ 3. explain how Asher creates the theme
✓ 4. talk about plot, character, and setting

Also ask yourself the following questions as you revise your response. Then make any needed changes.

___ Does the beginning include the name or title of the literature and the author?
___ Does the beginning give a clear focus statement?
___ Do the middle paragraphs support the focus?
___ Do I include specific details and quotes from the story?
___ Does the ending summarize my essay?
___ Do I use the proper voice to achieve my purpose?
___ Do I cover everything the assignment was asking for?

Editing and Proofreading Polishing Your Response

Check for Careless Errors ■ Quickly review your writing to correct errors such as missing words, run-on sentences, and incorrect or missing punctuation.

Responding Review

This quick summary can help you respond to a literature prompt.

1. **Analyze the prompt.** Use the **PAST** questions.

> **Purpose:** *Why am I writing? What is my goal?*
> **Audience:** *Who will read my writing?*
> **Subject:** *What literature should I respond to?*
> **Type:** *What form will my writing take?*

2. **Closely read the literature.** Take notes about the parts mentioned in the prompt.

3. **Plan your response.** Use the next 5 minutes for planning your response. List your details and arrange them quickly.

4. **Begin well.** Write sentences that lead to a focus statement that names your topic and specific focus.

5. **Support your ideas in middle paragraphs.** Start each paragraph with a main point. Support each point with evidence from the literature: examples, descriptions, and quotations.

6. **End in a meaningful way.** Restate your focus and summarize your main points.

7. **Revise using the checklist questions.** Use the last 5 minutes for revising and editing. (You can use the questions on page 242.) Make sure your writing answers the prompt.

8. **Edit your response.** Check for punctuation, spelling, and grammar errors.

Report Writing

Writing Reports

Reporters go to the scene of the action. They discover what's going on and investigate the situation. Once they have gathered enough information, they write a report.

Sometimes your teacher will ask you to act like a reporter. You'll learn about a subject from books, Web sites, videos, and even first-hand experiences. Then you'll write a report to share what you discover.

In this chapter, you will learn how to write a report—one that shares information in an interesting way.

What's Ahead

- Sample Report
- Writing a Report

Sample **Report**

The report that follows tells about a special cave from the Ice Age. (The Ice Age is a period when glaciers covered much of the earth.) The report includes interesting facts and details the writer discovered through his research. As you read, notice the writer's enthusiasm for the subject. He is obviously interested in his topic and presents colorful facts and details.

Ice Age Time Capsule
Carl Simmons

Beginning
The writer introduces the topic by sharing his personal interest in it.

Imagine being able to look into the past, directly into the last Ice Age that hit our planet. I've been interested in the Ice Age since I was a little kid, but a few years ago, an Ice Age cave was discovered near Springfield, Missouri. This time capsule got my head spinning.

Believe it or not, the discovery was an accident. A construction crew was working on a new road. After the first explosion to get a small hill out of the way, part of the hill vanished into the earth. The crew stared into the jagged opening. It turned out to be a 2,000-foot-long cave. Today the site is called Riverbluff Cave.

Middle
The writer gives specific details about the topic.

Exploration of Riverbluff Cave didn't happen right away. All sorts of permissions had to be granted. But once scientists got the okay and began exploring, they felt like they were walking back in time. Luckily, Riverbluff Cave had been sealed off long ago through the work of melting glaciers so that a lot of things were preserved.

Over time, scientists found all sorts of things. They discovered mammoth bones and beds clawed out of the clay by ancient short-faced bears. They also found tracks from herds of pig-like animals and large cats (maybe saber-toothed tigers or American lions). And a foot-long shell of an unknown turtle species was sticking out of one of the walls!

Ending

The writer shows where to find more information.

The exploration of Riverbluff Cave will go on for many years to come. Who knows what other ancient stuff they will find there? To keep up with new findings, you can go to www.riverbluffcave.com.

Carl's Notes:

My idea for the title of my paper comes from an article in the *Los Angeles Times:* "Ice Age 'Time Capsule' Is Discovered in a Missouri Cave."

Some of my information came from the book *Cave Detectives: Unraveling the Mystery of an Ice Age Cave* by David L. Harrison.

I also used information from a PBS special I saw on the cave a year ago.

Express Yourself When writing a report, use your own words as much as possible. It's okay to use some ideas and direct quotations from other sources, but be sure to give them credit.

Writing a Report

Prewriting *Choosing a Subject*

Carl's teacher allowed him to choose from a wide range of subjects. If you are given this choice, choose a subject that truly interests you.

Think of General Subject Areas ▪ If you are not sure what to write about, think about the subjects you are studying in your different classes. Can you think of an interesting topic related to any of these subjects? What about an interesting topic related to something in the news?

You could also review the following list of general subject areas. One of them may help you think of a specific topic. A subject like food may lead you to a specific type of food like yogurt.

animals	cities	families	laws
plants	school	food	technology
music	environment	friends	science
books	exercise	health	money
movies	clothes	houses	work

Choose a Specific Topic ▪ Your topic needs to be specific enough to be covered in a report. You couldn't cover the broad subject of "health" in a page or two, but you could cover the specific topic "walking for exercise." Here's how Carl chose a specific topic for his report:

Well, I knew a lot about the Ice Age already, so I thought maybe I would write about it. And then, when I heard about the cave they discovered in Missouri, I knew other students would be interested, too. That's when I decided to write about it for our classroom blog. I will learn what I can about the cave and share this information with my classmates.

Prewriting Gathering Information

Explore Your Topic ■ Once you have selected a specific topic, decide what you already know about it and what you still need to learn. Make a list of the details that you discover about your topic.

- The cave that was discovered in Springfield, Missouri, in 2001 is known as Riverbluff Cave.
- It was sealed by rocks and mud until a construction crew blasted a hole in one end while building a road.
- The remains in the cave date back at least 830,000 years, maybe even a million.
- The cave is over 2,000 feet long.
- Just under the surface, the finds so far include mammoth bones and beds clawed out of the clay by the short-faced bear.
- The cave shows how Ice Age animals lived.

Prewriting Organizing Your Information

Create a Writing Plan ■ Once you've gathered plenty of details, it's time to organize them. A writing plan can help you stay organized. You can use the **PAST** strategy to help you form a writing plan.

Purpose: To report useful and interesting information
Audience: Teacher and students at our school
Subject: Riverbluff Cave
Type: Report

 Tip Also consider the voice you will want to use. You will want to sound serious, but with a personal tone.

Create a Quick Outline ■ Next, you need to decide how you will arrange your details. Write a topic outline to organize your thoughts. (You can use single words and short phrases.)

I. Riverbluff Cave
   A. When it was discovered
   B. How it was discovered

II. Exploration
   A. Couldn't start right away
   B. Had to get permission

III. Findings
   A. What was found
   B. How to keep up with new findings

Writing Developing Your First Draft

Once you have organized your thoughts and details (in a list or outline), you can begin writing your first draft. Here are a few tips.

▶ Beginning

Begin with a Hook ■ Sharing your personal interest in the subject is one way to begin. Your interest in a topic will naturally draw your reader into your report.

Imagine being able to look directly into the past, into the last Ice Age that hit our planet. I've been interested in the Ice Age since I was a little kid, but a few years ago, an Ice Age cave was discovered near Springfield, Missouri. This time capsule got my head spinning.

Try Other Beginnings ■ Here are some other ways to start your report with a hook.

- **Use a quotation from something you've read.**
  One scientist calls Riverbluff Cave an "Ice Age time capsule."
- **Use a dramatic statement.**
  It's not every day a crewman building a road discovers an Ice Age turtle sticking out of a wall.
- **Introduce your subject.**
  Riverbluff Cave, discovered in 2001, is an ancient cave accidentally uncovered by a road crew near Springfield, Missouri.

▶ Middle

Use Different Text Structures ■ The writer uses *chronological order* to tell about the sequence of actions that led to the discovery of the cave. (See pages 24–26 for more about text structures.)

> Believe it or not, the discovery was an accident. A construction crew was working on a new road. Suddenly, after the first explosion to get a small hill out of the way, part of the hill vanished into the earth. The crew stared into the jagged opening. . . .

This part of his report is a *description* of what was found in the cave. He uses specific details like "ancient short-faced bears" in this section.

> Over time, scientists found all sorts of things. They discovered mammoth bones and beds clawed out of the clay by ancient short-faced bears. They also found tracks from herds of pig-like animals and large cats (maybe saber-toothed tigers or American lions). . . .

▶ Ending

End with a Strong Point ■ End your report in a way that helps the reader remember your topic and tells how to learn more about it.

> The exploration of Riverbluff Cave will go on for many years to come. Who knows what other ancient stuff they will find there? To keep up with new findings, you can go to www.riverbluffcave.com.

Revising Improving Your Report

Beginning

___ Do I start my report off with a "hook" that explains my topic and gets my readers' attention?

Middle

___ Do I add plenty of specific details to keep my readers interested?

___ Do I organize my details in clear, logical ways?

___ Do I connect my ideas from one paragraph to the next with transitions?

___ Do I use words and examples that are clear, colorful, and correct?

Ending

___ Do I leave readers wishing they could read more about this topic?

Editing Polishing Your Writing

Check your final paper for careless errors. (Use the "Editing and Proofreading Checklist" on page 66 as an editing guide.)

Writing Research Reports

Your teacher says, "Today we're going to begin our work on research reports about fish."

"Gee, another research paper," you think. "I hope this time we have a chance to pick our own topic and ask our own questions." Just then your teacher begins to speak, and you can hardly believe your ears.

"I want each of you to take your own personal angle on the subject. [Yes!] Maybe you've seen a cool fish documentary or a crazy thriller that has sparked your interest. Maybe you even have a personal fish story to tell. Whatever interests you, we want to hear about it."

What's Ahead

- Writing a Research Report
- Sample Research Report
- Citing Sources

Writing a Research Report

To write a good research report, you need to do four things: (1) choose an interesting and specific topic, (2) gather information about your topic, (3) make a plan, and (4) write an interesting and accurate essay to share what you have learned.

Choosing a Specific Topic

Choose a Topic ■ The first thing you have to do when you write a research report is to find a specific topic. (*Fish* is a general subject; *saltwater fish* is more specific. More about that later.) You also have to find a topic that works well for your assignment and for the students who will later be reading or listening to your report.

Create a Cluster ■ You may want to use a cluster to begin your topic search. First, put your subject in the middle. After looking over information about your subject, list specific questions that interest you.

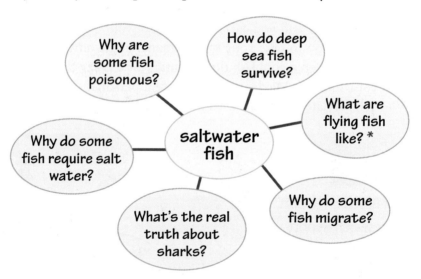

* Put a star next to the question(s) you want to answer in your paper. This will be your specific topic and focus.

Prewriting Gathering Information

Create a List ■ Once you have selected a topic (*flying fish*, for example), decide what you want to learn about it. Listing questions about your topic is one way to do this.

1. What is a flying fish?
2. How and why do they fly?
3. How fast do they go?
4. How many types are there?
5. How do people catch them?
6. How high can they fly?
7. How long have they been around?
8. What do they look like?
9. How far can they fly?

Tip   Avoid asking questions that can be answered with a simple "yes" or "no." Asking questions that begin with *what, how, who, when,* or *why* will lead to more interesting answers.

Review Your List ■ Readers expect certain qualities in a research report. Here are some of the characteristics readers expect to find in a scientific research report.

1. **A description of the subject** (*what it's like, where it lives*)

2. **Habits or characteristics** (*what it does or doesn't do*)

3. **Illustrations or photographs** (*what it looks like*)

4. **Diagrams or charts** (*how it compares to similar things*)

5. **Historical information** (*how it fits into our history or culture*)

Add to Your List ■ Always keep your list of questions in front of you and add questions that come to mind as you do your research. Remember to make sure that your questions cover the requirements for the assignment.

Find Good Sources ■ It's impossible to write a good research paper without good information.

- Look for books and magazines in the library.
- Search the Internet for articles and videos. (See pages 299–304.)
- Interview people who know a lot about your subject.

Mark Both Print and Digital Sources ■ When you "mark" a source, you are reminding yourself where you found important information. This can be done in many ways.

When Using Print Information

- Use book tabs to mark important sections of a book or article. You might choose different colored tabs for each question.
- Use highlighter tape or sticky notes to mark key ideas, words, or phrases. (If you have printed an article from the Internet, you can write directly on those pages.)

When Using Digital Information

- Gather and organize links to information and articles using a site or app your teacher recommends.
- Take notes using a word processor, your writer's notebook, or index cards.

Use a Gathering Grid ■ A gathering grid can help you organize the information you collect. (See the following page.)

- Write your **topic** in the upper left-hand corner.
- Write your **questions** down the left side of the grid.
- Write your **sources** across the top. (Sources are books, interviews, magazines, Web sites, and so on.)
- Search your sources and write your **answers** on the grid, or record where you can find your answers (such as in your writer's notebook, on numbered index cards, or in your electronic notebook).

Sample **Gathering Grid**

The following gathering grid was used by Marita Guttered, who wrote the sample research report on pages 264–267. This is only part of her grid, but it will give you a good idea of how a gathering grid works and how you can build one for your report.

Flying Fish	Books and Encyclopedias	Interviews	Magazine Articles	Internet Sites/Blog Posts/ Videos
What is a flying fish?	Specialized group of fish, The Amazing World, p.1		Flying, bony fish Ranger Rick	
How do they fly?	Fold in half, plus use pectoral fins, The Amazing World, p.12			Discovery Channel Video: Flying Fish Fly
Why do they fly?	To escape predators! The Amazing World, p.19			
How fast do they go?	20–40 mph The Amazing World, p. 17		More than 40 mph Ranger Rick	
Who has seen one?		Fisherman, Abe Short, interview in my writer's notebook		An amateur's account in The Log of the Snark, p. 84

Note   Part of this sample grid has been left out.

Prewriting *Recording Information*

Take Notes ■ There can be a lot of information to record for a research report. Your grid will help you keep track of key facts, but some facts may not fit. That's when you need to use your writer's notebook or note cards. Simply write the question at the top of the page or note card and then list the additional information. Record the source and page number.

How do they fly?
First they fold their bodies in half, and then they snap themselves forward. This gives them power.
The Amazing World, by Howell, p. 12

Write Down Quotations ■ When you read something that you want to use "word for word," copy the quotation just as it was written or spoken. (Place quotation marks before and after a quotation.)

Has anyone seen one fly?
"It came sailing through the air, and before I knew it, the fish was sticking into the side of my boat. Luckily it missed me by a few inches, or I would have been hurting for sure. The next thing I knew, it wiggled itself loose and was off again."
Interview with Abe Short, Jan 15, 2015

When you use exact words from books, magazines, the Internet, and interviews, you need to do two things: put quotation marks around the words, and tell the reader where you found the words you are quoting.

Prewriting *Organizing Your Information*

Create a Writing Plan ■ A writing plan can help you stay organized as you write your research report. You can use the **PAST** strategy to form a writing plan.

Purpose: To report about a subject
Audience: Teacher and classmates
Subject: Flying fish
Type: Research report

Develop an Outline ■ To organize the details you have gathered, use an outline like the one below. Think about your beginning, middle, and ending, as well as how you will organize specific details.

I. Beginning
   A. Set the stage with a chase.
   B. List questions that will be answered.
II. Middle
   A. What are flying fish?
     1. They are a specialized, bony fish.
     2. They are able to leave the water.
   B. Why and how do they fly?
     1. They need to escape predators.
     2. Explain how they take off. (Draw a picture.)

   E. Are they safe from becoming extinct?
     1. For now, they're all right.
     2. It's important to protect them.
III. Ending
   A. Tell readers that flying fish are doing okay.
   B. Comment on their possible future.

Writing Developing Your First Draft

▶ Beginning

Begin with an Interesting Lead ■ All writing needs a good lead or hook—something that will start the report with a bang. A short story or anecdote is one way to begin.

> In the ocean, two hungry dolphins pick up speed when they see a school of flying fish. Sensing danger, the fish swim faster and faster. Soon they are going 20 miles an hour. As the dolphins get closer, the flying fish break through the surface. Then they spread their side fins and take off. Amateur explorers have called them "dragonflies of the deep."

Tell What You're Going to Cover ■ Include a focus statement or a controlling idea that clearly states your topic and some subtopics you are going to cover.

> *How do flying fish do that —just take off and fly? And are they really fish? Why do they fly? How do they fly? How fast? How far? How high? What do they look like?* Read on to find out the answers to these questions and more.

Try Other Beginnings ■ You can also use a number of other ways to begin your report: a quotation from an interview, a surprising statement, a description of a character from your research paper—to name a few.

 Express Yourself Use your own words as much as possible. If you do use some direct quotations from other people, make sure to give them credit. (Not crediting sources is a mistake called *plagiarism*.)

▶ Middle

Connect Facts in Paragraphs ■ Simply listing the facts you've gathered would give you a research report like a shopping list—useful but very boring! You need to organize your facts into clear, colorful paragraphs.

You also need to include interesting information and carefully *elaborate* or explain each part with specific details. And, finally, be sure that the information is enjoyable to read. To turn your list into an interesting paper, follow these suggestions:

Adding Details: Elaboration

1. Use a variety of trustworthy sources.
2. Take good notes, double-check your facts, and always sort out fact and opinion.
3. Organize your paragraphs using different text structures (compare/contrast, problem/solution, cause/effect, and so on).
4. Use transitions or linking words to tie your ideas together throughout the paper. (See pages 24–26 for transitions to use with each text structure.)
5. Use headings, lists, quotations, illustrations, charts, and diagrams to make your key points stand out.
6. Link your ideas across paragraphs by restating an idea, building upon an idea you have already mentioned, or repeating important words or ideas.

Shaping Your Ideas: Craft

1. Include specific examples, definitions, and figures of speech (such as similes and metaphors) to help explain your ideas.
2. Vary your sentences by using different structures and beginnings. (See pages 469–470.)
3. Use a teaching tone—serious, but interesting.

▶ **Middle (continued)**

Explain the Key Points Clearly ■ Consider using questions, headings, or lists to make your key points stand out from the rest of the paper.

> **What are they?**
>
> Flying fish *are* fish. They are not dragonflies, or birds, or flying squid. They are a specialized group of bony fishes. . . .
>
> **Why and how do they fly?**
>
> Flying fish fly because they need to get away from predators such as other fish, water mammals, and birds that . . .

 Look at the middle section of the research report on pages 264–267. Notice how the writer builds her ideas and connects them from one paragraph to the next.

Add Information as Needed ■ After you develop each part, decide whether you need more details to explain an idea. If you do, try adding quotations, illustrations, or charts. These can add interest as well as information to your paper.

▶ **Ending**

End with a Strong Point ■ End your report with a summary of your main idea or a strong point about your subject. Also consider taking a look into the future or giving your readers a final idea to think about.

> Flying fish are successful creatures because they have developed ways to escape their enemies. They just glide away! They have been around since the days of the dinosaurs. Their special skill will probably keep them gliding for ages to come. One day, I hope to see one with its wings spread. Maybe I'll even see a disappointed dolphin that was chasing it!

Revising and Editing Improving Your Research Paper

Use a Checklist ■ Use the following checklist as a guide when you review and revise your report. Use the "Editing and Proofreading Checklist" on page 66 when you are ready to check for spelling, punctuation, capitalization, and grammar.

Overall

____ Does my research report follow the requirements for the assignment?

____ Do I have three main parts: a beginning, a middle, and an ending?

____ Do I organize my main ideas in a logical way?

Beginning

____ Does the introduction help readers understand and become interested in my subject?

____ Does a focus statement or controlling idea clearly state what I intend to cover in my paper?

Middle

____ Do I use information from reliable sources and give proper credit to each source?

____ Do I arrange my details according to familiar patterns (compare/contrast, problem/solution, cause/effect) and tie the details together effectively?

____ Do I connect my ideas from one paragraph to the next with transitions or headings?

____ Do I present or clarify my points in a variety of ways: charts, lists, quotations, definitions, and illustrations?

____ Do I use an interesting, teaching tone?

Ending

____ Do I offer a final summary or thoughtful question for my readers to consider?

Sample **Research Paper**

Flying Fish, Ocean Acrobats

Beginning
The lead
hooks the
reader with
a story
about the
topic.

In the ocean, two hungry dolphins pick up speed when they see a school of flying fish. Sensing danger, the fish swim faster and faster. Soon they are going 20 miles an hour. As the dolphins get closer, the flying fish break through the surface, spread their side fins, and take off. Amateur explorers have called them "dragonflies of the deep."

The writer
states the
focus and
identifies
what will be
covered.

How do flying fish do that—just take off and fly? And are they really fish? Why do the fly? How do they fly? How fast? How far? How high? Read on to find the answer to these questions and more.

What are they?

Middle
The writer
uses
headings to
identify
each new
part.

Flying fish *are* fish, not dragonflies or birds or flying squid. They are a specialized group of bony fishes that can stay in the air—sometimes as long as 45 seconds. While dolphins, rays, and whales can leap into the air for a few seconds, flying fish can leap and stay there, and leap again!

Why and how do they fly?

Flying fish fly because they need to get away from predators such as other fish, water mammals, and birds. Tuna, swordfish, dolphins, and birds love to have them for dinner. Humans eat them, too. To catch them, people have to use specialized nets.

Flying fish don't have wings. They have two sets of fins. Front or *pectoral* fins help them get airborne. Back or *pelvic* fins help them glide through the air. To leave the water, flying fish begin by folding their bodies in half. Then they snap themselves forward. This powers their flight. Next, their tails start to whip back and forth like propellers. As their tails beat, the flying fish leave the water. Finally, their pectoral fins spread open like wings. Their pelvic fins help them soar above the surface.

The writer clarifies specialized vocabulary.

A helpful graphic follows a description of the topic.

How fast and far can they fly?

The way flying fish take off is very interesting, but facts about how they fly are, too! While they can't fly long distances like birds, they can move through the air as fast as 40 miles per hour, and they can glide as far as three football fields. Most glide about four feet above the water, but if they have to, they can soar as high as 45 feet. That's high enough to sail over a house!

The first sentence of this paragraph links with the previous paragraph.

Sometimes flying fish land in fishing boats. One fisherman, Abe Short, recalled the day a flying fish dropped right out of the sky into his boat. "It came sailing through the air, and before I knew it, the fish was sticking into the side of my boat. Luckily it missed me by a few inches, or I would have been hurting for sure. The next thing I knew, it wiggled itself loose and was off again."

What do they look like?

Flying fish are fairly small—just 6–12 inches long. Their coloring is dull silver and white. Their coloring serves as perfect camouflage. This means that their body color helps them hide from their enemies. But, flying fish have beautifully colored fins, too, that span as long as 9–18 inches. When their fins open, people who have seen them say that they make a beautiful sight.

Are they safe from becoming extinct?

Many people are very concerned about animals becoming extinct. For now, it seems that flying fish are doing all right, but some overfishing and pollution are problems. The United Nations Council on the Law of the Sea is working tirelessly to keep flying fish abundant. So is Steven Howell. Howell wrote *The Amazing World of Flyingfish*, and he's worked hard to find out all the different types there are. He writes, "When humans start to recognize and name things, we have entered the first stage of understanding, which may help us to protect the oceans. . . . "

The writer quotes an expert to make a point.

Conclusion

Flying fish are successful creatures because they have developed ways to escape their enemies. They just glide away! They have been around since the days of the dinosaurs. Their special skill will probably keep them gliding for ages to come. One day, I hope to see one with its wings spread. Maybe I'll even see a disappointed dolphin that was chasing it!

Ending
The writers concludes with his thoughts about his topic.

Note

The bibliography page (or works-cited list) is not shown for this sample. If your teacher wants you to include a list of your sources, use the guidelines on page 268.

Citing Sources

Your teacher may ask you to make a list of the materials (sources) you used to write your research report. In that case, you will need to include a bibliography page or works-cited list at the end of your paper. Follow the examples below.

Tip

- List the author by last name, then first name.
- In a handwritten paper, use <u>underlining</u> instead of *italics*.

- **Book:** Author (Last Name, First Name). *Book Title*. City where the book is published, Publisher, Copyright year.

  Howell, Steve N. G. *The Amazing World of Flyingfish*. Princeton, NJ, Princeton University Press, 2014.

- **Magazine:** Author. "Article Title." *Magazine Title*, Date (day month year), Article page numbers (if numbered).

  Bolton, Mary. "Fish in the Air." *Marine Life*, June 2008, pp. 34–35.

- **Dictionary or Encyclopedia:** "Article Title." *Book Title*, edition or volume, Year published, Article page numbers.

  "Flying Fish." *World Book Encyclopedia*, vol. 7, 2011, p. 412.

- **Film/Movie:** *Title*. Director Name, Company, Year.

  Where the Yellowstone Goes. Directed by Hunter Weeks, Spinning Blue, 2012.

- **Personal Interview:** Person Interviewed (Last Name, First Name). Personal interview. Date (day month year).

  Short, Abe. Personal interview. 15 Jan. 2019.

- **Web Page:** Author (if listed). "Page Title." *Site Title*, Sponsor or publisher, Post date or last update, URL. Date accessed.

  Thomas, Bob. "Flying Fish: Missiles of the Sea." *Loyola Center for Environmental Communication*, Loyola University New Orleans, 25 June 2010, www.loyno.edu/lucec/natural-history-writings/flying-fish-missiles-sea. Accessed 12 Jan. 2019.

Writing Summaries

Think of all the reading you do in school: handouts, chapters, stories, reports, projects. And on top of that, you are expected to understand and remember the important ideas you have read.

Studies show that writing summaries may be the best way to remember what you have read. A summary is a short retelling of information using your own words. It should include the main ideas and important details in the same order in which you read them. Writing a summary is a little like squeezing out toothpaste. You squeeze out just what you need.

What's Ahead

- Developing a Summary
- Sample Summary and Original Selection

Developing a Summary

Planning Your Summary

Skim and Take Notes ■ Learn as much as you can about your reading selection before you try to summarize it.

- **Skim it.** Look at the title, table of contents, headings, pictures, and so on to get the general meaning. Then read the selection more carefully.

- **Take notes.** While reading and taking notes, follow these important rules:

> 1. **Write down headings.** Note headings and topic sentences, which often contain the main points.
>
> 2. **Use the 5W's questions.** Write down answers to the following: *Who? What? Where? When? Why?*
>
> 3. **Note repeated ideas.** Authors often say important things several times. Pay attention to words and phrases that are repeated.
>
> 4. **Record repeated ideas just once.** Avoid repetition in your notes and summary.
>
> 5. **Ignore trivia.** Don't write down details that are of little importance. Many details will be interesting, but if they are not key to the meaning of the text, do not include them in your notes or summary.
>
> 6. **Summarize lists.** If you see a long list, use a word or phrase to summarize it. For example, in the sample summary on page 273, the author wrote "Colorful" instead of "Red, orange, and yellow."

Annotate the Reading ■ Another way to take notes is to *annotate* your reading. Annotating means marking up a text as you read. Just make sure you own the text or are reading from a photocopy or a print out. Here's how one student annotated a text before writing a summary about it.

Need to find an answer to this question.

Why Do Leaves Change Color?

Even though leaves may look pure green in summer, they have other colors, too. Red, orange, and yellow pigments, which protect the leaves by blocking the harmful ultraviolet rays in sunlight, are hidden by the leaves' (chlorophyll.) It is this green (chlorophyll) that produces food for the tree.

* key word

In autumn, shorter days and cooler nights cause the green (chlorophyll) pigment in the leaves to break down and flow back into the tree. As the leaves' green color fades, the other colors begin to show themselves.

Here's why leaves change colors.

After the (chlorophyll) breaks down, leaves cannot make food anymore. Tubes (called *xylem* and *phloem*) that carried water to the leaf and food back to the tree become plugged. A layer of cork forms between the stems of the leaves and the tree branches.

Shortly after that, the leaves die and hang from their stems by a few strands. Cold autumn winds dry and twist the leaves until they become separated from the tree and float to the ground.

Writing | Developing Your First Draft

Use Your Own Words ■ Write your summary in clear and complete sentences. Use your own words, except for key terms.

1. **State the main idea.** The first sentence in your summary is a topic sentence. It should state the main idea (and the title and author if they are available). The sentences that follow must support the topic sentence.

2. **Choose important information.** Include only the most important information in the rest of your summary. (Follow the rules on page 270.)

3. **Place details in order.** Arrange your ideas in the same order they occurred in the original text. Pay attention to the overall organization (problem/solution, cause/effect, process, and so on).

The article says that leaves change color because chlorophyll flows back into the tree. This is a cause/effect relationship. The summary uses "because" in the first sentence to show this cause/effect relationship.

4. **Wrap-up the summary.** Add a concluding sentence if one seems necessary.

Revising and Editing | Improving Your Writing

Review Carefully ■ Ask yourself the following questions when you revise your summary. (Use the checklist on page 66 as an editing guide.)

___ Do I include the most important ideas and details?
___ Do I state these ideas briefly and in my own words?
___ Can another person get the main idea of this selection by reading my summary?

Sample **Summary**

The article "Why Do Leaves Change Color?" reports that autumn leaves change because they lose their green pigment. Colorful pigments are in the leaves, too, but they are hidden by the green. When cooler weather comes, the green chlorophyll breaks down, and the other colors can be seen. Then the leaves dry up, and the wind blows them off the trees.

Original Selection

Why Do Leaves Change Color?

Even though leaves may look pure green in summer, they have other colors, too. Red, orange, and yellow pigments, which protect the leaves by blocking the harmful ultraviolet rays in sunlight, are hidden by the leaves' chlorophyll. It is this green chlorophyll that produces food for the tree.

In autumn, shorter days and cooler nights cause the green chlorophyll pigment in the leaves to break down and flow back into the tree. As the leaves' green color fades, the other colors begin to show themselves.

After the chlorophyll breaks down, leaves cannot make food anymore. Tubes (called *xylem* and *phloem*) that carried water to the leaf and food back to the tree become plugged. A layer of cork forms between the stems of the leaves and the tree branches.

Shortly after that, the leaves die and hang from their stems by a few strands. Cold autumn winds dry and twist the leaves until they become separated from the tree and float to the ground.

Writing Plays and Poems

Writing Plays

Do you enjoy pretending—imagining you're someone you're not, making up conversations, and solving unusual problems? If so, try writing a play. You'll need some characters, a problem for them to solve, lots of conversation, and some creative thinking.

Ideas for plays can come from real life or from your imagination. Think about what happens to you and to other people. These experiences are good starting places for plays. You can also use ideas from stories, books, or TV shows. This chapter will help you turn one of your ideas into an effective play, one you and your classmates can act out in class.

What's Ahead

- Sample Play: Act 1
- Writing a Play
- Sample Play: Act 2

Sample Play: Act 1

You can begin your play by introducing the main characters and setting up a problem for them to solve. In the sample below, Dave and Jessica are in trouble, and they need a way out.

What Will We Tell Mom and Dad?

Characters: DAVE, 12 years old   JESSICA, 11 years old
DAD, their father   MOM, their mother

ACT 1

(The room is empty. Suddenly, JESSICA bursts through the door closely followed by DAVE.)

DAVE: *(pushing her)* It's all your fault!

JESSICA: *(pushing him back)* It's not! You're the one who couldn't wait till Mom and Dad got home from the store. You just had to go fishing the minute we got to this cabin. I should never have let you talk me into it.

DAVE: I just wanted to surprise them with a fish for dinner. And anyway, you're the one who borrowed Dad's new fishing rod.

JESSICA: Yeah, but I'm not the one who broke it, am I?

MOM: *(calling from offstage)* Jessica? Dave? Come help with these groceries.

DAVE: Oh, no! They're home! What are we going to do?

JESSICA: We'll just have to tell them we broke . . .

DAVE: *(interrupting her)* Tell them? Are you kidding? This vacation will be over before it's even begun. All we have to do is keep Dad's mind off fishing.

JESSICA: But how?

Writing a Play

Prewriting Planning Your Play

Find the Main Parts ■ You'll need at least two characters, a problem, and a place (the setting) for the action. Your characters can be based on people you know. The problem and action in your play can depict actual events that made you laugh or cry. Your setting may be a familiar place. You may also use your dreams and imagination to give you ideas.

Gather Details ■ Use a collection sheet or checklist to help you plan the details of your play. But don't make your plan too complicated. Sometimes your characters can take over and almost "write" the play for you!

Collection Sheet

Main Characters #1 and #2:
(Give each character a name and an age that fits. Briefly describe how your characters look and act.)

Other Characters:
(Identify and describe all other characters.)

Setting:
(Describe the place—or places—where your play happens. If it's important, also tell when the play takes place.)

Problem or Goal:
(State the problem or goal facing the main characters.)

Action:
(Describe your characters' actions as they try to solve their problem or achieve their goal.)

Solution:
(Have your characters solve the problem.)

Writing Developing the First Draft

Set Up the Play ■ Before you begin writing your play, you must let the reader know the title of the play, the names of the characters, and the setting in which the play takes place. (See page 276.)

Start the Play ■ For the opening dialogue, you can have the characters talk about the scene they are in or have them discuss the problem or goal of the play. Each time a person talks, you must write the name of that person, followed by a colon.

Solve the Problem ■ In the middle of the play, have the characters work at solving the problem or reaching their goal. This is where most of the action takes place. It is the talking and actions of the characters that make the play move ahead. In the sample that begins on page 276, Dave and Jessica plan all sorts of fun activities to keep their dad from fishing.

Note To create excitement—and maybe a little fun— your main characters can disagree about how to solve the problem.

End the Play ■ End your play by showing how the main characters solve their problem or reach their goal. You may also choose to have your characters fail at their solutions, just as sometimes happens in real life.

Be certain your ending is believable. Unless Dave and Jessica are millionaires, they shouldn't hop into a private jet, fly to the factory, and buy their dad a new fishing rod! They'll have to find a realistic solution to the problem.

Revising Improving Your Writing

Read Aloud ■ Read your first draft aloud. Decide if the play moves along smoothly and clearly from beginning to end. See if any parts should be cut out or if anything needs to be added. Pay attention to each line. Put a check next to any lines that you want to rewrite.

Write Dialogue ■ Dialogue is what your characters say to each other. You want them to sound like real people talking. Listen to how your family, friends, and other people talk, and use the words they use. Which of these lines sounds more real?

> Lee: Shar, please give me a call when you
>   arrive home from school today.
>
>   OR
>
> Lee: Shar, call me after school, okay?

Make a Point ■ Plays often share a theme or make a point about life. This message is carried through the characters' actions and words. By the end of *What Will We Tell Mom and Dad?*, the audience learns, along with Dave and Jessica, that it is best to tell the truth. Check to see that the point of your play comes through clearly.

Tip   Ask several classmates to read your play out loud. Listen carefully to find any dialogue that doesn't sound real or actions that aren't believable. Change them to better fit the rest of the play.

Editing Polishing Your Play

Check for Errors ■ Review your writing for spelling, capitalization, and grammar errors. Then write a neat final draft of your play, following the form of the sample. Proofread the final draft again before sharing it. (See page 66 for an "Editing and Proofreading Checklist.")

Sample **Play: Act 2**

In the first act of this play on page 276, Dave and Jessica break their father's new fishing rod. They don't want him to find out. Here, in Act 2, student writer Faith Brawley continues the action and adds a little suspense.

ACT 2

(The family has just finished dinner and is chatting in the living room.)

MOM: So, what did you guys do while we went grocery shopping?

JESSICA: *(in a shaky voice)* Well, we . . . um . . .

DAVE: *(interrupting JESSICA)* We played a game of cards.

JESSICA: *(glaring at DAVE)* We also went to the beach. I pushed Dave in the water. I thought he could use a cooling off.

DAD: Oh, that reminds me. Do you guys want to go fishing tomorrow, or would you rather go on a nature walk?

DAVE & JESSICA: *(at the same time)* NATURE WALK!

DAD: Okay, that settles that. We'll go on a nature walk.

MOM: *(yawning)* It's getting kind of late.

JESSICA & DAVE: *(leaving the living room)* Okay, Mom, we'll see you tomorrow.

JESSICA: That was a close one!

DAVE: You're telling me!

JESSICA: *(feeling horrible)* You know, I can't keep this a secret any longer. I'm going to tell Dad!

DAVE: *(in a panic)* You can't tell him. He'll be very upset. Remember, he hasn't had a vacation in three years.

JESSICA: I suppose so. . . .

Writing Poems

Poems are different from other kinds of writing. They have a special shape and sound. If you read enough poetry, you'll get better and better at understanding—and writing—poems. You'll even make friends with some of them. Here's how:

- Read the poem to yourself several times.
- Read the poem aloud; listen to what it says.
- Read it with feeling to friends or classmates.
- Talk or write about the poem.
- Copy the poem in a special notebook.

Words

Words! said the earth.
And the cloud
bumping into the hilltop
said back, Words!
And the words
were born
on a high wind
at the tail end of June,
when the sun brights
the sky so hard
no one can stop laughing.

—Anne-Marie Oomen

What Makes Poetry Special?

Poetry is different from prose (the regular writing you do). Here are some things that make poetry special.

1 Poetry looks different.

It's easy to recognize poems. They are written in lines and stanzas (groups of lines). Some poems are short enough to fit on the inside of greeting cards, and some poems go on for many pages. Here is a one-stanza, eight-line poem written by Phil Ryan.

My Ancestor
I look in the mirror
And what do I see?
I see an image of someone
That looks a little like me.
Could it be the face
Or maybe the hair?
I know who it is now:
It's my great-great-grandma Claire.

2 Poetry speaks to the mind and heart.

You can like a poem for what it says (that's the mind part), and you can like a poem for how it makes you feel (that's the heart part). It's the "heart part" that really separates poetry from other forms of writing.

3 Poetry says a lot in a few words.

Poets create word pictures using details about the sights, sounds, smells, tastes, and physical feelings connected with a subject.

I was standing on the street when . . .
The rusty old black station wagon (sight)
grunted rack-a-bump-she-bang, (sound)
and heated up my cool spot of air, (physical feeling)
and spewed oily smoke (smell)
all over my mustard-covered foot-long hot dog. (sight)
—Anne-Marie Oomen

4 Poetry says things in special ways.

Poets will sometimes create special word pictures by making comparisons. They may write a metaphor or a simile, like "I climbed slow as an old fly." Can you figure out which two things are being compared in the following examples?

Rain

Rain Rain
Wet Little Chicken Pox
On the Window . . .

—Cassie Hoek

A gentle wind at night is
my wispy grandmother.

—Tim Capewell

5 Poetry pleases the ear.

Poets carefully arrange words until their poems sound just right. Sometimes they use words that rhyme. Sometimes they repeat certain vowel and consonant sounds to make their poems sound pleasing. Notice how this repetition of sounds works in the poem called "Purple Poems."

Purple Poems

Quiet purple clouds rolled in.
Purple rain drops drip from
the clouds.
Smooth purple shells wash
in with the waves.
Purple lightning strikes a tree.
Purple poems litter the field.

—Katlyn McKalson

Express Yourself You will find pleasing sounds, sensory details, similes, and metaphors in regular writing, too. They just stand out more in poetry.

Writing a Free-Verse Poem

The following guidelines will help you write a free-verse poem. Free-verse poetry does not follow a specific form, or pattern, and it usually does not rhyme.

Prewriting Planning Your Poem

Choose a Subject ■ Write your poem about a subject that truly interests you. This could be a special room, a close friend, a favorite animal, a strong feeling, and so on.

Gather Your Thoughts ■ Freewriting about your subject can be a good way to begin. Here is poet Anne-Marie Oomen's freewriting about an old dog she once knew.

I knew an old alley dog. My stepmom said to never touch him. But once I tossed him half my butter sandwich, and he danced around. And once I climbed down our fire escape, and he crept up next to me. We sat near each other and watched the sunset on the brick wall. We stayed there until it was dark.

Writing Developing the First Draft

Create a Poem ■ The next step is to turn your freewriting into a poem. Begin by copying down the words, making line breaks where you hear pauses in the sentences. As you do this, you can also change some of the words or move them around.

Add New Words ■ This is a good time to add new words and phrases as you develop your poem. Here is how Anne-Marie used her freewriting to create a poem.

The writer changed the first line into a title.

She made the line breaks where she heard pauses in the sentences.

She added and changed some words to make the poem more interesting.

The Alley Dog

My stepmom said
to never touch him.
But once I tossed him
half my butter sandwich,
and he danced around.
And once I climbed
down our fire escape,
and he crept up next to me.
We sat near each other
and watched how the sun shined
on the brick wall
until it was dark.

Revising Improving Your Poem

Now you can turn your basic poem into a very special poem by doing some revising.

Add Word Pictures ■ Ask yourself what words you can add to brighten your poem. Try using word pictures like *personification, similes,* and *metaphors.* (See "The Sounds of Poetry" on page 289.)

Create a Shape ■ Think about writing the words in ways that make them look and sound like the topic of your poem.

Sample **Free-Verse Poem**

Anne-Marie moved words and added similes.

She wrote her words in the shape of a fire escape.

She also used personification.

The Alley Dog

Never touch him! my stepmom
shouted loud as a train. But once
I tossed him half my butter sandwich,
and he danced like loose litter in wind.
And once I climbed
slow as an
old fly
down our fire escape,
and he crept up,
stop
and go
like a car in bad traffic,
and we sat near each other,
and watched how the sun pushed
the cracked brick wall
into the dark.

Revising Different Versions

"The Alley Dog" is a good example of a free-verse poem. But sometimes poets like to create rhythms and rhymes in their poems. Poems with rhythms and rhymes are fun to say aloud. What's more, adding rhythm and rhyme helps people remember them!

Create Rhyme ■ Rhyme is important because it gives sound and a musical quality to a poem. Our brains like sounds that are similar but also a bit different—Like *beat* and *feet*. These sounds are friendly to each other.

Rhyme doesn't have to be perfect to be interesting. *Feet* and *beat* are **perfect** rhymes because only one sound changes, the first letter. You can also use **slant** rhyme and **internal** rhyme.

Perfect rhyme	Words at the end of a line that sound exactly alike except for the first letter or letters, like *frog* and *dog*, or *stutter* and *butter*.
Slant rhyme	Words that sound similar but are not perfect rhymes, like *litter* and *stutter* or *crate* and *safe*.
Internal rhyme	This is a rhyme that happens inside a line, or before the end of a line, like *disappear* and *fear* in the first part of the version of "The Alley Dog" on the next page.

Develop Rhythm ■ Rhythm comes from the Greek word *rhythmos*, meaning "to flow." In speech, it is the natural rise and fall of the language that creates the rhythm. Some syllables are stressed, or said with more force, than others. If you say the nursery rhyme "Old Mother Hubbard" aloud, you will hear yourself stressing some words more than others. That's rhythm!

Old mother Hubbard,

went to the cupboard,

to give her poor dog a bone. . . .

Sample Rhymed Poem

Anne-Marie added rhyme and rhythm to "The Alley Dog." Read the poem aloud. Do you hear how the rhythm falls on certain parts?

Anne-Marie changes the simile from *train* to *fog* to add rhyme.

She adds *perfect, slant,* and *internal* rhymes.

She uses city words to help set the scene.

She also uses personification, to prepare for the friendship at the end.

The Alley Dog

"Do not touch that strange dog,"
my stepmom whispers, soft as fog.
Though she's quiet, he hears.
He turns to disappear,

all fear.

So I toss him my bread and butter.
And he dances like let-loose litter,
and his paws stutter and sputter,
as he gobbles his treat,

watching me.

I climb down the fire escape and wait.
Slow as a car in a backed-up street,
he belly-scrapes down our alleyway
and stops near me, but not to bite,

so polite.

He eases up close, curls next to me,
like we were always meant to be.
We watch the sun push the alley bricks
into shadow. No tricks.

Real cool.
Friends rule.

Tip You can vary the rhythm by saying some words louder or faster than others. A fast rhythm can suggest excitement, and a slow rhythm can suggest laziness or sleepiness.

Editing and Proofreading

- **Make sure your poem reads well.** Do you stumble over certain words or lines in the poem? If so, change them.
- **Review the form.** Does the shape of your poem truly reflect what you are trying to say?
- **Check for errors.** Use the checklist on page 66 as a guide.
- **Write a final copy of your poem.** Make all of the corrections in the final copy and proofread this copy before sharing it.

The Sounds of Poetry

Here are some special writing devices used in poetry.

Alliteration: The repetition of beginning consonant sounds in words like *dance, dare,* and *drop.*

Assonance: The repetition of vowel sounds in words like *rain, makes, pavement,* and *wavy.*

End Rhyme: The rhyming of words at the ends of two or more lines of poetry.

Metaphor: A comparison without using the words *like* or *as. The full moon is a shiny balloon.*

Onomatopoeia: The use of words that sound like the noise they name, as in *buzz, thump,* and *snap.*

Personification: A comparison in which something that is not human is described with human qualities. *The sunflowers smiled at us.*

Repetition: The repeating of a word or phrase to add rhythm or emphasis. *The wind hissed, hissed down the alley.*

Rhythm: The pattern of sounds and beats that helps poetry flow from one idea to the next.

Simile: A comparison using the words *like* or *as. Granny's house looks like a dollhouse.*

Traditional Poetry

Traditional poetry has been around for a long time. Here are some examples:

Ballad ■ Ballad poems tell a story. The ballad is written in four-line stanzas. Often the second and fourth lines rhyme. (Here is the first stanza of "Ballad of Skull Rock.")

> We miners long ago did find
> the skull rock on the lake.
> The silver lay in open veins,
> all shining for the take.

Cinquain ■ Cinquain (*SIN-kane*) poems are five lines long with a specific purpose and number of syllables or words for each line. Here is one type of pattern for a syllable cinquain, followed by an example.

Pattern for a Syllable Cinquain

Line 1:	Title	(2 syllables)
Line 2:	Description or example of the title	(4 syllables)
Line 3:	Action about the title	(6 syllables)
Line 4:	Feeling about the title	(8 syllables)
Line 5:	Synonym for the title	(2 syllables)

Example of a Syllable Cinquain

Line 1:	Seashells
Line 2:	Cockles and clams
Line 3:	Collecting on beaches
Line 4:	Waiting for me to pick them up
Line 5:	Treasures.

Couplet ■ A couplet is a two-line verse form that usually rhymes and expresses one thought.

> Back and forth the dancer whirled,
> A butterfly with wings unfurled.

Free Verse ■ Free verse is poetry that does not include patterned rhyme or rhythm. (See the sample on page 286.)

Haiku ■ Haiku (*hi-KU*) is a traditional Japanese poem about nature. In English haiku, the first line is five syllables; the second, seven; the third, five.

Sun shines on sidewalks,	*(5 syllables)*
weeds grow sideways in small cracks,	*(7 syllables)*
ants take treasures home.	*(5 syllables)*

Limerick ■ A limerick is a funny verse in five lines. Lines one, two, and five rhyme, as do lines three and four. Lines one, two, and five have three stressed syllables; lines three and four have two stressed syllables.

There once was a chef named Maurice
Who always used way too much grease.
His chicken was fine;
His fries were divine,
But his dinners could make me obese.

Lyric ■ A lyric is a song-like poem that uses sensory details. Add a tune, and it can become a song.

Up! Up! Bright kites fly, oooh,
maroon, and yellow, and easy blue
over the evening park.
I like to think they pull me, too,
up into that blue, that easy blue,
far away from the dark.

Quatrain ■ A quatrain is a four-line stanza. In this sample, the first two lines rhyme, and the last two lines rhyme. (In some quatrains, the first and third and the second and fourth lines rhyme.)

The buses in cities are hot
And I have to ride them a lot.
But sometimes I get a good seat
And guess who is happy? My feet!

Playful Poetry

Poets have fun inventing new forms of poetry. Here are some invented forms to try.

Alphabet Poetry ■ An alphabet poem uses a part of the alphabet (such as *d, e, f, g*) to create a list poem.

> **D**elightful
> **E**vergreen
> **F**orever
> **G**reen

Concrete Poetry ■ Concrete poetry takes on a special shape that expresses the poem's meaning or feeling.

> The way to school is d$_{o_{w_n}}$
> **WIDE** streets
> FULL OF **BIG** PEOPLE!!!

Definition Poetry ■ Definition poetry tells the meaning of a word or an idea creatively.

> **FRIENDSHIP**
> Friendship is like the moon and stars,
> hanging around together,
> walking across the Milky Way.

Five W's Poetry ■ A 5 W's poem answers *Who? What? Where? When?* and *Why?*

> I *(Who?)*
> Love to skate *(What?)*
> Along Venice Beach *(Where?)*
> In the middle of the day *(When?)*
> Because people are friendly and get out of my way. *(Why?)*

List Poetry ■ A list can be a poem. Often the title says what the list is about.

What's in the box under my bed?
eight marbles and a shoestring
a shiny bubblegum ring
two valuable baseball cards
some chocolate candy bars
a letter my friend wrote . . .

Name Poetry ■ A name poem, or acrostic poem, uses the letters of a name or a word to begin each line in the poem.

Friendly	**C**alm eyes
Remarkable	**O**utgoing
Energetic	**O**pen
Dude	**L**aid-back

Telephone-Number Poetry ■ You can "find" a poem in your phone number. Each number can represent either syllables or whole words. Let's say your phone number is 362-4814. The first line of your poem will have three syllables (or words), the second will have six, the third will have two, and so on. Here's an example:

Our cat starts	*(3 syllables)*
his mornings on my lap	*(6 syllables)*
before	*(2 syllables)*
stalking stuffed mice	*(4 syllables)*
or dashing downstairs to explore.	*(8 syllables)*
He	*(1 syllable)*
likes things the same.	*(4 syllables)*

Terse Verse ■ Terse verse is short and humorous—two words that rhyme and have the same number of syllables. The title is the subject.

Joke Books	Lemonade	Candy
Smile	Pink	Sweet
File	Drink	Treat

Using Technology

Communicating Online

We love to communicate. We talk, text, phone, blog, Tweet, and Skype. We chat face to face, with video, or with text. The fact is that we are very social, and much of our socializing happens online.

When you communicate online, you need to think about each communication situation. What are you saying and why? Who is receiving your message? What is the best medium for sending it?

You'll find answers to these questions and more in this chapter. Think of this chapter as your driver's manual for communicating online.

What's Ahead

- Understanding the Situation
- Choosing Online Media
- Communicating Emotion Online

Understanding the Situation

Whether you are writing an instant message, sending an email, creating a video, or posting other media, you need to think about the situation. To do that well, you need to consider these elements:

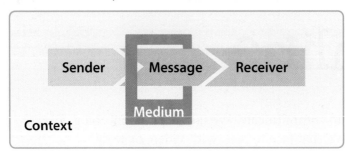

Sender: As the sender of the message, are you a student, a friend, a relative, a storyteller, a musician? What role do you have in sending this message?

Message: What is your message about (*topic*), and why are you sending it (*purpose*)? Make sure you understand what you are saying and why you are saying it—or your audience won't understand.

Medium: What is the best medium for your message?
- A *video chat* lets you chat, but it may intrude on someone.
- A *text message* doesn't intrude, but you can't say much.
- An *email* is more detailed, but it might not get a quick reply.
- An *online post* is more visible, but it is also less private.
- A *slide show* or an *animation* is impressive, but it takes work.

Receiver: Who is the receiver of the message? Writing for someone you know is easier than writing for someone you don't know. Whenever possible, have a classmate or family member respond as a first receiver before you send a message.

Context: What is the context? What came before, and what will come after? What will success look like for this message? Also, how formal should it be? Personal messages can use casual language, but school and public messages must be more formal.

Choosing Online Media

Once you've considered all of the elements in the situation, you are ready to choose a medium for communicating your message.

Voice or Video Chat

In a voice or video chat, the sender and receiver can interact to make the message clear. This medium is almost like talking face to face.

Text Chat

A text chat is almost as flexible as voice or video, and you may be able to save the conversation as a file.

What should we name our pet exercise story?

How about "Hot Dogs"?

LOL. Will people think it's about food?

How about "Hot Dogs and Cats"?

Text Message

Sending a short text is like sticking a note to your refrigerator: "Mom, we're out of corn flakes." The other person can read it anytime.

Email

Email is great for longer messages to one person or a small group. Schools and other groups use email for most important messages.

Blog or Wiki Post

Your class may have a blog or wiki where school reports, stories, poems, and drawings can be shared. Classmates, parents, and friends of the school can see these things. Follow the rules to protect your privacy.

Communicating Emotion Online

Sometimes *how you feel* about a message is at least as important as the message itself. The best way to communicate emotion is face to face:

- **Facial expression** lets people see how you feel.
- **Tone of voice** lets people hear how you feel.
- **Gesture, posture, and body language** express emotion.

If you need to convey emotion online, choose a medium that includes some of these clues. For example, a video chat includes all of them, but a phone call includes just tone of voice. Email includes none.

Communicating Emotion in Email

Email doesn't communicate emotion well. Receivers often think an email message is less positive than it was meant to be. To communicate emotion in email, raise your positivity one notch.

Delighted   Happy   Okay   Annoyed   Furious

If you are feeling happy, try to sound delighted. If you are feeling okay, try to sound happy. If you are feeling annoyed, try to sound okay. If you are feeling furious—walk away and cool off. In other words, never communicate online when you are very upset.

Using Emoticons

In casual online writing, emoticons can help express emotion:

- A colon, hyphen, and end parenthesis make a smiley face. :-)
- You can also make other faces.   ;-)   :-(8>D
- A left karat and the number three make a sideways heart. <3

Note: Do not use emoticons or text abbreviations (lol) in schoolwork or other formal writing.

Researching Online

When you need information for a project or report, you can find a whole world of it online—on the World Wide Web. In addition to discovering a treasure trove of amazing facts, however, you'll also find information that is out of date, inaccurate, or just not true.

This chapter helps you find the information you need. You'll learn *where* to look and *how* to judge the quality of a resource, as well as how to avoid research problems. Use this chapter and guidance from trusted adults to safely and effectively do research using computers.

What's Ahead

- Finding Information
- Evaluating Results
- Avoiding Research Pitfalls

Finding Information

Good research skills help you find the best information. Effective searching starts with knowing what to look for, where to search, and how to find it.

Knowing What to Look For

The best research starts with the best questions. You can use the *5 W's and H* to focus your research.

Who do I want to learn about?	*or*	**Who** is an expert on my subject?
What do I know about this?	*and*	**What** do I want to know?
When did this happen?	*or*	**When** was it written about?
Where did this happen?	*or*	**Where** should I start my search?
Why did it happen?	*or*	**Why** do people study it?
How did it happen?	*or*	**How** does it work?

Example: I want to know *how* author Norman Bridwell *(who)* invented Clifford the Big Red Dog *(what)*.

Knowing Where to Search

Finding answers means looking in the best places.

- **Start with search tools:** A search tool helps you find information. (On the next page, you'll learn tips for using search tools.)
- **Check out Web sites:** Most information on the Internet appears in Web sites. Sites are built out of pages—with text, pictures, videos, audios, and other media.
- **Consider ebooks:** Many books are available in digital form. They are searchable to help you find what you need.
- **Search library collections:** Use computer catalogs to find resources available through your library.
- **Ask experts:** At trusted Web sites, you can ask questions of experts. Get permission from your parent or guardian first. Do not post personal information!

Knowing How to Search

Search tools use *keywords* to find information about your topic. You can brainstorm keywords for your search. Write your topic in the middle of a piece of paper. Then list related words around it.

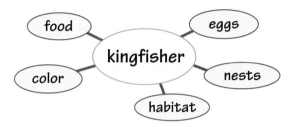

Using Keywords

Once you have brainstormed keywords, experiment with them in different groups to find the information you need.

- Searching for the word *kingfisher* by itself brings results for the bird, the city of Kingfisher in Oklahoma, an airline, and more.

- Searching for the words *kingfisher* and *food* brings up the bird and what it eats, but also restaurants named after it.

- Adding a minus sign, *–restaurant*, removes those businesses.

- Using a plus sign focuses on a specific word. Searching for *kingfisher +nest* focuses on nests made by kingfisher birds.

- Quotation marks mean exact words: *"kingfisher habitat"* will find those two words in that order.

- Some search tools have "advanced options" to help you fine-tune your search. ***Example:*** A library catalog may have a form with a space for subject words, another for title, another for author, and another for publisher.

Tip Check your search tool's screen or "Help" file to see if it has any special instructions or advanced search options.

Evaluating Results

Not all search results are valuable. Some may not fit your needs, and others may not be trustworthy. Use the communication situation to evaluate or judge your results.

Communication Situation

Each part of the communication situation reveals something about your search results.

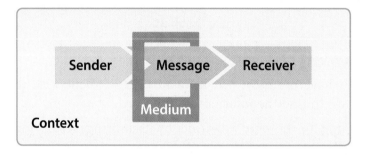

Sender: All information is sent by someone. Some senders are more trustworthy than others. Whenever you read, view, or hear information, ask who is sending it and whether the sender is reliable.

Message: Every message has a subject and a purpose. What is the message saying and why? Some messages are just providing information. Others are trying to sell something.

Medium: The medium is the way that the message is sent. For example, information about butterflies can come in articles, videos, FAQs (frequently asked questions), maps, photographs, or emails from experts. Each medium has its own strengths and weaknesses.

Receiver: Messages are meant for different audiences. Whenever you use a source, think about its intended audience. Who is supposed to use this information?

Context: Every message is created for a specific time and place. Ask yourself when and where information was created and whether it is still up to date.

Checking Extensions

Different Web sites have different endings, or extensions. They can help you judge whether a site is trustworthy.

.gov means a federal or state government site., and **.mil** means a military site. These sites provide reliable information, which usually can be used freely. (Give credit to your sources.)

> usa.gov   nasa.gov   alaska.gov   navy.mil

.edu means an education site, run by a school or college. Most often the information is reliable. Sometimes the information is free, but check with the site to make sure.

> wisc.edu   harvard.edu   purdue.edu   usc.edu

.org means an organization. Some are nonprofit. Others are not. Double-check their information elsewhere.

> habitat.org   moma.org   cancer.org   pbs.org

.com, .biz, .name, and others are commercial sites or personal pages. **.net** often means a network. Some of these sites give reliable information, but others are trying to sell you something, so be careful.

> minecraft.net   monkey.biz   smithsonianmag.com

.au (Australia), **.ca** (Canada), **.mx** (Mexico), **.uk** (United Kingdom), and most other two-letter domains refer to nations. Some sites with these extensions are government sites. Some others are businesses, and some are personal pages. Find out the kind of site you are viewing.

> canada.ca   amazon.co.uk   gutenberg.net.au

Avoiding Research Pitfalls

"The trouble with Internet quotations is that many of them are fake."
—Abraham Lincoln

Avoid the following research pitfalls, which can lead you in the wrong directions.

- **Don't rely on Wikipedia.** It makes your research seem lazy. Also, not everything on that site is trustworthy. Remember, good research compares more than one source.

- **Avoid clicking on advertisements and "sponsored" results.** Businesses pay to list those first. Their information may not be what you need. If you search for "Lincoln," you may see a car ad:

> **Lincoln.com - Official Lincoln® Site** ◄——— Sponsored Result
> [Ad] www.lincoln.com/ ▾
> Visit the Official **Lincoln** Site Now for Complete Vehicle Info.
> The Lincoln Motor Company · Luxury Cars, Crossovers
>
> **Abraham Lincoln - Wikipedia, the free encyclopedia**
> en.wikipedia.org/wiki/Abraham_Lincoln ▾ Wikipedia ▾
> **Lincoln** grew up on the western frontier in Kentucky and Indiana. ... In 1860 **Lincoln** secured the Republican Party presidential nomination as a moderate from a ...

- **Don't rely on just the first results that come up.** What you need may be several pages deep. One secret for effective searching is to keep digging until you find the best sources.

- **Don't use the same search terms over and over.** Use your first results to fine-tune your search terms. What you find early on can help focus your search.

 Tip Not every source is for all ages. Whether searching online, in a library catalog, or even in an electronic encyclopedia, don't click on anything you're not sure of. Ask an adult for help.

Staying Safe Online

Imagine living in a glass house. You could see everything outside, but everything and everyone outside could see you, too. The online world is like a glass house. It can show you lots of information, but it can also share secrets. Learn to protect yourself.

This chapter focuses on ways that you can keep yourself safe online. You'll learn about safety habits and rules as well as questionable things to watch for. When in doubt, check with a trusted adult before doing anything online.

What's Ahead

- Develop Safe Habits
- Follow Safety Rules
- Understand Dangers

Using Computers Safely

The World Wide Web provides many opportunities for education and entertainment, but also some dangers. If you develop safe habits, follow safety rules, and understand the dangers, you'll be better able to keep yourself safe online.

Develop Safe Habits

These important practices can help protect you.

- **Log out when you leave.** Many programs and apps have you sign in. That lets them remember details to help you work or play. When you leave the program, always sign out. Then someone else can't see your details, change your files, or pretend to be you.

- **Use safe passwords.** You wouldn't set your locker or bicycle lock to "1-2-3." If your computer password is easy to guess, it isn't safe either. Choose a mix of letters, numbers, and punctuation you can remember. If your cat's name is Sheila, a good password could be 5h3i!a.

- **Keep private details private.** Never post your photos, phone number, address, or other private information where strangers can see them.

- **Don't fall for tricks.** A pop-up message on a Web page might say your software is out of date. An email might claim you have won something. A quiz for fun might ask your cat's name (to guess your password). Don't fall for these tricks.

Pop-Up Example

Always ask an adult before installing anything.

● ● ●

Warning!

Your antivirus software may be out of date! Click "Yes" to install the latest antivirus protection for free!

Yes   Cancel

Follow Safety Rules

Learn the following rules that are meant to keep you safe.

- **House rules:** Follow technology rules set up by your parent.
- **School rules:** Follow the rules your teachers provide.
- **Online rules:** Obey age guidelines for technology use.

Understand Dangers

Watch for and avoid the following types of dangers.

- **Viruses** are software made to infect your device, steal your information, and spread to other computers. Email attachments and online ads may have viruses.
- **Bloatware** is software that takes up lots of computer memory. Many free programs contain hidden software to change your computer settings or give unwanted advertisements. Always ask an adult before installing a new app or program.
- **Pop ups** are windows that "pop up" when you visit some Web pages. Many pop ups link to viruses or bloatware.
- **Spam** refers to unwanted messages with ads or viruses. Keep your email and social media accounts private to avoid spam.
- **Phishing** is a type of spam that asks for personal information. It may pretend to be from a trusted company. Do not respond to such requests. Tell an adult about it.

Phishing Example

Never click links in unexpected emails.

● ● ●

Dear Sir,

Your Brooster Community Bank account is about to be closed. To avoid closure penalties, please fill out the www.broostercommunitybank.com/complaints-form.

Sincerely,
Complaints Department

Reading and Spelling Skills

Reading Strategies for Fiction

Reading fiction is different from reading informational books and articles. Short stories and novels are imaginary. They can be funny, exciting, serious, and everything in between. The basic strategies in this chapter can help you enjoy and understand fiction. They guide you through each step in the reading process—before, during, and after you read. Or stated in another way, they keep your reading right on course.

What's Ahead

- Before Reading
- During Reading
- Model Short Story
- After Reading

Before Reading

Before you start to read a story, preview it. Previewing is taking a peek at a novel or short story to get a sense of what to expect. Who are the characters? What is the setting? What problem or event is the story about? Previewing allows you to read with purpose.

Tips for Previewing

1 Consider basic elements of fiction.

- **Characters:** Who is the story about?
- **Setting:** Where and when does the story take place? What is the setting like?
- **Conflict:** What problem or event gets the story rolling?
- **Plot:** What happens in the story? How do the characters respond to the conflict?
- **Theme:** What is the author's major message or statement about life?

2 Think about other elements.

- **Narration:** Who is telling the story? Is the story told about the characters (third-person point of view), or is it told by the characters (first-person point of view).
- **Description:** How does the author describe the characters? How does the author describe the settings?
- **Dialogue:** Do the characters speak a lot, or only a little? What do their words reveal about them?

Tip Previewing a story can be very helpful if the story is difficult or complicated. Simple stories can usually be read without any need for previewing. You will have to decide from one story to the next.

3 Preview the story or the novel.

Strategies for previewing a story may vary, based on its length.

Short stories: Though short stories often have no pictures or chapter titles to give you clues, you can still preview stories. Here are a few tips:

- Look at the title and author.
- Check out the author on the Internet. Ask, *What types of stories does the author write?*
- Read the first few paragraphs. Look for hints about the setting, the main characters, and the event or problem they face.

Novels: Use these tips to get a general idea of the plot, characters, setting, and theme of a novel.

- Notice the title and author.
- Look at the book's cover.
- On the back cover and on the first few pages, search for and read *summaries, information about the author, a preface,* or *an introduction.*
- Read the chapter titles and look at any illustrations.

During Reading

As you read a story or a novel, read actively. The tips that follow will help you do just that:

Tips for Reading

1 Read with purpose.

Answer these questions about the elements of fiction: character, setting, conflict, and narration.

___ Who is the main character?

___ What is the setting (time and place)?

___ What problem is the main character facing?

___ Who is telling this story (narrator)?

2 Read actively and record your thoughts.

Use the following ideas. (See "The Truth About Rowf" on pages 313–316 for examples.)

- **Predict upcoming events.** Predicting what may happen next will keep you focused on the story.
- **Infer.** Use what you've read so far to grasp an idea that is not specifically stated by the author.
- **Check your understanding.** Stop reading from time to time and think about what you have just read. Reread when necessary.
- **Summarize.** When you're through reading for the day, write a short summary of your thoughts. (See pages 269–273 for summarizing suggestions.)
- **Visualize scenes.** To do this, reread part of the story and ask yourself these questions about it:

  ___ What am I seeing?   ___ What's the shape?

  ___ What's the color and size?   ___ What do I hear, smell, taste, touch, feel?

  ___ How many?   ___ When is this happening?

- **Evaluate.** Ask yourself . . .
  How does the author make the story come alive?
  What seems to be really entertaining, informative, or useful?
  Could the author have done anything differently?

Express Yourself When you visualize a scene, use your own experience and knowledge to add details to your mental picture. You should also share your ideas with other students. Their responses may give you other interesting thoughts about the scene.

Sample **Short Story**

The Truth About Rowf
by Sandy Asher

The beginning introduces Rowf and Jessica and sets up the problem (she is tactless).

Rowf is a dog with problems. Don't get me wrong. I love him just the way he is. But I'm a very honest person, and if my dog has problems, I say so. Mrs. Krebs across the hall will tell you how honest I am. She told me a couple of weeks ago. Boy, did she ever!

"Jessica Gentry, you are a tactless person," she said. "You'd better watch that mouth of yours, or it will get you into trouble."

Details describe the setting.

I'd just told her that her cabbage soup was stinking up the whole building. Well, it was! We live on the 7th floor, and I could smell it in the lobby. But I did look up "tactless." It means "lacking a sense of what to do or say to maintain good relations with others or avoid offense."

The main character narrates the story.

That is not the truth about me. I have the "sense." I know the answer to Mom's "Do you like my new hairdo?" shouldn't be "No." She can't paste the cut parts back on. And I know the answer to a friend's "Are these jeans too baggy?" shouldn't be "Yes." She can't leave school to change them.

But I know these things too late—after my mouth opens and the truth pops out.

How do you watch your mouth?

Back to Rowf, my dog with problems. Mom and I adopted him from the shelter two years ago. He was a

Sensory
words
describe
Rowf.

stray, so there's no telling how old he is, but his sight and hearing are not good. And he's slow. And ugly. Big, grayish brown, shaggy, nearly deaf and blind, slow, probably old, definitely ugly.

We just had to take him home.

Rowf loves everybody, but we get some funny looks when we're out walking together. (Slowly.) The best look we've ever gotten was on the face of Rags Dugan last week when he tried to get tough with my best friends, Vic and Val Tasca. Vic and Val are twins. They live across the hall, next to Mrs. Krebs, and they're my age, fifth grade. Rags doesn't live in our building or go to our school. He's older. And mean.

Vic, Val, and I were trying to earn some money. We do that a lot—try to earn some money. Not easy when you're too young to babysit and other people prefer to walk their own dogs. So, we decided to have a rummage sale.

Dialogue
moves the
plot
forward.

"We must have tons of useless stuff around our apartments," I said. "We could set up a table outside."

"Great idea!" Vic said.

"We'll see what we can find," Val agreed.

"I'll bring the table," I told them.

Up the elevator we rode.

"Mom," I called, "have we got any old clothes?"

"Only what we're wearing," she said.

"I mean, really old clothes. Or other stuff we don't need. The twins and I want to have a rummage sale."

"You have that junk jewelry Aunt Rose gave you. I've

been trying to throw that out for years."

"It is not junk jewelry," I said, for the millionth time. "It's costume jewelry. Aunt Rose said so."

Dialogue also reveals who the characters are.

"And then gave it all to you," Mom pointed out, "when you were three. How long has that box been gathering dust?"

Ages.

I found the box and carried it over to the Tascas.

"We found our baby toys," Val announced.

"Great," I said. "And look at this jewelry. Some of it's chipped, but I'll bet it'll sell if we don't ask too much."

We maneuvered the folding table onto the elevator, set it up outside the front door of our building, and spread out our stuff. In the sun, it all looked pretty good! Then we waited for customers. Lots of people walked by. A few stopped. One young woman bought two pairs of earrings (not chipped), and a gray-haired man bought a set of alphabet blocks — even though I almost blew it when I told him three letters were missing.

Jessica struggles again with her problem (holding back).

Twin looks from Vic and Val: Too much information!

"Still plenty left for when the grandchildren visit," the man said.

Lucky for me! The twins did not mind one bit when I had to go upstairs and get Rowf. It was time for his walk.

By the time I got back, everything had changed. Vic and Val had another customer— kind of. Rags Dugan was swinging one of my necklaces around his finger.

"You give that back!" Val yelled. "You'll break it!"

"Put it down or pay for it!" Vic shouted.

Rags grinned, dangling the necklace high overhead.

Just then, Rowf yanked me forward in his big, slow way, and bumped into the table. He wanted to walk.

Rags dropped the necklace. Val caught it mid-fall.

"Call off your dog!" Rags demanded.

"I can't," I said.

Rowf pushed forward, smack into Rags. Rags began backing away. Slowly.

"Call him off!" he said again, in a voice that had gone kind of squeaky.

The voice in my head was much louder: Rowf may be big and ugly, it said, but he's also deaf and harmless. Rowf loves everyone, it said. That's the truth, it said.

I bit my lip, wishing my mouth would stay shut. Then I noticed the look on Rags's face —all wide-eyed and wild, the way he often made other kids look. Younger kids. Like my best friends Vic and Val.

"I . . . can't," I repeated.

Rowf inched forward. Rags stumbled backward. Then, he turned and ran. The twins, Rowf, and I stood frozen until he disappeared around the corner.

"Our hero!" cried Val, kneeling beside Rowf.

"That was so clever," Vic told me, "saying you couldn't call him off."

"It was the truth," I said.

I'd told the truth and watched my mouth!

It was smiling.

The action reaches a climax, when the character confronts her problem head on.

The falling action and resolution bring the story to a close.

After Reading

When you finish a story, complete the following types of strategies.

Tips for Reflecting

1 **Reflect by asking yourself some questions.**

___ Do I understand everything that happened?
___ Can I describe the personalities of the main characters?
___ Does the end come as a surprise? Why or why not?
___ Does anything in the story confuse me?
___ What is the main point or theme of the story?

 Tip You may need to do some rereading to answer these questions.

2 **Create a plot diagram.**

Skim the story to review the important parts:
(1) the main characters, (2) the conflict or problem they struggle with,
(3) their response to the problem, (4) the "aha" moment (the climax),
(5) the follow-up action, and (6) the way the story ends.

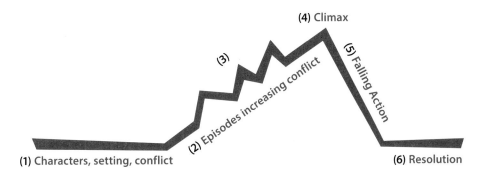

(4) Climax

(3)

(2) Episodes increasing conflict

(5) Falling Action

(1) Characters, setting, conflict

(6) Resolution

3 Fill out a character map.

Consider what the characters say, do, and feel. Also consider what you and others think and feel about them.

Sample **Character Map: Jessica**

What She Says and Does	What Others Think
• She loves her dog. • Honest things come out of her mouth, regardless of how they make other people feel. • She wants to earn money.	• Mrs. Krebs thinks she's tactless. • Val and Vic like her a lot!

Feelings About Herself	How I Feel About Her
• She does have the sense to know when "the truth" will be "tactless," but it's usually too late.	• She seems to have a fun personality. • She'd make a good friend.

4 Chart character development.

What a character says, does, and thinks at different points can show how he or she changes. This may reveal the story's theme.

Sample **Character Development Chart: Jessica**

Beginning	Middle	End
Jessica is a bit out of step. She doesn't sense how her words make people feel.	Her friends help her sense when she's saying too much. She begins to change.	She discovers when to hold back, and this makes all the difference in the story's outcome.

Theme: The theme is "Think before you speak."

5 Fill in a fiction organizer.

To help you reflect even more on the story you have just read, you can record important information about the *characters, setting, plot,* and *theme* on a "fiction organizer." You can also include information about the *narrator,* the *author's style,* the *sentence style,* and the *key features* of the storytelling. This should help bring everything together.

Sample **Fiction Organizer: "The Truth About Rowf"**

Characters	Setting
• Jessica Gantry • Vic and Val Tasca • Rags Dugan	• Apartment building • Rummage sale in front • Modern day

Plot	Theme
• Jessica needs to hold back. • She and friends have a sale. • Rags tries to take necklace. • Jessica lets Rowf scare Rags.	• Jessica learns that she should not just blurt out the truth when it is wiser or kinder not to.

Narrator	Author Style
• Jessica is the narrator. • She says "I" and "me," using first-person. • She uses past-tense verbs.	• The voice is friendly. • She uses clear description, lively dialogue, and action.

Sentence Style	Key Features
• She uses short sentences. • Long sentences show excitement. • Some are fragments: "Twin looks from Vic and Val: Too much information!"	• Sensory adjectives describe Rowf: slow, ugly, big, grayish brown, shaggy, nearly deaf and blind. • Characters are likable and seem real.

6 Reread the story.

If you are still confused or unclear about some part of the story, you may want to reread all or part of it. You can also reread simply to enjoy favorite parts or to study any special techniques that the author uses.

Note Sometimes you may get distracted while you're reading. Other times, you may need to think more about a story. These are good reasons to reread.

A Rereading Process

If you do decide to reread the story, the following tips can help to make it a worthwhile experience:

- **Scan the story.** Now and then, *stop, think,* and *retell* the story to yourself. If you have trouble retelling a part, think about why:

  1. Do you need to find out the meanings of any words?

  2. Did you miss signal words like "because" or "nevertheless"?

  3. Did you get lost because of the pronouns *(he, him, they, she)?* Are you unsure of who did what to whom?

  4. Did you miss an inference? (An inference is an idea you figure out from your own knowledge and experience. It is not directly stated in the story.)

- **Reread favorite parts of the story.** Think about why you like those parts so much. Does the author use just the right words? Does a part surprise you? Can you relate to one or more of the characters?

- **Scan the story one last time to identify the elements of fiction.** Think about characters, setting, plot, and narration (point of view). Then look for the author's big idea, or theme. (You can use the "Tips for Previewing" on pages 310–311 to help you scan or review the story.)

Reading Strategies for Nonfiction

Reading nonfiction is one of the main ways that you learn in most of your classes—including science, social studies, math, and language arts. As a result, you can improve in all these classes by learning the basic reading strategies for nonfiction covered in this chapter. These strategies will help you later in life as well. Adults read a lot of nonfiction for their jobs and to keep track of what is happening in the world. This chapter helps you take charge of your nonfiction reading.

What's Ahead

- Before Reading
- During Reading
- Model Nonfiction Article
- After Reading

Before Reading

When you read nonfiction, you should always preview the text first. Previewing gives you a general idea of what an article or a book is about. It gets your mind ready for the new information you'll be learning.

Tips for Previewing

1 Review the basic parts of the text.

That means looking at the beginning, middle, and ending. The beginning introduces the topic; the middle gives more information about it; and the ending repeats or summarizes the main idea about the topic.

2 Predict what the text is about.

To make an accurate prediction, you need to look at the title and first paragraph. You should also look at the headings, graphs, illustrations, and other cues. (See the sample cue chart below for the article starting on page 326.) Also look over any questions at the end of each chapter.

Cue	Prediction
Title	This article is about Superman. Cool!
First paragraph	It talks about comic book superheroes.
Headings	• This part must be about how Superman got started. • This part maybe talks about the first Superman comic book. • Here I'll find out why Superman became so popular.
Highlighted/repeated words	The article talks a lot about "comic books" and "superheroes."
Last paragraph	The main point is that Superman was and still is a superhero!

Brainstorm what you already know about the topic.

Make a list, freewrite, or cluster your ideas about the topic.

> Superman helps people. He is strong and brave. Everyone has heard of this guy. His clothes stand out: a blue and red cape with a huge "S" on front. And Superman is an alien from Krypton! He's a two-in-one character: Superman, the superhero; and Clark Kent, the reporter.

During Reading

As you read your text, read with a purpose. Find the most important information, take notes, and ask, "Do I understand this?"

Tips for Reading

1 **Pick out the key sentences in each paragraph.**

This sentence gives the topic of the paragraph: Superman's secret identity.

> <u>Like other heroes of the period, Superman came with a secret identity.</u> When not leaping over tall buildings, Superman is a timid newspaper reporter named Clark Kent. Clark's character was drawn from the author's own experiences. "The concept came to me that Superman could have a dual identity." He would be a superhero in one identity. But in the other, he would "be meek and mild as I was, and wear glasses, the way I do."

2 Identify the most important facts and details.

Most key facts and details are set off in some way. Look for these clues:

- **Typestyle:** Pay attention to print size, *italics*, **bold**, and color. Also notice ideas set off by bullets (•, ▪, *) or numbers.
- **Illustrations and photographs:** Look at visual details closely. They can help you understand information in a whole new way.
- **Graphics:** Review any diagrams, cutaways, cross sections, overlays, maps, word bubbles, tables, graphs, and charts.
- **Captions or labels:** Read captions and labels to gather more details and deepen your understanding.
- **Parts of a book:** Look at each part of a nonfiction book. An *appendix* gives extra information, an *index* lists every topic, a *glossary* defines special words, and so on.
- **Organization:** Learn about the patterns of organization—cause/effect, question/answer, compare/contrast, and problem/solution. You will understand ideas best when you know how they are arranged.

3 Take notes.

- Look at your preview predictions, read the text, and jot down ideas and details. Do your notes match your predictions?
- Mark the text with these symbols (if it's allowed).

> * I knew this.
> ? I wonder, or
>   I don't understand.
> + This is new information.
> ! This is very interesting.

> + Finally, Superman made his debut in Action Comics #1 in 1938. In that first issue, Superman comes from an unnamed distant planet. He shows extraordinary powers. He can leap* great distances, and he has super strength. His eyes give him heat vision, X-ray vision, and telescopic vision. ?

■ Create an outline.

> "Superman Takes Off"
> I. A Superhero Is Born
>   A. Jerry Siegel is a high school kid.
>   B. He wants to be reporter and do something special.
>   C. He discusses a new character with Joe Shuster.

4 Check your comprehension.

■ Read a passage.

■ Then stop and ask, "What does this mean?" Use your own words to write or say aloud the main idea of the passage. If you cannot figure out what the passage means, try one of these four fix-up strategies.

Problem	Fix-Up Strategy
I don't know the meaning of these words.	Check the context of the words to figure out their meaning. If necessary, use a dictionary or ask for help from someone.
I can't figure out how this text is organized.	Look for signal words that tell you how the ideas are related.
The author seems to have left something out here. I can't follow this.	Try to infer what the author means. Use your own knowledge and experience to understand what the author is saying. If you still can't figure things out, talk about the text with others.
I don't know much about this topic.	Find out more about the topic—read about it in a reference book or on the Internet, or ask someone for help.

Nonfiction Article

This article is about Superman.

The first paragraph talks about comic book super-heroes.

Superman Takes Off
by Stephen Krensky

American comic books became popular in the 1930s. One type of character especially—the superhero—struck a chord with comic book readers. Superheroes are characters who often use special powers or extraordinary abilities to fight injustice and defend the weak.

A Superhero Is Born

In the early 1930s, young Jerry Siegel was an ordinary high school student. Someday, he thought, he might become a reporter. As he remembered later, he had several crushes on "attractive girls who either didn't know I existed or didn't care if I existed."

What could he do about that? He wasn't sure. But at least he could use his imagination. "What if I was really terrific?" he wondered. "What if I had something special going for me, like jumping over buildings or throwing cars around or something like that?"

Siegel and his friend Joe Shuster attended high school in Cleveland, Ohio. They were both science-fiction fans. They also loved reading about the jungle man Tarzan, who was already a comic-strip star.

After graduating, the two friends began discussing an idea for a new character. His name was Superman. Siegel even published a story about him called "The Reign of Superman." However, this Superman was a

This part explains how Superman got started.

villain. He used his mental powers to further his own evil purposes. In a 1983 interview, Siegel recalled what happened next. "A couple of months after I published this story, it occurred to me that Superman as a hero rather than as a villain might make a great comic strip character."

Like other heroes of the period, Superman came with a secret identity. When not leaping over tall buildings, Superman is a timid newspaper reporter named Clark Kent. Clark's character was drawn from Siegel's own experiences. "The concept came to me that Superman could have a dual identity." He would be a superhero in one identity. But in the other, he would "be meek and mild as I was, and wear glasses, the way I do." Siegel also decided that Clark Kent is in love with another reporter, Lois Lane. But Lois does not return Clark's feelings. In fact, Lois is madly in love with Superman.

Superman Makes His Debut

This part talks about the first Superman comic book.

In the mid-1930s, Siegel and Shuster got jobs at DC Comics (then called DC-National). They worked as a team. Siegel wrote adventure and crime-fighting comic book stories, and Shuster illustrated them. They tried several times, with no success, to convince DC to publish Superman stories. But as their reputations grew, DC took their proposal more seriously.

Finally, Superman made his debut in Action Comics #1 in 1938. In that first issue, Superman comes from an unnamed distant planet. He shows extraordinary powers. He can leap great distances, and he has super strength. His eyes give him heat vision, X-ray vision, and telescopic vision.

After a few months, Superman's popularity erupted. At that time, one issue of a successful comic book might sell one hundred thousand copies. Superman was soon selling more than one million. As the series continued, readers learned that Superman was the last survivor of the doomed planet Krypton. He was an infant when his planet exploded. But he escaped just in time. How? His parents Jor-El and Lara sent him to Earth in a small spaceship. The spaceship crashed in a field in Smallville, Kansas. Farmers Jonathan and Martha Kent found the ship with the healthy baby inside. They adopted him and named him Clark.

Why Did Superman Catch On?

This part explains why Superman became so popular.

Well, first, his many powers were exciting to fantasize about. Who wouldn't like to fly and see through walls? Second, Superman used those powers to do good deeds and to battle crime. In the 1930s, gangsters roamed the streets of many big cities, and people wished for a hero to save the day. Third, Superman confronted injustice. In Europe and other parts of the world, dictators loomed as a growing menace. The comics overflowed with these dangers. And when society is turning ugly, the idea of Superman is comforting. He gave people a sense of hope about the future.

This part tells about radio's impact on Superman.

Superman was immediately popular, the first hero ever to get his own comic book. Soon, he went on to bigger things. He was the subject of a newspaper comic strip and appeared on radio. It was the radio program that introduced the famous phrases describing Superman as "faster than a speeding bullet" and "more powerful than a locomotive." It also included the famous lines: "Look! Up in the sky! It's a bird! It's a plane! It's Superman!"

From 1938 to the present, Superman has been one of Earth's guardians. He remains on the lookout for the next bad guy with evil on his mind.

After Reading

When you finish reading, you can respond to the text using these strategies.

Tips for Reflecting

1 Keep track of new vocabulary words.

Write down words you come across you don't know. (See page 346 for vocabulary notebook ideas.)

2 Reflect on the text in a learning log.

Write down main points about the topic, interesting supporting details, and any ideas that surprised you. (See pages 121–124 for tips on keeping a learning log.)

> Krensky compared the number of comics that Superman sold to the previous best-sellers: 1,000,000 to 100,000. Wow! Ten times as many!

3 Summarize the text.

Review your notes and write a summary of the text.

> "Superman Takes Off," by Stephen Krensky, is a short article about the very beginning of the comic book hero Superman. It also explains how Superman made his debut and why he, literally, took off.

4 Write a blog post to share what you've learned.

Create a short review of the reading. It's a good way to connect with students who care about the same topic.

Review of "Superman Takes Off"

It's not every day that you learn how a superhero was born. But when you read Stephen Krensky's "Superman Takes Off," you sure do! Who would have thought having a crush on someone could lead to a world-famous comic book hero? What's more, who could imagine that a superhero could sooth a whole country during a war? Did you know that Superman started off as a villain? If these questions interest you, read "Superman Takes Off"!

Express Yourself Talk with your classmates about what you've read. Very often, they will have read the same text you did, so you can compare your thoughts and impressions.

Reading Graphics

Did you know that the first writing ever invented used pictures instead of words? Five thousand years ago, Egyptian children learned by "reading" a kind of picture writing called **hieroglyphics:**

Cleopatra

Native American tribes also used picture writing to "talk" to other tribes that didn't speak their language. That's one useful thing about simple pictures—they mean the same thing to everybody. "Bear" is *oso* in Spanish, *ours* in French, and *honaw* in Hopi, but everybody understands . . .

What's Ahead

- Symbols
- Diagrams
- Graphs
- Tables
- Reading Graphic Information

Symbols

The drawings used in picture writing are called "symbols." A **symbol** is a simple picture or drawing that stands for something else.

Picture Symbols ■ It's easy to tell what a symbol means when it looks just like the thing it stands for.

Signs and Symbols ■ Sometimes symbols stand for things that you can't really draw a picture of—like the equal sign. In this case, the symbol stands for an idea; everybody who knows basic math knows that = means "equals." Here are a few examples of signs and symbols used in different subjects. How many do you know?

Math:	≠	>	⊥
Weather:	✳	▲	▥
Science:	Ω	⇄	↑

 If you see a symbol and you don't know what it means, look for "Signs and Symbols" in the table of contents of your dictionary.

Diagrams

Diagrams are simple pictures that usually include words (labels). Diagrams can show everything from the parts in your computer to the bones in your hand.

Cycle Diagram ■ A cycle diagram shows how something happens over time. It shows a series of events that happen over and over again, always leading back to the beginning.

Line Diagram ■ A line diagram helps you see how one thing fits in among other things; for example, how a certain animal fits into a group of animals.

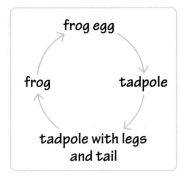

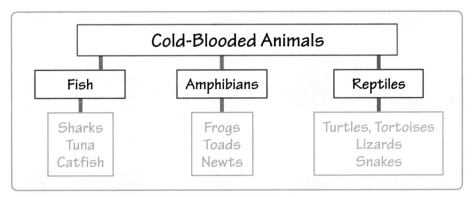

Picture Diagram ■ A picture diagram uses drawings to show how something is put together, how parts relate to one another, or how the thing works.

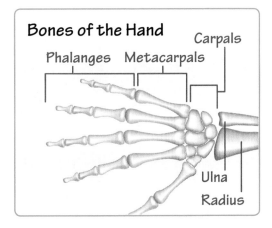

Graphs

Graphs share information about how things change over time or about how things compare to one another. They give you a picture related to the words on a page. They also help you see information "at a glance." There are different kinds of graphs for different kinds of information. There are **bar graphs**, **line graphs**, and **pie graphs**.

Bar Graph ▪ A bar graph compares two or more things at one point in time—like a snapshot. The bars of the graph can go up and down or sideways. Both bar graphs below compare the number of guppies in the 4th-grade aquarium to the number in the 5th-grade aquarium at the end of the school year.

Sample **Bar Graphs**

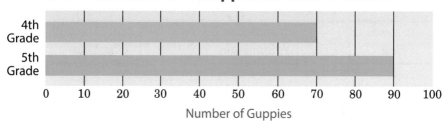

The Total Number of Guppies in Grades 4 and 5

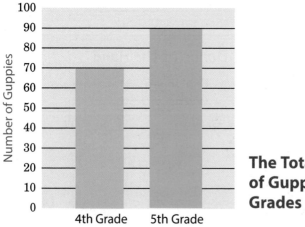

The Total Number of Guppies in Grades 4 and 5

Line Graph ■ A line graph is drawn on a "grid." The horizontal (left-to-right) side of the grid shows time passing. The vertical (top-to-bottom) side shows the subject of the graph. The line drawn through the grid lets you see the subject as it passes through time.

The line graph below shows how many guppies were in the 5th-grade aquarium in each month of the school year. "Number of guppies" is the subject of this graph, and time is measured in months (September through June).

Sample **Line Graph**

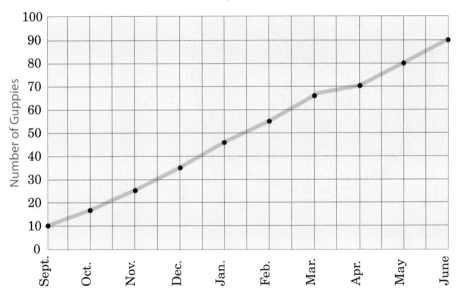

Number of Guppies in the 5th-Grade Aquarium Each Month

Note ■ Sometimes a line graph has dots or points on the line to make it easier to read. (See the graph above.) Other times, the line has no markings on it, and you must picture the points in your mind's eye.

Pie Graph ■ A pie graph shows how each part of something compares to the other parts and to the whole "pie." The graph below shows what part (or percentage) of the total number of guppies is contained in each grade's aquarium. For example, if there were 100 guppies in the whole school, the 5th-grade class would have 62 guppies, because 62% of 100 is 62.

Sample **Pie Graph**

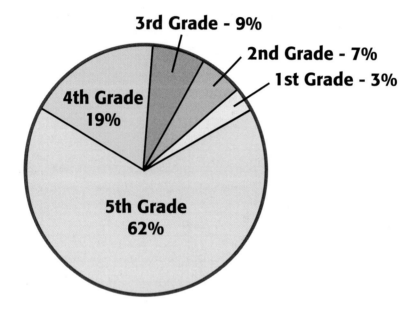

Quick Guide to Graphs

■ Every graph has a subject—just like a paragraph.

■ A **bar graph** compares things at the same time.

■ A **line graph** tells you how things change over time.

■ A **pie graph** shows how the parts of something compare to one another and to the whole.

■ Some graphs repeat information you already read somewhere on the page; other graphs tell you more about a topic.

Tables

Like diagrams and graphs, tables share information in "picture" form. **Tables** have *rows* (going across) and *columns* (going down). Rows show one kind of information, while columns show another kind of information.

Schedule ■ The table below is a bus schedule. The rows show days of the week; the columns show times of day. A check mark means a bus leaves on that day, at that time.

Bus Departures	8 a.m.	Noon	6 p.m.
Mon.–Fri.	✓	✓	✓
Saturday	✓	✓	
Sunday		✓	
Holidays	✓	✓	✓

Distance Table ■ Another common kind of table is a distance or mileage table. To read a distance table, find the place you're starting from. Then find the place you're going to in the opposite part of the table. Finally, look at the number where the row and the column meet—that's how far it is from one place to the other.

Can you use this table to figure out how many miles it is from New York to Seattle? (The answer is shown below the table.

Distance in Miles	Los Angeles	Seattle	Baltimore
Los Angeles	0	1,141	2,701
New York	2,787	2,912	197
Tampa	2,591	3,096	997

(New York to Seattle is 2,912 miles.)

Conversion Table ■ Conversion tables help you convert (change) information from one form to another. The chart below shows certain American measurements that have been converted into other American and metric measurements.

AMERICAN MEASUREMENTS		METRIC
1 inch	1/12 of a foot	2.54 centimeters
1 foot	12 inches	0.3048 meter
1 yard	3 feet	0.9144 meter
1 pint	2 cups	0.4732 liter
1 quart	2 pints	0.9463 liter

Custom-Made Tables ■ You can make your own table to show any kind of information you choose. Imagine that for your science project you need to guess the weight of certain animals or people, and then weigh them to find out how well you guessed. You could make a table like the one below.

Things I weighed	Guessed weight	Actual weight	Difference over (+) under (−)
my hamster	1 pound	7 ounces	+9 ounces
my cat	5 pounds	8 pounds	−3 pounds
my dog	50 pounds	68 pounds	−18 pounds
my friend	100 pounds	75 pounds	+25 pounds
my mom	150 pounds	118 pounds	+32 pounds
me	90 pounds	75 pounds	+15 pounds

Reading Graphic Information

When you look at a graphic, you want to first see the big picture. That means that you will want to know what the topic is, what the graphic is saying, and whether the information adds something new or is just there to clarify. Here are some guidelines you can use when you are trying to read graphics.

Quick Guide to Reading Graphics

1. First, look at the graphic as a whole and try to get the big picture.
2. Next, read the title, labels, and headings to get a better idea of what the graphic is about.
3. Read what it says inside the graphic and look for important information.
4. Read the "key" or any special notes included with the graphic.
5. Finally, read the paragraph above or below the graphic to gather more information.

Reading Graphics in Advertisements

Graphics that are used to promote or advertise a product or idea require special attention. Sometimes these ads purposely leave information out or tilt things to convince you. This is common in both political and product ads.

Here are some questions you can ask:
- What is the purpose of the graphic?
- What does the graphic tell me (or not tell me)?
- What is the source of the information? Is it reliable?
- Are any parts of the graphic misleading?
- Overall, how trustworthy is the graphic?

Reading Product Labels

As you know, many of the food products you buy have a special label listing the "Nutrition Facts" for a serving of their product. If you read the labels closely, you can pick up important information that can help you purchase the product that's right for you.

Look at the "Nutrition Facts" for milk. Can you find an answer to each of the following questions?

1. How many calories are in each serving?

2. How much fat does each serving contain?

3. What percentage of your daily need of calcium is included?

4. How much protein is contained in each serving?

Nutrition Facts

Serving Size 1 cup (110g)
Servings Per Container About 6

Amount Per Serving

Calories 250   Calories from Fat 30

	% Daily Value*
Total Fat 7g	**11%**
Saturated Fat 3g	**16%**
Trans Fat 0g	
Cholesterol 4mg	**2%**
Sodium 300mg	**13%**
Total Carbohydrate 30g	**10%**
Dietary Fiber 3g	**14%**
Sugars 2g	
Protein 5g	

Vitamin A	7%
Vitamin C	15%
Calcium	20%
Iron	32%

* Percent Daily Values are based on a 2,000 calorie diet. Your daily value may be higher or lower depending on your calorie needs.

	Calories:	2,000	2,500
Total Fat	Less than	55g	75g
Saturated Fat	Less than	10g	12g
Cholesterol	Less than	1,500mg	1,700mg
Total Carbohydrate		250mg	300mg
Dietary Fiber		22mg	31mg

Express Yourself Be on the lookout for questionable graphics in everything you read or see on television or the Internet. Use the questions on the previous page as a helpful guide.

Building Vocabulary Skills

Suppose your friend Sean says to you, "Jim *donated* $10 for our clubhouse, but now he says he only *lent* us the money!" If you don't know what *donated* and *lent* mean, you won't know why your friend is upset: Sean thought the money was a gift, but Jim is telling Sean he has to pay it back.

Unfortunately, you can't use a crane or any other machinery to help you build your vocabulary. Instead, you must rely on the strategies covered in this chapter, such as reading and keeping a personal dictionary.

What's Ahead

- Strategies for Building Your Vocabulary
- Prefixes, Suffixes, Roots
- Using Vocabulary Words Correctly

Strategies for Building Your Vocabulary

1 Read and check.

When you are reading and you come to a word you don't know, check the surrounding words (the *context*) to help figure out its meaning. Here are some ways to do this:

- Study the sentence containing the word, as well as the sentences that come **before and after it.**

- Search for **synonyms** (words with the same meaning).

  Because I plan to be an actor, Dad calls me a thespian.
  (A *thespian* is an "actor.")

- Search for **antonyms** (words with the opposite meaning).

  Dad says fishing is tedious, but I think it's exciting.
  (*Tedious* means "boring," the opposite of "exciting.")

- Search for **a definition** of the word.

  We saw yuccas, common desert plants, on our drive to the Grand Canyon. (*Yuccas* are "common desert plants.")

- Search for **familiar words in a series** with the new word.

  In the South, many houses have a veranda, porch, or patio.
  (A *veranda* is a large, open porch.)

- Watch for words that have **multiple meanings.**

  He charged me 50 cents for the candy bar.
  My mom charged the battery on my go-cart.

- Watch for **idioms** (words that have different uses from their dictionary meanings).

  "I'm cutting out." (This phrase is an idiom that means "leaving a place.")

- Watch for **figurative language** like similes and metaphors. (See pages 101–104.)

2 Use a dictionary.

You can always use a dictionary to find the meaning of new words. A dictionary can also help you with the following:

Spelling ■ If you don't know how to spell a word, try looking it up by how it sounds.

Capital Letters ■ A dictionary shows if a word needs to be capitalized.

Syllable Division ■ A dictionary shows where you can divide a word. Heavy black dots (•) divide a word into syllables. A hyphen (-) shows that the word is hyphenated.

Accent Marks ■ An accent mark (´) shows which syllable should be stressed when you say a word.

Pronunciation ■ To remember a word and its meaning, it helps if you know how to say it. A dictionary spells each word phonetically (as it sounds).

Parts of Speech ■ A dictionary tells what part of speech (*noun, verb,* etc.) a word is. Some words can be used in more than one way.

Word History ■ Some words have stories about where they came from or how their meanings have changed through the years. This information appears inside brackets [ ].

Synonyms and Antonyms ■ Synonyms (words that have the same or similar meaning) are listed, and some words are used in sample sentences. Antonyms (words with opposite meanings) may be listed last.

Meaning ■ Some words have only one meaning, while other words have several meanings. You will have to choose the best one.

Tip There may be a dictionary and a thesaurus on your computer. When you come to a word you don't know, finish the sentence first. Then, if you're using a computer, go back and check out the "tools" bar. If you're using an e-reader, simply touch the word, select it, and request a definition.

Sample **Dictionary Page**

Guide ——— **muscular ◆ mushroom**
words
—————————— Pronunciation

mus•cu•lar (**mŭs′** kyə ler) *adj.* 1. Having or being characterized by muscle: *muscular leg.* 2. Being characterized
by strength: *muscular argument.* **–mus′•cu•lar′•i•ty**
(mŭś kyə **lăr′** ĭ te) *n.* **–mus•cu•lar•ly** *adv.*

Synonyms ——— Synonyms: **athletic, beefy, brawny, buff, burly, lean,
ripped** *(slang)*, **sinewy, toned**. Each of these adjectives
refers to strength. The words *athletic, lean, sinewy,* and *toned*
refer to a lighter, more slender muscularity. A ballet dancer
will often be *lean* and *toned.* The words *beefy, brawny, buff,
burly,* and *ripped* refer to a bulkier, heavier muscularity. A
football linebacker will often be *beefy* or *burly.*
Antonyms: scrawny, weak, feeble —————— Antonyms

muscular dys•tro•phy (**dis′** trə fē) *n.* An inherited condition that causes slow but permanent muscular
deterioration; early stages result in weakness; later
stages result in disability.
—————————— Parts of speech
Syllable ——— **mus•cu•la•ture** (**mŭs′** kyə lə chŏŏr′) *n.* The arrange-
division ment of muscles in part or all of a creature.

muse (myōōz) *intr. v.* **mused, mus•ing, mus•es**. Think
about carefully; reflect; predict; imagine: *musing on her
options for a career.*

Spelling ——— **Muse** (myōōz) *n.* **1.** One of nine divine sisters in Greek
and mythology guiding science and art. **2. muse.** Anyone
capitals who guides, inspires, or advocates for an endeavor.
[Appeared first in a Middle English text in 1380; ——— Word history
derived from the Greek *Mousa.*]

Sound- ——— □ *Homophones:* **Muse, mews** (alley), **muse** (consider). ——— Accent mark
alike **mu•se•um** (myōō ze′ əm) *n.* Institution that gathers,
words curates, and exhibits works of art, history, science, technology, nature, or other fields of interest. [Appeared
first in a Modern English text in 1615; derived from the
Greek *Mouseion,* which refers to a place of worship for
the Muses.]

mush[1] (mŭsh) *n.* **1.** Corn meal boiled in milk or water to
create a breakfast porridge. **2.** A pasty material. **3.**
Usage label ——— *Informal.* Overly emotional material: *That old song
from the 1970s is such mush.* [Appeared first in
American English in 1671; derived from *mash.*]

mush[2] (mŭsh) *intr. v.* **mushed, mush•ing, mush•es. 1.**
Drive a dogsled over snow. **2.** *interj.* Command shouted
to sled dogs, telling them to start running or to run
faster. [Appeared first in American English in 1862;
originally spelled *mouche;* derived from the French
marchons, meaning "let's go!"]

mush•room (**mŭsh′** rōŏm *or* **mŭsh′** rōŏm′) *n.* **1.** The
flowering part of a fungus, generally with a fleshy stalk
and cap; a growth that assists in the breakdown of
decaying material. **2.** An object that has a shape similar
to a mushroom. **3.** *intr. v.* Grow upward and spread
outward: *The expenses for this project mushroomed out
of control.*

mushroom
|
Caption

Pronunciation key

ă	cat	oi	toy
ā	say	ou	out
âr	dare	ōŏ	book
ä	father	ōō	root
ĕ	set	ŭ	nut
ē	we	ûr	urge
ĭ	sit	th	think
ī	die	th	then
îr	pier	hw	who
ŏ	dot	zh	fission
ō	toe	ə	anew
ô	saw	n	French bon

3   Use a thesaurus.

A thesaurus is a book of words and their synonyms (other words that mean the same thing). A thesaurus also lists antonyms (words that have the opposite meaning). You can use a thesaurus to build your vocabulary and improve your writing. Go to a thesaurus when you know the meaning of a word but want a new word to express an idea.

Sample Thesaurus Entry

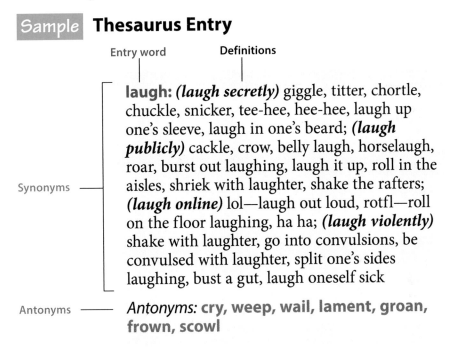

Entry word   Definitions

laugh: *(laugh secretly)* giggle, titter, chortle, chuckle, snicker, tee-hee, hee-hee, laugh up one's sleeve, laugh in one's beard; *(laugh publicly)* cackle, crow, belly laugh, horselaugh, roar, burst out laughing, laugh it up, roll in the aisles, shriek with laughter, shake the rafters; *(laugh online)* lol—laugh out loud, rotfl—roll on the floor laughing, ha ha; *(laugh violently)* shake with laughter, go into convulsions, be convulsed with laughter, split one's sides laughing, bust a gut, laugh oneself sick

Synonyms

Antonyms — *Antonyms:* **cry, weep, wail, lament, groan, frown, scowl**

Choose a Word:

In some thesauruses, the words maybe listed alphabetically, like a dictionary; in other thesauruses, you may need to look up your word in the index. The sample thesaurus above was used to help a student find different ways to express his laughter in a blog post.

> Comedy Sportz was so funny last night. At first, we were just snickering, but soon, we were shrieking with laughter and shaking the rafters! My dad roared like a bear. I never knew there were so many ways to laugh.

4 Keep a personal dictionary.

You can improve your vocabulary by keeping a personal dictionary and adding new words as you read or hear them.

1. **Look up each new word** in a regular dictionary to learn what it means and how to say it.

2. **Write the word** and its part of speech on a note card or in a notebook.

3. **Write the word's meaning** (or meanings).

4. **Write a sentence** using the word.

5. **List some synonyms** and antonyms, too.

---

chuck (verb)
1. To toss or throw
2. To pat or tap lightly

He chucked his old ragged shirt.

synonyms: flip, fling, heave
antonyms: keep, retain

---

trite (adjective)
• Something that isn't original

Robert wrote a trite poem
about spring.

antonyms: authentic, unused, original
synonyms: common-place,
           old-hat, stale

5 Learn about word parts.

You can figure out the meanings of new words by learning about the three basic word parts:

- **prefixes** (word beginnings),
- **suffixes** (word endings), and
- **roots** (word bases).

Learn the meanings of some of the most common prefixes, suffixes, and roots.

The prefix **sub** means "under."

The root **terra** means "earth."

Look for those word parts whenever you meet a new word.

The story is about a **subterranean** city.

(If you know that *sub* means "under" and *terra* means "earth," you can figure out that *subterranean* means "under the earth.")

6 Watch for word families.

Word families are groups of words that are built from the same basic word. If you know the meaning of the basic word, you can often figure out the meanings of other words in the same family. The basic word *astro* or *aster* means "star." Can you use that knowledge to figure out the meaning of any of the following words?

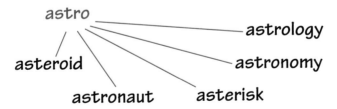

On the pages 348–357, you will find a list of the most common prefixes, suffixes, and roots in the English language. Take some time to look them over. It can be both fun and educational.

Prefixes

Prefixes are word parts that come before the root or word base (*pre = before*). Prefixes can change the meaning of a word.

ambi, amphi *[both]*
ambidextrous *(skilled with both hands)*
amphibious *(living on both land and water)*

anti *[against]*
antifreeze *(a liquid that works against freezing)*
antipollutant *(designed to work against pollution)*

astro *[star]*
astronaut *(star or space traveler)*
astronomy *(study of the stars)*

auto *[self]*
autobiography *(writing about yourself)*
autonomy *(self-government)*

bi, bin *[two]*
binocular *(using both eyes)*
biweekly *(every two weeks)*

circum *[around]*
circumference *(the line that goes around a circle)*
circumnavigate *(to travel completely around)*

co *[together, with]*
coauthor *(one who writes with at least one other person)*
copilot *(one who flies with and assists the main pilot)*

ex *[out]*
exit *(the act of going out)*
expel *(drive out)*

hemi, semi *[half]*
hemisphere *(half of a sphere)*
semicircle *(half of a circle)*

hyper *[over]*
hyperactive *(overly active)*
hypersensitive *(overly sensitive)*

inter *[among, between]*
intermission *(a pause between the acts of a play)*
international *(of or between two or more nations)*

macro *[large]*
macroclimate *(general climate of a large area)*
macrocosm *(the entire world)*

mal *[badly, poorly]*
maladjusted *(poorly adjusted)*
malnutrition *(poor nutrition)*

mono *[one]*
monochrome *(one color)*
monorail *(one-rail train)*

non *[absence of, not]*
nonfat *(absence of fat)*
nonfiction *(not fiction)*

oct *[eight]*
octagon *(a shape with eight sides)*
octopus *(a sea animal having eight armlike tentacles)*

penta *[five]*
  pentagon *(a figure or building having five angles and sides)*
  pentameter *(a line of verse composed of five metrical feet)*

poly *[many]*
  polychrome *(many colors)*
  polygon *(a figure having many angles or sides)*

post *[after]*
  postscript *(a note added at the end of a letter)*
  postwar *(after a war)*

pre *[before]*
  premature *(happening before the proper time)*
  preview *(showing something before the regular showing)*

pseudo *[false]*
  pseudonym *(false name)*
  pseudopod *(false foot)*

quad *[four]*
  quadrant *(one quarter of a circle)*
  quadruple *(four times as much)*

quint *[five]*
  quintet *(group of five musicians)*
  quintuplet *(one of five children born in a single birth)*

re *[again, back]*
  return *(to come back)*
  rewrite *(to write over again)*

sub *[under]*
  submerge *(put under)*
  subsoil *(layer under the topsoil)*

trans *[across, beyond]*
  transoceanic *(crossing the ocean)*
  transplant *(to move something)*

tri *[three]*
  triangle *(a figure that has three sides and three angles)*
  tricycle *(a three-wheeled vehicle)*

un *[not]*
  uncomfortable *(not comfortable)*
  unhappy *(not happy)*

uni *[one]*
  unicycle *(a one-wheeled vehicle)*
  unique *(one of a kind)*

Numerical Prefixes

Prefix	Symbol	Equivalent
deca	*da*	tenfold
hecto	*h*	hundredfold
kilo	*k*	thousandfold
mega	*M*	millionfold
giga	*G*	billionfold
tera	*T*	trillionfold

Prefix	Symbol	Equivalent
deci	*d*	tenth part
centi	*c*	hundredth part
milli	*m*	thousandth part
micro	*u*	millionth part
nano	*n*	billionth part
pico	*p*	trillionth part

Suffixes

Suffixes are word parts that come at the end of a word. Sometimes a suffix will tell you what part of speech a word is. For example, many adverbs end in the suffix *ly*.

able *[able, can do]*
   agreeable *(willing to agree)*
   capable *(able to do something)*

ed *[past tense]*
   called *(past tense of* call*)*
   learned *(past tense of* learn*)*

er *[one who]*
   baker *(one who bakes)*
   teacher *(one who teaches)*

er *[used to compare things]*
   neater *(more neat than another)*
   tougher *(more tough than another)*

ess *[female]*
   lioness *(a female lion)*
   princess *(female royalty)*

est *[used to show superiority]*
   fastest *(most able to move fast)*
   hottest *(highest temperatures)*

ful *[full of]*
   careful *(full of care)*
   helpful *(full of help)*

ing *[an action or process]*
   talking *(to talk)*
   writing *(to write)*

ist *[one who]*
   artist *(one who creates art)*
   chemist *(one who specializes in chemistry)*

less *[without]*
   careless *(without care)*
   hopeless *(without hope)*

ly *[in some manner]*
   bashfully *(in a bashful manner)*
   quickly *(in a quick manner)*

ment *[act of, result]*
   achievement *(result of achieving)*
   movement *(act of moving)*

ness *[state of]*
   carelessness *(state of being careless)*
   restlessness *(state of being restless)*

ology *[study, science]*
   biology *(study of living things)*
   geology *(study of the earth, rocks)*

s *[plural, more than one]*
   books *(more than one book)*
   trees *(more than one tree)*

sion, tion *[state of]*
   action *(state of doing something)*
   infection *(state of being infected)*

y *[inclined to]*
   cheery *(inclined to be cheerful)*
   itchy *(inclined to itch)*

Roots

A **root** is the main part of a word. If you know the root of a difficult word, you can most likely figure out the word's meaning. This can be very useful when learning new words in all your classes.

acid, acri *[bitter, sour]*
    acrid *(bitter taste or odor)*
    antacid *(works against acid)*

act, ag *[do, move]*
    action *(something that is done)*
    agent *(someone who acts for another)*

ali, alter *[other]*
    alias *(a person's other name)*
    alternative *(another choice)*

am, amor *[love, liking]*
    amiable *(friendly)*
    amorous *(loving)*

anni, annu, enni *[year]*
    anniversary *(happening at the same time every year)*
    annually *(yearly)*
    centennial *(every 100 years)*

anthrop *[man]*
    anthropoid *(humanlike)*
    anthropology *(study of human beings)*

aster *[star]*
    aster *(star flower)*
    asterisk *(starlike symbol)*

aud *[hear, listen]*
    audible *(can be heard)*
    auditorium *(a place to listen)*

bibl *[book]*
    Bible *(sacred book of Christianity)*
    bibliography *(list of books)*

bio *[life]*
    biography *(writing about a person's life)*
    biology *(study of life)*

centri *[center]*
    centrifugal *(moving away from the center)*
    concentric *(having a common center)*

chrom *[color]*
    chromatics *(scientific study of color)*
    monochrome *(one color)*

chron *[time]*
  chronological *(in order of time)*
  synchronize *(together in time)*

cide *[kill]*
  genocide *(race killer)*
  homicide *(human killer)*

cise *[cut]*
  incision *(a thin, clean cut)*
  precise *(cut exactly right)*

cord, cor *[heart]*
  cordial *(heartfelt)*
  coronary *(relating to the heart)*

corp *[body]*
  corporation *(a legal body)*
  corpulent *(having a large body)*

cosm *[universe, world]*
  cosmos *(the universe)*
  microcosm *(a small world)*

cred *[believe]*
  credit *(belief, trust)*
  incredible *(unbelievable)*

cycl, cyclo *[wheel, circular]*
  bicycle *(a cycle with two wheels)*
  cyclone *(a circular wind)*

dem *[people]*
  democracy *(people rule)*
  epidemic *(on or among the people)*

dent, dont *[tooth]*
  denture *(false teeth)*
  orthodontist *(someone who straightens teeth)*

derm *[skin]*
  dermatology *(the study of skin)*
  epidermis *(outer layer of skin)*

dic, dict *[say, speak]*
  dictionary *(a book of words people use or say)*
  predict *(to tell about something in advance)*

dynam *[power]*
  dynamite *(powerful explosive)*
  dynamo *(power producer)*

equi *[equal]*
  equilibrium *(a state of balance; equally divided)*
  equinox *(day and night of equal length)*

fac, fact *[do, make]*
  factory *(a place where people make things)*
  manufacture *(to make by hand)*

fer *[bear, carry]*
  conifer *(a cone-bearing tree)*
  ferry *(carry from place to place)*

fide *[faith, trust]*
  confident *(trusting oneself)*
  fidelity *(faithfulness to a person or cause)*

fin *[end]*
  final *(the last or end of something)*
  infinite *(having no end)*

flex *[bend]*
  flexible *(able to bend)*
  reflex *(bending or springing back)*

flu *[flowing]*
  fluid *(flowing, waterlike substance)*
  influence *(to flow in)*

forc, fort *[strong]*
  force *(strength or power)*
  fortify *(to make strong)*

fract, frag *[break]*
  fracture *(break)*
  fragment *(a piece broken from the whole)*

gastr *[stomach]*
  gastric *(relating to the stomach)*
  gastritis *(inflammation of the stomach)*

gen *[birth, produce]*
  congenital *(existing at birth)*
  genetics *(study of inborn traits)*

geo *[earth]*
  geography *(study of the earth)*
  geometry *(measuring the earth)*

grad *[step, go]*
  gradual *(step-by-step)*
  graduation *(taking the next step)*

graph *[write]*
  autograph *(self-writing)*
  photograph *(light-writing)*

greg *[group, herd]*
  congregation *(a group that is functioning together)*
  segregate *(tending to group apart)*

hab, habit *[live]*
  habitat *(the place in which one lives)*
  inhabit *(to live in)*

hetero *[different]*
  heterogeneous *(different in birth or kind)*
  heterosexual *(with interest in the opposite sex)*

homo *[same]*
  homogeneous *(of same birth or kind)*
  homogenize *(to blend into a uniform mixture)*

hum *[earth]*
  exhume *(to take out of the earth)*
  humus *(earth; dirt)*

hydr *[water]*
  dehydrate *(take water out of)*
  hydrophobia *(fear of water)*

ject *[throw]*
  eject *(to throw out)*
  project *(throw forward)*

leg *[law]*
  legal *(related to the law)*
  legislature *(persons who make laws)*

log, ology *[word, study]*
  psychology *(mind study)*
  zoology *(animal study)*

luc, lum *[light]*
  lumen *(a unit of light)*
  translucent *(letting light come through)*

magn *[great]*
  magnificent *(great)*
  magnify *(increase to a greater size)*

man *[hand]*
  manicure *(to fix the hands)*
  manufacture *(to make by hand)*

mania *[madness]*
  kleptomania *(an abnormal tendency to steal)*
  maniac *(a mad person)*

mar *[sea, pool]*
  marine *(related to the sea)*
  marsh *(a wet, grassy area)*

medi *[middle, between]*
  Mediterranean *(lying between lands)*
  medium *(in the middle)*

mega *[great]*
  megalopolis *(great city or an urban region)*
  megaphone *(great sound)*

mem *[remember]*
  memo *(a note; a reminder)*
  memorial *(a remembrance)*

meter *[measure]*
  meter *(a unit of measure)*
  voltmeter *(instrument to measure volts)*

migra *[wander]*
  emigrant *(one who leaves a country)*
  migrant *(someone who wanders from place to place)*

mit, miss *[send]*
  emit *(send out; give off)*
  missile *(an object sent flying)*

mob, mot *[move]*
  mobile *(capable of moving)*
  promotion *(to move forward)*

mon *[warn, remind]*
  admonish *(warn)*
  monument *(a reminder of a person or an event)*

morph *[form]*
  amorphous *(with no form or shape)*
  metamorphosis *(change of form)*

mort *[death]*
  immortal *(something that never dies)*
  mortuary *(a place for the dead)*

multi *[many, much]*
  multicultural *(including many cultures)*
  multiped *(an organism with many feet)*

nat *[to be born]*
  innate *(inborn)*
  nativity *(birth)*

neur [nerve]
   neuritis (inflammation of a nerve)
   neurologist (a physician who treats the nervous system)

nov [new]
   innovation (something newly introduced)
   renovate (to make like new again)

numer [number]
   enumerate (to find out the number)
   innumerable (too many to count)

omni [all, every]
   omnipresent (present everywhere)
   omnivorous (all-eating)

onym [name]
   anonymous (without a name)
   pseudonym (false name)

ortho [straight]
   orthodontist (someone who straightens teeth)
   orthodox (straight or usual belief)

pac [peace]
   Pacific Ocean (peaceful ocean)
   pacify (make peace)

path, pathy [feeling, suffering]
   empathy (feeling with another)
   telepathy (feeling from a distance)

patr [father]
   patriarch (the father of a family)
   patron (special guardian or father figure)

ped [foot]
   pedal (lever for a foot)
   pedestrian (a traveler by foot)

pend [hang, weigh]
   pendant (a hanging object)
   pendulum (a weight hung by a cord)

phil [love]
   Philadelphia (city of brotherly love)
   philosophy (love or study of wisdom)

phobia [fear]
   acrophobia (fear of high places)
   agoraphobia (fear of public, open places)

phon [sound]
   phonics (related to sounds)
   symphony (sounds made together)

photo [light]
   photograph (light-writing)
   photosynthesis (action of light on chlorophyll)

pop [people]
   population (the number of people in an area)
   populous (full of people)

port [carry]
   export (carry out)
   portable (able to be carried)

proto [first]
   protagonist (the first or leading character)
   prototype (the first model made)

psych [mind, soul]
   psychiatry (healing of the mind)
   psychology (study of the mind)

rupt *[break]*
interrupt *(break into)*
rupture *(break)*

sci *[know]*
conscious *(knowing or being aware of things)*
omniscient *(knowing everything)*

scope *[see, watch]*
kaleidoscope *(instrument for viewing beautiful forms)*
microscope *(instrument for seeing tiny objects)*

scrib, script *[write]*
manuscript *(written by hand)*
scribble *(write quickly)*

sen *[old]*
senile *(the weakness of old age)*
senior *(an older person)*

sequ, secu *[follow]*
consecutive *(following in order, one after another)*
sequence *(one thing following another)*

spec *[look]*
inspect *(look at carefully)*
specimen *(an example to look at)*

sphere *[ball, orb]*
hemisphere *(half of a sphere)*
stratosphere *(the upper portion of a sphere)*

spir *[breath]*
expire *(breathe out; die)*
inspire *(breathe into; give life to)*

strict *[draw tight]*
constrict *(draw tightly together)*

tact, tag *[touch]*
contact *(touch)*
contagious *(transmission of disease by touching)*

tele *[far]*
telephone *(far sound)*
telescope *(far look)*

tempo *[time]*
contemporary *(those who live at the same time)*
tempo *(rate of speed)*

tend, tens *[stretch, strain]*
extend *(to make longer)*
tension *(tightness caused by stretching)*

terra *[earth]*
terrain *(visible earth or ground)*
terrestrial *(relating to the earth)*

therm *[heat]*
thermal *(related to heat)*
thermostat *(a device for controlling heat)*

tom *[cut]*
anatomy *(cutting apart a plant or animal to study it)*
atom *(cannot be cut or divided)*

tox *[poison]*
  intoxicated *(poisoned inside)*
  toxic *(poisonous)*

tract *[draw, pull]*
  traction *(the act of pulling or gripping)*
  tractor *(a machine for pulling)*

trib *[pay]*
  contribute *(give money to)*
  tribute *(pay honor to)*

turbo *[disturb]*
  turbulent *(violently disturbed)*
  turmoil *(very disturbed condition)*

typ *[print]*
  prototype *(first print)*
  typo *(a printing error)*

vac *[empty]*
  vacant *(empty)*
  vacuum *(a space empty or devoid of matter)*

val *[strength, worth]*
  equivalent *(of equal worth)*
  evaluate *(find out the worth)*

vert, vers *[turn]*
  divert *(turn aside)*
  reverse *(turn back)*

vid, vis *[see]*
  supervise *(oversee or watch over)*
  video *(what we see)*

viv *[alive, life]*
  revive *(bring back to life)*
  vivacious *(full of life)*

voc *[call]*
  vocal *(calling with your voice)*
  vocation *(a calling)*

vor *[eat greedily]*
  carnivorous *(flesh-eating)*
  herbivorous *(plant-eating)*

zo *[animal]*
  zodiac *(circle of animals; the constellations)*
  zoology *(study of animal life)*

Using Vocabulary Words Correctly

When you learn new vocabulary words, it's important to use them correctly. There are formal and informal ways to use words.

Formal Language

You use formal language when you write informational essays, research papers, and business letters. Here are some tips (and a sample) to help you use words in a formal way:

- Pay careful attention to the words you choose.
- Follow the rules of grammar.
- Use a serious tone.

> Large cows line the streets of downtown Chicago. Each cow is actually a work of art decorated in a clever or artistic way. The cows will be auctioned to buyers around the country. The money will benefit local charities.

Informal Language

You use informal language when you write friendly letters, personal narratives, character sketches, and personal blogs. Here are some guidelines and a sample:

- Use everyday language.
- Follow the basic rules of grammar.
- Write with a friendly tone.

> Cows have invaded downtown Chicago. But these are fake cows that are decorated from head to hoof. They'll soon be auctioned off for charity. Who knows, one may show up on your front lawn!

Becoming a Better Speller

When you write, you work hard to share your best ideas. You try to use vivid, descriptive words and words that clearly communicate your ideas. So take care to also spell those words correctly.

Why? *Beecus speling erers ar harrd tu rede. Besides, people won't know how smart you really are ef yew spel lack thes.* And each time you correct a spelling error, you're more likely to spell the word correctly the next time you write it.

In this chapter, you'll learn five strategies for improving your spelling.

What's Ahead

- Design a Personal Spelling Dictionary
- Analyze Words Carefully
- Use Word Families
- Learn to Proofread for Spelling
- Learn Some Basic Spelling Rules

1 Design a personal spelling dictionary.

- Get a notebook, electronic or otherwise.
- Label the pages or columns with letters of the alphabet.
- Then each time you have to look up a word, or when you notice that your spell checker corrects it for you, write it—and its meaning—in your notebook.
- Use your notebook as your own personalized reference tool.

Sample **Personal Dictionary**

A	B	C
alligator - (remember the two "ll's") reptile	byte - computer measurement	calf - baby cow
afford - to be able to do something, or pay for something without bad consequences	breeze - (use "z" not "s") wind	choir - singing group
	bleacher - flat bench for sitting at sporting events	congruent - math term for numbers that agree
askew - something that is out of line or uneven		curtain - window fixture
amendment - an official change to the Constitution		confrontation - a face-to-face disagreement with another person

2 Analyze words using "The 7 Steps."

1. **Look** at the word and say it aloud. *(imperfection)*

2. **Write** the word and say it slowly—syllable by syllable. *(im/per/fec/tion)*

3. **Study** the word for "meaning units," which would include prefixes, suffixes, base words, and word roots: *(im* means *not)*, *(perfect* is the base word), *(tion* means *state of)*.

4. **Find** the base word or word root and say it slowly. *(per/fect)*

5. **Listen** for the number of sounds you hear in each syllable versus the number of letters. If the numbers are different, figure out why. *Double consonants? Silent letters?*

6. **Say** the word again, syllable by syllable, and write it without looking at it. *(imperfection)*

7. **Check** to make sure you have spelled the word correctly.

 Tip Using "The Seven Steps" can obviously help you with your spelling, but it can also help you with the pronunciation and meaning of a word as well. That makes it well worth using.

3 Use word families.

You can spell some words more easily when you place the words in their families. Note how the difficult **LETTERS** in the first words below are easy to hear and spell in the second words.

To spell ...	Relate it to ...	Listen for ...
muSCle	muSCular	the *S* and *C* sounds
expreSSion	expreSS	the *SS* sound
compEtition	compEte	the *E* sound
gEnetic	gEne	the *E* sound
resIGN	resIGNation	the *I*, *G*, and *N* sounds

4 Learn to proofread for spelling.

After you have revised your writing, you should check it for punctuation, grammar, and spelling errors. (We suggest that you check your spelling last.) Here are some suggestions.

Read from Bottom to Top ■ Start with the last line of your draft and read from bottom to top. This will force you to concentrate on each individual word.

Tip Hold an index card or a half sheet of paper right beneath the line you are studying. After checking one line, move the index card up and check the next line.

Correct the Misspellings ■ Cross out each misspelled word and make the correction above it. (**Remember:** Skip every other line when you write your draft; it will be much easier to make corrections.)

Circle the Puzzlers ■ If you are not sure about a spelling, circle it. Double-check the circled words when you have finished checking your entire paper.

Use a Spell Checker ■ When you write with a computer, you may use a spell checker. Just remember that a spell checker can't replace a human proofreader. It can't tell you how to spell a name, and it sometimes misses when you use the wrong word (for example, *by* instead of *buy*).

Ask for Help ■ Finally, have a friend or classmate check your corrections and look for other spelling errors in your writing.

Note For more help, check out the following pages:
- Checking Your Spelling (pages 452–455)
- Possessives and Plurals (pages 439, 448–449)
- Using the Right Word (pages 456–465)

5 Learn some basic spelling rules.

You can avoid some spelling errors by learning a few basic rules. As you will see, most of these rules deal with adding endings to words.

Words Ending in Y ■ When you write the plurals of words that end in *y*, change the *y* to *i* and add *es*.

bully, bullies   country, countries

Except: If the word ends in a vowel plus *y*, just add *s*.

boy, boys   monkey, monkeys

Consonant Ending ■ When a one-syllable word with a short vowel needs the ending *ed*, *er*, or *ing*, the final consonant is usually doubled.

bat, batted   drop, dropper   get, getting

I Before E ■ For words spelled with i and e together, repeat this: "*i* before *e*, except after *c*, or when rhyming with *say*, as in *neighbor* and *weigh*."

believe, receive, sleigh

Except: Here are some exceptions:

either, neither, their, height, weird, and seize

Silent E ■ If a word ends with a silent *e*, drop the *e* before adding an ending (suffix) that begins with a vowel.

use, using, usable

believe, believing, believable

Except: Do not drop the *e* when the suffix begins with a consonant (*-ful, -ty, -teen*)

nine, ninety, nineteen

Tip Many other spelling rules exist, but these are used most often. When you are unsure of a word's spelling, check to see if any of these four rules can help.

Speaking, Viewing, and Listening Skills

Giving Speeches

How do you feel when you are asked to speak in front of others? Do you get nervous and excited? Or do you enjoy sharing your feelings and ideas? Some people just naturally like speaking to groups of people. Others have to get used to it, just like a horse has to get used to wearing a saddle.

Whichever way you feel, giving a speech is easier if you talk about topics that interest you. That's why it's important to select the right topic and research it whenever you are asked to give a speech in class. This chapter will help you develop classroom speeches from start to finish—from selecting an effective topic to presenting your final speech.

What's Ahead

- The Steps in the Process
- Sample Speech
- Evaluating a Speech

The Steps in the Process

Whenever you are asked to prepare a speech, follow these nine steps, and you'll do just fine.

1 Decide which kind of speech you will give.

First, ask yourself, "Why am I giving this speech?" Is it to share information, to demonstrate something, or to change people's minds?

Speech to Inform

An **informational speech** gives interesting or important facts and details about a topic. You might inform your audience, for example, about a new discovery that uses recycled plastic to make roads hold up better in harsh winter climates.

Speech to Demonstrate

A **demonstration speech** shows how to do something. You might show your audience how to wash and wax a car or how to make peanut-butter fudge.

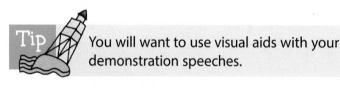 **Tip** You will want to use visual aids with your demonstration speeches.

Speech to Persuade

A **persuasive speech** tries to convince listeners to agree with your opinion about a topic. You might try to persuade your audience that there should be a law that all school buses must have seat belts.

2 Pick your topic carefully.

Once you know what kind of speech you'll be giving, you need to choose an appropriate topic. Ask yourself these questions:

- What do I know a lot about?
- What would I like to know more about?
- What do I enjoy doing?
- What do I like to read about?
- What do I talk about with my friends?

(See "Selecting and Collecting" on pages 35–44 for more help.)

3 Narrow your topic.

Let's say that because you love horses, you've chosen "horses" as the general subject of your speech. Next, you need to narrow your subject to a specific topic that's just right for the speech. Here are some examples:

Speech to Inform

For an **informational speech**, you could describe how to take care of a horse, or you could talk about different kinds of horses.

Speech to Demonstrate

For a **demonstration speech**, you could show your audience how to saddle and bridle a horse, or you could show them how to braid a horse's mane for a horse show.

Speech to Persuade

For a **persuasive speech**, you could try to convince your listeners that anyone can enjoy horseback riding, even if you don't own a horse.

Tip   Consider your audience when you choose a subject, just as you consider your guests when you plan a party. If you invited grandparents, would you play rap music? If you invited your friends, would you play waltzes?

4 Gather information.

Begin gathering information for your speech by looking through books and checking out articles on the Internet. Then look further.

- **Observe** and take notes on people, places, and events around you.
- **Talk or write** to experts in your school, family, or neighborhood.
- **Watch** videos, visit Web sites, and read articles.
- **Recall** past experiences.

 **Note** Remember to use drawings, photos, props, or video clips during a demonstration speech.

5 Prepare an exciting introduction.

After you've gathered enough information, write the beginning of your speech. Here are some good ways to begin:

- **Use a famous quotation.**

  " . . . forbid that I should go to a heaven in which there are no horses."
  —Theodore Roosevelt

- **Tell a story.**

  One day two summers ago, I was riding my horse in the field near our house when suddenly . . .

- **Refer to a recent incident.**

  At the last Olympics, the U.S. basketball team won a gold medal. So did the U.S. horse-jumping team.

- **Make a striking statement.**

  Horses understand body language better than people do. The slightest twitch of your body can tell a horse to move.

- **Ask an interesting question.**

  Did you know that horses have a language of their own?

6 Write an outline.

After writing your introduction, construct an outline of your speech either on note cards or on paper. Use short phrases—just enough words to remind you of what you want to say. It's a good idea, however, to write out your introduction and conclusion word for word. And don't forget to add reminders (in parentheses) about using pictures or props.

Sample Note Cards

Introduction: #1
The average horse weighs between 1,000
and 1,600 pounds. When you consider that I
weight just a small fraction of that, it seems
amazing that I can climb onto a horse and get
him to take me where I want to go. One thing
that helps me is knowing the personality
of each horse, but I also depend on my
equipment: a saddle, saddle pad, bridle, bit,
and reins.

Show and Tell the Following: #2
    I. Prepare the horse for the saddle.
        A. Talk to the horse.
        B. Rub under his mane.
        C. Stroke his neck.
        D. Stand left of the horse.
        E. Place saddle pad on horse.
            (Use diagram)

                                                        #3
    II. Saddle the horse.
        A. Place saddle on top of pad.
        B. Check and straighten girth.
        C. Tighten girth from left.
        D. Later, tighten a second time.

7 Write your speech.

You may give your speech using your outline, or you may write out your speech word for word. If you decide to write out your speech, review "Steps in the Writing Process" on pages 9–12 and then do the following:

- Keep your purpose (to inform, to demonstrate, to persuade) in mind and also remember who your audience is.
- Include specific details: examples, stories, facts, and figures.
- Choose the best words and arrange your thoughts and details into clear, interesting sentences.
- Use transitions to tie everything together.

8 Practice your delivery.

Practice your speech on at least two different days. You've heard that practice makes perfect: That is especially true when it comes to giving a speech. Do one or more of the following:

- Practice in a quiet place where you can listen to yourself.
- Practice in front of friends or parents. Ask for their suggestions.
- If possible, record yourself. Play it back and watch and listen to see how you can improve your speech.
- Review the points in step 9 below and keep them in mind as you practice.

9 Present your speech.

When you are ready to give your speech, remember these points:

- Look at your audience.
- Stand up tall; don't slump, sway, or lean.
- Speak loudly—use your "outside" voice.
- Speak clearly; don't mumble or use expressions like *ah* or *um*.
- Speak slowly and don't rush.

Sample Speech

If you follow the steps in the process, you should end up with a speech that is interesting to your listeners. (Add reminders so you don't forget to use your props.)

Saddle Up!

The average horse weighs between 1,000 and 1,600 pounds. When you consider that I weigh just a small fraction of that, it seems amazing that I can climb onto a horse and get him to take me where I want to go. One thing that helps me is knowing the personality of my horse, but I also depend on my equipment: a saddle, saddle pad, bridle, bit, and reins.

The first step is to prepare the horse for the saddle. I talk to my horse, rub under his mane, and stroke his neck to help him relax. I always stand on the left side of my horse as I place the saddle pad just below his withers, which is the ridge between his shoulders. (Show visuals.)

Next I place the saddle on top of the pad. From the right side, I check and straighten the girth, the strap that fastens the saddle on the horse. Then I tighten the girth from the left side. Just before I mount, I will tighten it a final time. (Show visuals.)

Now I'm ready for the bridle, bit, and reins. They are all connected. (Show props.) I hold the bridle from the top with my right hand with my arm resting over my horse's head. Then I guide the bit into the horse's mouth with my left hand. Next I pull the bridle up over his ears and buckle it under his throat. I make sure his mane is not caught under the bridle. That would hurt, just like it hurts when something pulls your hair.

All I have to do then is collect the reins. That just means that one rein is on each side of the horse's neck, and the ends are in my hand. After I mount, I'm ready to ride.

Evaluating a Speech

Use the following checklist to prepare and evaluate your speeches. You can also use this checklist to evaluate the speeches of others.

The Speech

___ Does the speech focus on an important or interesting topic?

___ Are the main points presented clearly from start to finish?

___ Does the speech move smoothly from one point to the next?

___ Does the speech include accurate and appropriate facts and figures?

___ Is everything tied together effectively at the end?

The Voice

___ Is the speaker loud enough to be heard by everyone?

___ Does the speaker speak slowly and clearly?

___ Does the speaker use plain, conversational language?

___ Is the speaker's voice colorful and pleasant to listen to?

The Delivery

___ Does the speaker stand straight and tall?

___ Does the speaker make eye contact with the audience?

___ Does the speaker avoid swaying, rocking, or other distracting movement?

___ Does the speaker use visual aids to clarify or emphasize information?

___ Does the speaker hold the audience's attention throughout the speech?

Improving Viewing Skills

According to a recent survey, young people between 8 and 11 years old spend an average of 19 hours and 49 minutes a week watching television or using the Internet. If you're average, that means you spend nearly 20 hours a week viewing something. That's a lot of time!

All of this viewing shapes . . .

- What you know about the world
- What you believe about people, places, and events
- What you buy (thanks to commercials)

Because viewing plays such an important role in your life, you need to become a thoughtful viewer. This chapter can help.

What's Ahead

- Watching the News
- Watching Documentaries
- Watching for Fun
- Watching Commercials
- Viewing Online Sites

Watching the News

1 Watch for completeness.

Whenever you watch the news, you need to make sure it's telling the complete story. A news story must answer the 5 W's and H about an event.

Who was involved? ...... *park ranger*
What happened? .... *reported a wildfire*
When did it happen? .... *this morning*
Where did it happen? .... *in Yosemite National Park*
Why did it happen? ...... *the extra dry underbrush*
How did it happen? ...... *exploded into flames, and fire spread*

2 Watch for correctness.

A news story should report only facts. If the reporter doesn't know all the facts yet, the story should say something like this:

<u>**We are getting reports**</u> that the fire may have been caused by a tossed cigarette, but <u>**official sources have not confirmed this**</u>.

Tip The underlined words tell you that the report may not be correct. You should watch for news updates.

3 Watch for balance.

A news story should tell all sides of the story.

What facts and pictures are included? ■ Let's say there's a story about the possible need for a new school. The old school has a leaky gym roof and not enough classrooms. A news story that showed only the leaky roof would not be balanced.

Who is interviewed? ■ The story should include reliable people who have different views. A balanced story would refer to board members and community members for *and* against the new school.

Watching Documentaries

A documentary is a special program that gives detailed information about one particular subject. Here is a plan to help you view and analyze any documentary you watch.

Before Viewing

- Think about what you already know about the subject.
- Write down questions you may have about the subject.

During Viewing

- Watch and listen for the answers to your questions.
- Write down interesting facts and any new questions you have.
- Watch for completeness, correctness, and balance. (See page 374.)

After Viewing

- Compare notes with someone who also saw the special.
- Write a summary of the program in your learning log.

Notes from TV Special
Saturday, January 3, 2015
Lake Baikal—The Deepest Lake in Russia

It's so deep and so cold, it has life in it that's found nowhere else in the universe! That's because it was formed millions of years ago. Here are some animals you can find only in Lake Baikal:
- Golomyanka and other rare fish
- Baikal seals

It's beautiful and wild—336 rivers flow into it, but only one flows out. The lake is frozen from January to May. That's a long time!

Watching for Fun

Even when you just want to have fun, it's important to think about what you're watching on television or online.

Is it real or staged? ■ Medical, crime-fighting, and family shows may be based on real-life situations, but they often exaggerate emergencies, chase scenes, or jokes. Remember that such shows are designed just to entertain you. They are not real life.

Documentaries often re-enact important historical events, like the Lewis and Clark Expedition. Because this event took place over 200 years ago, nothing new or modern should show up in any of the scenes. Watch and listen carefully. Try to tell the difference between what is real and what is staged.

Is it fact or opinion? ■ A movie star on a talk show may say, "It's time for everyone to become a vegetarian." Keep in mind that celebrities are not necessarily experts on nutrition and food. Their opinions are just that: opinions.

Is it showing stereotypes? ■ A stereotype is an unfair generalization or prejudice. It is like saying, "If *one* _____ is a certain way, then *all* _____ are that way." Here are two examples of stereotypes:

Doberman Pinschers are always mean.

Boys can't draw.

It's true, some Doberman Pinschers are mean, but others are as nice as can be. And some boys can't draw, but many boys are great artists. Watch out for stereotypes in TV shows. Make sure you don't judge people (or anything else) by an unfair generalization or stereotype.

BE AWARE: Watching Commercials

Commercials have one main purpose—to get you to buy things. Here are five selling methods that commercials use to persuade you.

Slice of Life ■ These commercials often look like home videos. The people in them are happy because they are drinking Brand X cola or wearing Brand X shoes.

> **BE AWARE:** The people in these commercials are actors. They're being paid to look like they're happy.

Famous Faces ■ These commercials use athletes and other famous people. If you want to be like a famous athlete, you'll want to eat the same fast food he or she eats, right?

> **BE AWARE:** Famous people may not really use the products they sell on TV. They are paid to be in the ads.

Just the Facts ■ These commercials quote facts and figures. Let's say a commercial says, "Nine out of ten fourth graders asked for our cereal!" Where did those figures come from?

> **BE AWARE:** The survey of fourth graders may not have been fair. The cereal company may have asked, "Which would you rather have for breakfast: peas and carrots or our cereal?" That's a silly example, but you get the idea!

Problem-Solution ■ These commercials show someone with a problem. Then they show Brand X solving the problem. For example, Janet hates to do her homework. Her parents buy her a new computer with lots of software. Suddenly, Janet loves doing homework.

> **BE AWARE:** Very few problems can be solved just by buying something.

Infomercials ■ These commercials look like TV shows (usually half an hour long). They give a lot of information to get you to believe their products are the best you can buy.

> **BE AWARE:** Infomercials are just long commercials. The presenter (and the audience) have been hired to sell the product.

Viewing Online Sites

Like television, the Internet is a popular source of information. When you look for something online, try to answer these questions:

Who publishes or develops the Internet site? ■ The publisher may be a company, a school, a person, a club, or some other group. Knowing who publishes the site can help you answer these questions:

- **Is the information from a reliable source?** Imagine that you're looking for information about tornadoes. A Web site published by the National Weather Service has information from experts you can trust. A Web site published by someone who chases tornadoes as a hobby may not be as trustworthy.

- **Is the information balanced or biased?** Let's say you're looking for information about good eating habits. An Internet site published by a respected health magazine will most likely have balanced information. A Web site published by a company that produces breakfast cereal may be biased, making its products sound more healthful than they really are.

Who pays for it? ■ Whoever pays for a site gets to decide what is posted there. The Internet site is paid for by the companies that place ads on the Web site.

How often is the site updated? ■ Many Internet sites are updated every day or every week. But some sites may have information that is weeks, months, or even years out of date.

How does the information compare to other sources? ■ When you search for information on the Internet, look at more than one site, or check the information with a book or magazine. This comparison will help you check for accuracy.

Improving Listening Skills

Since this page and the next are about listening, find a partner to read them out loud—while you listen. If that isn't possible, do the next best thing: Listen to yourself read.

Did you know that we spend more time listening than we do speaking, reading, and writing combined? Our ears make it possible for us to hear, but our minds make it possible for us to listen. Listening is more than just hearing—it is thinking about what we hear. This chapter will help you to *hear* as well as *listen*.

What's Ahead

- Becoming a Good Listener
- Avoiding Listening Problems

Becoming a Good Listener

Because we are human, we don't always listen. We get distracted. We daydream. We sometimes hear people without actually *listening* to them. So how can you become a better listener, both in and out of school? Here's a whole page of suggestions.

- **Listen with a positive attitude;** you'll learn more.

- **Listen with your eyes as well as your ears;** you'll hear more if you look at the speaker.

- **Listen for the main ideas;** you'll stay on track.

- **Listen for the speaker's tone of voice;** you'll get the true meaning.

- **Listen for specific directions;** you'll know what you're supposed to do.

- **Listen for key words (first/second, before/after, next/then);** you'll keep things in the right order.

- **Take notes or make drawings;** you'll remember things longer.

- **Think about what you hear;** you'll understand better if you relate new ideas to what you already know.

> *Good listeners are not only popular everywhere, but after a while they get to know something.*
> —Wilson Mizner

Express Yourself After listening carefully to what others have to say, ask questions and share your thoughts. Also listen carefully when you are working in a group. (See page 415.)

Avoiding Listening Problems

When you listen, especially in groups, you will want to avoid the following bad habits or pitfalls.

- **Daydreaming.** Don't think about what you'll be doing after school or what to get your friend for his birthday. Keep your mind on the person speaking.

- **Becoming emotional.** Sometimes you may get distracted by what the speaker is saying. Maybe it sounds like a great idea, and you want to talk about it rather than continue to listen. Or maybe it upsets you, and you want to disagree or holler. Keep your cool and keep listening.

- **Interrupting.** Sometimes it's necessary to interrupt the speaker. Maybe you are confused and need to ask for clarification. That's okay, but do it politely. If it can wait, however, don't interrupt.

- **Taking too many notes.** It's actually possible to take too many notes. It's important to take good notes, but that means writing down only the essential information, not every last detail.

- **Taking too few notes.** Just as taking too many notes is not a good idea, neither is taking too few. Sometimes listeners get so caught up in what is being said that they forget to take notes. That can be a problem, especially when it comes to reviewing for tests.

- **Doing other things.** When you are supposed to be listening, give the speaker your full attention. Don't work on your math assignment when a classmate is giving a report or draw cartoons when the teacher is giving a history lesson (unless the cartoon is about the topic).

 Tip   The best advice to listeners: "Listen to others the same way you would want them to listen to you."

Thinking Skills

Using Graphic Organizers

Thinking is the most important thing you do in school. You think when you read, write, listen, and speak. In short, you are thinking whenever you are learning.

It's no surprise, then, that the better you think, the more you learn. This chapter shows you how to use graphic organizers to arrange your thoughts about your coursework. You can use these organizers to record your reading notes, plan what you will write, and show what you know.

What's Ahead

- Kinds of Graphics
- More Graphic Organizers

Kinds of Graphics

Graphic organizers come in many different shapes and sizes. On these two pages, you'll find some common graphic organizers and tips on how and when to use them.

Web Organizer ■ Use a web organizer whenever you gather facts and details for reports, personal narratives, stories, and poems.

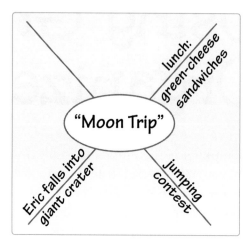

5 W's Organizer ■ Use the 5 W's to gather details for newspaper stories and personal narratives.

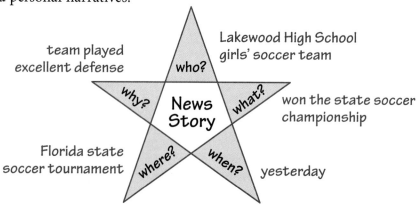

5 Senses Organizer ■ Use the 5 senses organizer to gather details for observation reports and descriptive paragraphs.

Sight	Sound	Smell	Taste	Touch
bright Ferris wheel	people laughing	popcorn	nachos with warm cheese	Carmen spilled wet, sticky soda on me

Compare/Contrast Organizers ■ The organizer shown below is called a Venn diagram. It can be used to organize your thoughts when you need to compare or contrast two subjects. Put the specific details for one of your subjects in area **1**. Put the details for the second subject in area **2**. In area **3**, list the details the two things have in common. Then you can clearly see the similarities and differences. (Also see page 50.)

Venn Diagram

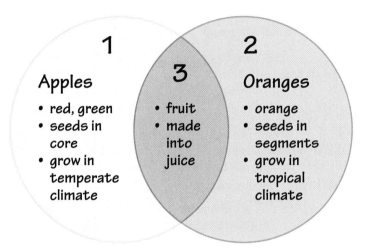

Cause/Effect Organizers ■ You will use one of two different organizers when you record cause-and-effect details. It depends on your subject and how many causes and effects it has. Use these organizers when you gather details for explanations of science and history topics.

Many causes, one effect

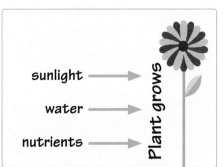

One cause, many effects

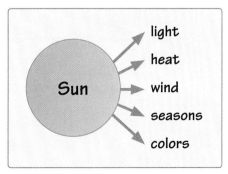

More Graphic Organizers

There are many other kinds of graphic organizers throughout your handbook. Check them out and think about how you could use each one to help you organize your thoughts.

Outline ■ An outline helps you organize information for book reviews, explanatory or persuasive essays, classroom reports, and so on. (See pages 49, 170, 200, and 259.)

Gathering Grid ■ Use this type of grid when you gather information from several sources. (See pages 44 and 257.)

Reading Strategies ■ Consider using one of these two organizers to record details from your reading.

- **Cluster** Use it when you want to gather details. (See page 39.)
- **Plot line** Use it when you are reading or planning a story. (See pages 241 and 317.)

Graphics ■ Diagrams, graphs, and tables are all helpful graphic organizers. Some diagrams work best for specific kinds of information:

- **Cycle diagram** Use this organizer when you read and write about science. (See page 333.)
- **Picture diagram** A picture diagram uses simple drawings. Use it to show how something is put together, how parts are related to one another, or how something works. (See page 333.)

Time Line ■ A time line shows the order in which things happened. Use it when you read or write about history. (See pages 50 and 177.)

Tips for Using Graphic Organizers

- Think about which organizer will work best for the kind of reading, writing, or thinking you are doing.
- Try several kinds of organizers. Seeing information in two or three different ways can help you learn and remember better.
- Invent your own graphic organizer! You may think of a whole new way to organize and record your thoughts.

Thinking and Writing

Writing is one of the best ways to think about the subjects you are studying in school. The physical act of writing one word after another focuses your attention on your subject so you can think carefully about it. No other activity helps you concentrate and think as much as writing does.

This chapter explains six kinds of thinking: *recalling, understanding, applying, analyzing, evaluating,* and *creating*. It also shows you how writing can help you think in each of these different ways.

What's Ahead

- Guidelines for Thinking and Writing
- Recalling/Remembering
- Understanding
- Applying
- Analyzing
- Evaluating
- Creating

Guidelines for Thinking and Writing

This chart reviews the important types of thinking you will use in school assignments and tests.

Use **recalling / remembering** when you are asked to . . .
- fill in the blanks
- define terms
- list facts or words
- label parts of something

Use **understanding** when you are asked to . . .
- explain something
- summarize something
- tell how something works
- tell if something is true or false
- choose the best answer

Use **applying** when you are asked to . . .
- use information in your own life
- solve a problem

Use **analyzing** when you are asked to . . .
- compare things
- contrast things
- put things in order
- divide things into groups
- give reasons for something
- tell why something is the way it is

Use **evaluating** when you are asked to . . .
- judge something
- rate something
- give your opinion of something

Use **creating** when you are asked to . . .
- make something
- imagine something
- combine things
- predict what will happen

Recalling / Remembering

When you *recall*, you remember information you talked about in class or read about in a book.

You *recall* when you . . .

- write down facts and definitions
- study information until you know it well
- answer basic test questions

This test question asks you to recall.

Directions: List in complete sentences five important facts you have learned about acid rain.

1. Acid rain is caused by pollution from cars and some electric-power plants.

2. When acid rain is still in clouds, it can blow far away from where the pollution started.

3. Acid rain kills plants and trees.

4. When acid rain falls on lakes and rivers, it kills fish.

5. The worst acid rain contains as much acid as lemon juice.

Tip

- Listen in class and read your assignments carefully.
- Write things down and illustrate those things that are difficult to describe in words.
- Use graphic organizers and memory aids.

Understanding

When you *know* information well enough to talk or write about it, you understand what it means.

You *understand* when you . . .

- explain what you have learned
- give specific examples
- tell how something works

This assignment asks you to show understanding.

Directions: In a paragraph, explain acid rain.

Acid rain is a form of pollution. It starts when exhaust from cars and chemicals from power plants go into the air. In the atmosphere, the chemicals mix with the tiny drops of water that make up clouds. When rain falls from the clouds, the acid chemicals are in the rain. The acid rain falls back to earth where it kills plants, trees, and fish.

Tip

- Write a summary of the information in your own words.
- Review the information out loud with a friend or family member.
- Explain what you know to someone else, using a drawing, a chart, or a graphic organizer.

Applying

When you *apply* information, you are able to use what you've learned.

You *apply* when you . . .

- use what you've learned in art, music, or sports to help you practice or perform.
- use information you've learned to solve problems

This test question asks you to apply information to your own life.

Directions: In a letter to the director of a power plant in your area, explain what you've learned about acid rain. Ask this person to write to you about what is being done at your local power plant to prevent acid rain.

Dear Mr. Gray:

In school, I learned that electrical power plants that burn coal are a major cause of acid rain. They release chemicals that mix with clouds and can be blown far away, even to other countries, before the acid rain falls. When it falls, it can kill plants and animals.

Please write to let me know if your power plant releases these chemicals. If it does, what are you doing to stop this pollution?

Sincerely,

 Tip In a learning log or journal, write about what you've learned and tell how it applies to your past, present, or possible future experiences.

Analyzing

When you *analyze* information, you break it down into parts.

You *analyze* when you . . .

- tell how things are alike or different
- tell which parts are most important
- tell how the parts fit together
- give reasons for something

This assignment asks you to analyze what you know.

Directions: In a paragraph, discuss the causes of acid rain.

Acid rain is caused by air pollution. But not all air pollution causes acid rain. It is caused only by certain chemicals. When coal or gasoline is burned, nitrogen oxides and sulfur dioxide are some of the chemicals released into the air. They mix with the water droplets in the clouds. When the water droplets fall as rain, the acid chemicals are still there. The acid in acid rain kills trees and fish.

Tip

- Consider what different parts make up the whole.
- Think about how the parts work together. (See the cause-and-effect organizers on page 385.)
- Decide whether the parts could best be described in order of importance, time order, or order of location. (See page 47.)

Evaluating

When you *evaluate*, you judge what you have learned. You explain the value of something—how good or bad it is.

You *evaluate* when you . . .

- give your opinion about something
- tell the good points and bad points about something
- explain the strengths and weaknesses of something

This assignment asks you to evaluate something.

Directions: Evaluate the latest attempts to stop acid rain.

The latest attempts to stop acid rain are not strong enough. In most places, the main chemical in acid rain is sulfur. Sulfur forms a gas (sulfur dioxide) when it is burned at electric-power plants. Many new power plants have "scrubbers" to keep sulfur from getting into the air. That helps prevent acid rain. But, if we want to do more to prevent acid rain from getting worse, all coal-burning power plants need scrubbers.

Tip Before you can evaluate something, you must understand it very well. Then you can judge it, form your opinion, and share your opinion with others.

Creating

When you *create*, you use what you already know to develop new information.

You *create* when you . . .

- add some new ideas to the information
- use the information to imagine something new or different
- predict what will happen in the future based on this information

This assignment asks you to create something new.

Directions: Write a title-down paragraph about acid rain. Use the letters in the words "acid rain" to begin each sentence.

Acid rain starts with air pollution.

Cars are one source of air pollution that causes acid rain.

Industry is another source of air pollution that causes acid rain.

Damage from acid rain lasts for years.

Rain that is polluted kills plants and animals.

Acid snow is just as harmful as acid rain.

In Canada, forests and lakes are dying from acid rain caused by
     pollution from the United States.

Nitrogen oxides are chemicals that cause acid rain.

Tip Thinking creatively is an important learning tool. More and more, employers are looking for people who are imaginative thinkers and creative problem solvers—people who can think in new ways.

Thinking Clearly

You don't have to be a brain to use your brain. In fact, as you read this page, you are already using your brain. You are observing, comparing, analyzing, and evaluating. Plus, you've been doing these things since you were very young, without even "thinking" about it.

Even though you've been practicing a long time, there's still more to learn about the thinking process. You need to think clearly in order to make good decisions, express and support an opinion, and solve everyday problems. This chapter can shed new light on how to do just that.

What's Ahead

- Becoming a Clear Thinker
- Using Facts and Opinions Correctly
- Avoiding Fuzzy Thinking
- Making Good Decisions
- Solving Problems
- Basic Thinking Moves

Becoming a Clear Thinker

There is no magic formula for becoming a clear thinker. Like everything worthwhile, it takes practice. However, the suggestions that follow should help you.

Be patient. ■ Don't expect quick solutions to every problem or challenge you face. Clear thinking often takes time and requires you to plan, listen, and discuss.

Set goals. ■ Separate the tasks you can do now (short-term goals) from those you need to work on step-by-step to accomplish (long-term goals).

Get involved. ■ Read books, magazines, and newspapers; watch films, view documentaries; participate in sports, join a club; look at art, create your own art.

Think logically. ■ Think beyond your feelings and emotions. Don't accept the first answer that pops into your head. Look at all sides of a problem and consider all the possible solutions.

Ask questions. ■ Be curious about what you read, what you hear, even what you see. If you think you know "what" it is, then ask *why, who, when, where, how, how much, why not, what if?*

Be creative. ■ Do not settle for the obvious answer or the usual way of doing things. Look at things in a new way—redesign, reinvent, rearrange, rewrite.

Make connections. ■ Pay attention to the details and how they are tied together. Use what you have learned to help you solve new problems. Make comparisons and connections.

Write things down. ■ Writing can help you clarify ideas and remember them longer. It can help you discover things you didn't know you knew.

Writing can help you sort through your thoughts and see them in a whole new light.

Using Facts and Opinions Correctly

A **fact** is something that is true—something that really happened. An **opinion** is something that someone believes; it may or may not be true. Facts tell us the way things are; opinions tell us how a person thinks or feels.

Opinion: Recycling paper should be a requirement.

Fact: If paper is not recycled, trees must be cut down to make more paper.

Fact: We are running out of places to dump our trash, and much of our trash is paper.

Writing an Opinion Statement

First, you must decide what your opinion is. Then you need to put your opinion into words that others will understand. Follow this basic formula to help you write a good opinion statement.

Formula: A specific topic (Recycling paper)
+ your opinion (should be a requirement)
_____
= a good opinion statement
(Recycling paper should be a requirement.)

Tip   Opinions that include very strong positive or negative words such as *all, best, every, never,* or *worst* are difficult to support.

Recycling all paper should be a requirement.

Supporting Your Opinion

Use clear, specific facts to support your opinion. Readers are more likely to agree with an opinion based on facts.

Opinion Based on a Fact

Recycling paper should be a requirement because it would save trees.

Opinion Based on Another Personal Opinion

Recycling paper should be a requirement because it is the right thing to do.

Avoiding Fuzzy Thinking

When you're trying to get others to agree with you, it's important to think clearly, write clearly, and stick to the facts! There's really no room for lazy or fuzzy thinking. Here are some suggestions to help you keep your thinking clear and logical.

■ **Don't make statements that jump to conclusions.**

> **"Because ozone is a gas found in smog, ozone is bad."**
>
> This statement jumps to a conclusion. It says that ozone is bad because it is part of smog, which is bad. But ozone can be good. The natural ozone in the atmosphere protects the earth from the sun's rays.

■ **Don't make statements that compare things that aren't really like each other.**

> **"When acid rain falls, it's like liquid fire falling on the earth."**
>
> This statement compares acid rain to something that is really much worse. The worst acid rain is about as acidic as lemon juice. That's bad for the earth, but not as bad as liquid fire.

■ **Don't make statements that are based on feelings instead of facts.**

> **"All big factories should be shut down because they cause air pollution."**
>
> This statement is based on feelings, and there are no facts to back it up. First, not all big factories cause air pollution. Second, there are other ways to stop air pollution besides shutting down factories.

■ **Don't make statements that are half-truths.**

> ### "Acid rain is 2,000 times more acidic than unpolluted rain."
>
> This statement makes it sound like all acid rain is 2,000 times more acidic than unpolluted rain. Some is, but some is only 10 times more acidic. The statement makes part of the truth sound like the whole truth.

■ **Don't make statements that make things seem worse—or better—than they are.**

> ### "Americans recycle tons of paper, so we're saving millions of trees that would have to be cut down to make new paper."
>
> This statement makes things sound better than they are. It sounds like most paper is recycled, so only a few trees need to be cut down to make paper. But only about half of all paper is recycled, so a lot of trees still need to be cut down.

■ **Don't make statements just because most people agree with them.**

> ### "Acid rain is not a bad problem because most people I talked to don't think it is."
>
> This statement is based on the idea that if most people believe something, it must be true. But "most people" can be wrong. They may not know how bad acid rain really is.

Note After you have read each of the six **Don't** statements, go back and read them again. Then rewrite each of the "fuzzy" examples so that they are clear. Compare your examples with the examples written by your classmates.

Making Good Decisions

You make decisions every day. You decide what to wear to school, where to sit at lunch, what book to read for your next report. Many of these decisions can be made quickly and easily.

Other decisions are much more difficult and take time and thought. Here are some guidelines you can use when you are facing a tough decision.

1 Define your goals.
- What are you trying to figure out or accomplish?
- What decision do you have to make?

2 List your options or choices.
- What options have already been tried?
- What other things could be done?

3 Study your options.
- Think carefully about each option.
- Write down the pluses and minuses of each one.

4 Rank the options.
- Put your options in order from best to worst, from easiest to most difficult, from quickest to longest.
- Ask for help from someone who knows about this issue.

5 Choose the best option.
- Consider all your options carefully.
- Select the best option. (The best option for you might not be the best option for someone else.)

6 Review all the steps.
- Let some time pass.
- Repeat the process to see if your thinking has changed.

Solving Problems

Just like doctors and teachers and moms and dads, you have to solve problems every day. Some problems are small and easy to solve. Other problems are big and hard to figure out. For big problems, you need a step-by-step plan to find the best solution.

 1 Identify or name the problem.
- What is the problem?

2 List what you know about the problem.
- What exactly is wrong or needs to be done?
- What caused the problem?
- Has this problem happened before?

3 Think of possible solutions.
- What could you do right now?
- What could you do a little at a time?

4 Try out the solutions.
- Imagine each solution in action.
- Imagine the result of each solution. What will happen?
- Try out different solutions if you can.

5 Choose the best solution.
- Think of what's best for others as well as for you.
- Put your plan into action.

 6 Evaluate the result.
- How did things work out?
- If you had it to do over again, would you choose the same solution?

Basic Thinking Moves

This chart shows you the kinds of "thinking moves" you can use to help you gather, organize, re-examine, and evaluate your thoughts.

Observe

Watch	Listen	Taste	Feel	Smell

Gather

Use personal experiences	Freewrite, cluster, list	Brainstorm with others	Talk to others	Read, write, draw

Question

Ask *who, what, when, where, why?*	Ask *how, how much?*	Ask *what caused it?*

Organize

Put in the right order	Compare, contrast	Give reasons	Group, define	Argue for or against

Imagine

Create new ideas	Experiment, invent	Wonder *what if...*	Predict, guess

Rethink

Re-examine (Is this the best *way?*)	Rearrange (Is this the best *order?*)	Revise (Is this the best *wording?*)	Restructure (Is this the best *form?*)

Evaluate

Judge (Is it accurate?)	Criticize (Is it interesting?)	Persuade (Is it worthwhile?)

Thinking Creatively

It's magic! At least that's what some people say when they talk about creativity. It's magical, wonderful, exciting—but they're not really sure how it happens. It's a kind of mystery how musicians, designers, and artists create their work.

But thinking creatively isn't magic, and it isn't a mystery. All you need is an active imagination, a little time to spare, and a strategy or two to get you started. In this chapter, you'll learn about the things you can do to become a creative thinker. More specifically, you'll learn about bringing out your hidden creativity, trying some creative strategies, and seeing creativity in action.

What's Ahead

- Becoming a Creative Thinker
- Strategies for Creative Thinking
- The Creative Mind in Action
- Assessing Your Creative Thinking

Becoming a Creative Thinker

One of the first questions you might ask is, "How will becoming a more creative thinker help me—especially in school?" Here are some of the ways.

Creative thinking will . . .

- Expand both your curiosity and your imagination
- Help you to find connections between things that aren't exactly alike
- Turn you into a visual thinker
- Help you see things in a whole new way
- Make you a more interesting person

Bringing out your creativity . . .

There is no magic formula for becoming a creative thinker. Like most things, it takes patience and practice. Here are some suggestions that can help you bring out the creativity waiting inside of you.

1. **Be patient.** Creative thinking often takes time. So don't settle for the first thought that pops into your head. Keep on thinking.

2. **Be curious.** Play with ideas. Imagine all the possibilities. Some of your best ideas will come to you when you least expect them.

3. **Ask questions.** *Who? What? (What if?) Where? Why? (Why not?) When? How?*

4. **Observe closely.** Look at details and think about how they are connected or tied together. Compare them to similar items.

5. **Talk to others.** Ask other people what they think. Ask them why.

6. **Make predictions.** Think about the way things are and imagine what they may be like later today . . . tomorrow . . . next year.

Strategies for Creative Thinking

Creative thinking is about discovering. It involves playing with ideas in order to make new ones. So how do you do that? Here are some specific strategies, guaranteed to improve your creative thinking skills.

1. **Think visually.**
   - Picture things in your mind.
   - Draw, doodle, and cluster.

2. **Brainstorm.**
   - Talk with other people and share ideas.
   - Ask them what they think about your ideas.

3. **Use off-beat questions.**
   - What object, place, word, or sport is this subject like?
   - What would happen if . . . ?

4. **Use reverse thinking.**
   - What is the exact opposite of this?
   - How could this be changed to make it better?

5. **Use nutshelling and predicting.**
   - In one sentence, write what have you discovered about . . .
   - In one sentence, write what you think will happen . . .

6. **Write about it.**
   - Write freely, quickly, and without stopping.
   - Write until you discover something that is beyond your imagination!

The Creative Mind in Action

If you're not thinking creatively, you might look at an object like a pencil and think, "There's a pencil. Something to write with. It's yellow. It looks brand new." But if you look at the same pencil with a creative mind, you'll see something completely different.

The No. 2 Pencil Meets a Creative Mind

- First, imagine the life of the pencil—how it was made—the wood, the glue, the "lead," the paint.

- Then, think of the tree the wood came from. Where did it grow? Where are the other parts of the tree now?

- Think about who else will use this pencil before it's worn out. What will be the most important thing it has ever written? The funniest thing?

- Look really closely at the pencil. What else does it look like? What does it feel like?

- Suppose it is being used as a pointer. Who is pointing it and what is the person pointing at? Why?

- Imagine the pencil as a pillar. What is it holding up?

- How strong is it? How much weight would be needed to break it?

- Imagine an occasion when this pencil might be given as a gift. What is the occasion, and why is it being given?

- Imagine a world in which no pencils (or pens) exist. What would that world be like?

Express Yourself Can you think of other ways of looking at a pencil? Make a list and share with it with a classmate. *Remember*, to be a creative thinker, you always want to think of new ways of looking at old objects and ideas. You want to see Velcro, not sandburs.

Assessing Your Creative Thinking

Use the statements below to test your awareness of your creative thinking skills. In your mind, answer *Always, Usually, Sometimes,* or *Never* to each statement.

1. I enjoy using my imagination.

2. I enjoy brainstorming with others.

3. I am able to visualize a problem or solution in my mind.

4. I keep a journal and write down or draw my creative ideas.

5. I ask "What if . . . ?" when I'm thinking.

6. I can think quickly and add new ideas in a discussion.

7. I try to imagine what life is like for other people.

8. I recognize the creative people around me, and I watch what they do and how they do it.

9. I listen carefully to the ideas of others.

10. I make connections between things I know and things I wonder about.

11. I enjoy explaining things to other people.

12. I use thinking strategies to improve my creativity.

How did you do? If you had some *Always* and *Usually* answers, good for you. If not, try using those strategies!

Tip As Albert Einstein once said, "Imagination is everything. It is the preview of life's coming attractions."

Learning Skills

Completing Assignments

How do you learn? Is learning easy for you? Do you sometimes wish it could be easier? Well, it can be if you first understand *how* you learn. How you learn depends on three things: you, your teachers, and your texts.

Your teachers start the learning process by introducing a unit of study. Your texts (this includes books, online articles, videos, and so on) give you information for the unit. Your job is to read and study this material until you become the best student you can be.

We'll help you do your job by showing you how to set goals, manage your time, and complete your assignments. It's as easy as 1, 2, 3.

What's Ahead

- Setting Goals
- Managing Your Time
- Doing Your Assignments

Setting Goals

Before you started school, you set goals for yourself all the time—like learning to ride a bike or dribble a basketball.

And you're still setting goals—like learning to play an instrument, earning money to buy something, or getting a good grade on your next test.

> **No one plans to fail; they just fail to plan.**

Some Helpful Guidelines

1 ## Be realistic.

Learn to set realistic goals. Can you learn to play a guitar in a day? Of course not. Some goals can be achieved only one step at a time. For example, your goal might be to learn one guitar chord a day for a week. Or if you play a sport, you might try to improve just one specific skill at a time.

2 ## Work toward your goals.

Continue working toward your goals—no matter what happens! If you choose to keep a journal, set aside a specific time each day to write in it. If you want to improve in a certain sport, talk to your coach, a parent, or a friend about how to do it. Then practice often.

 Tip Remember, there will be times when you won't be able to write or practice—when you are sick or on vacation, for instance. Find another time to make it up.

3 ## Reward yourself.

Whenever you reach a goal, reward yourself in some way. Let's say you've decided to keep a daily journal. When you have written in your journal every day for two weeks, do something special or share your success with a parent or teacher.

Managing Your Time

If you're like many students, you have a limited amount of time, and lots of things to do. The best way to make sure you get everything done is to use a planner.

Daily Planner ▪ In a daily planner, you can list assignments you have for each day. Your planner may be a simple list.

Monday, _____May 9, 2016_____   **Tuesday,** _____May 10, 2016_____

English	English
Read page 102. Write a topic sentence.	Write a paragraph using my topic sentence.
Math	**Social Studies**
Do workbook page 16. (Test tomorrow)	Finish question sheet for tomorrow.
Social Studies	**Science**
Answer question sheet by Wednesday.	Collect five different leaves; take to class.

Weekly Planner ▪ A weekly planner is a schedule of all the important things you have to do during a week.

	Before School	School	After School	Evening
Mon.	Make a lunch for field trip	Field trip	Open gym	Study math
Tues.	Take garbage out	Math test	Do homework	Guitar practice

Doing Your Assignments

Plan Ahead

- **Write down** exactly what your assignment is and when it has to be done.
- **Figure out how** much time you'll need to complete your assignment. Write down study times in your planner.
- **Get the phone number or email address** of one or two students in your class. Ask if you can contact them when you have a question about an assignment.
- **Gather all the materials you need** to complete your assignment: paper, pens, notebook, handouts, handbook.

Do the Work

- **Find a time** that works best for you.
- **Work in a quiet place** where you won't be interrupted.
- **Read over your assignment carefully** so that you know exactly what to do.
- **Set goals.** How much will you get done before you take a break? How much will you get done today? Tomorrow? Stick to your plan!
- **Keep a list of questions** to ask a classmate or your teacher.

Tip Remember to use reading strategies for your reading assignments. (See pages 309–320 and 321–330.)

Working in Groups

What was it like the last time you worked in a group? Did your teacher ask you to work with other students in the class? Did you work with a group of kids in the neighborhood to clean up a park? Did you play a team sport? Did you have a good time? Did you accomplish something?

Listening, clarifying, and cooperating are often called *people skills* because they help people work and learn better in groups. In this chapter, you'll learn how you can use people skills to make your next group work a success. You can begin by *making a plan*.

What's Ahead

- Making a Plan
- Skills for Listening
- Skills for Cooperating
- Skills for Clarifying
- Making a Group Decision
- Evaluating Your Work
- Sharing Books

Making a Plan

Every group project should begin with a plan. The members of the group should ask themselves these questions:

- What is our project or assignment?
- What jobs do we need to do to complete it?
- What job or jobs will each group member do?
- What deadlines do we need to meet?

Try using an outline like the one below to help your group make its plan. Be sure everyone understands what he or she needs to do.

I. Group Plan

A. Our project is
(Is it to solve a problem, answer questions, research a topic?)

B. Things we need to do:
1.
2.
3.
(Add more lines if you need them.)

C. Jobs for each group member:
1. Name: Job:
2. Name: Job:
3. Name: Job:
(Some sample jobs: writer or recorder, researcher, artist, coordinator)

D. This is our schedule:
1. By this date (   ) we will have this done:
2. By this date (   ) we will have this done:

II. Results

Skills for Listening

Listening is very important when you work in groups. People can work together only if they listen to one another. Imagine a group of firefighters at a huge fire. If they didn't listen closely to one another, they could never cooperate well enough to put out the fire and remain safe in the process.

Just listen. ■ Listening means *thinking about* what is being said. So you can't truly listen and do something else at the same time. Don't doodle, write notes to your friends, or check your messages while you're listening.

Listen actively. ■ Try hard to keep your mind on what's being said. It's natural for your mind to wander from time to time. Because people can't talk as fast as you can think, your mind can race ahead and get off the track. To stay on track, do the following:

- **Look at the person who is speaking.** This helps you listen because your mind usually thinks about what your eyes see.

- **Listen for key words and phrases.** For example: "The best solution is . . . " or "Here's what I think we should do."

- **Write down a few notes.** Write down some of the main points or details, but keep it short and don't stop listening.

Ask questions. ■ If you don't understand something, ask about it. But don't interrupt the person who is speaking unless you're really lost. Wait until she or he is finished. Then ask a good, clear question, such as "Karen, you're saying we should do a report instead of making a model, because a report will be easier—right?"

Listening is not as easy as it sounds! To **hear**, you need only your ears. To **listen**, you need both your ears and your mind.

Skills for Cooperating

Cooperating means working together with others to solve a problem or reach a shared goal.

Give your ideas and opinions. ■ It's important to let other group members know what you think. When you like someone's idea, say so! Also say so when you don't. But don't say, "That's a bad idea!" Say, "I don't think that will work *because . . .* " (When you give your opinion, give your reasons, too.)

Be willing to change your opinions. ■ Listen to everyone's opinions with an open mind. Remember that you are trying to reach a decision everyone agrees with.

Don't get personal. ■ Try not to criticize or say anything too personal. And if you hear a personal comment, remind the speaker that this is a group project and everyone needs to work together.

Skills for Clarifying

Clarifying means "clearing up." If someone in the group is confused, the group can't work together toward its goal. Here are some ways you can help clear up confusion:

Remember your goal. ■ Remind everybody what the group's goal is, and suggest steps that will help you reach that goal. For example: "First, let's decide whether to do a report or make a model. Then let's decide what each person's job will be."

Re-explain it. ■ If someone doesn't understand something, re-explain it, or ask if anyone else can think of a new way to explain it.

Stay on track. ■ If someone gets off track, say something as simple as, "I think we should get back to the main point."

Making a Group Decision

Successful groups make decisions by *consensus*. Reaching a consensus means "getting the majority of the group to agree with the decision." How do you get everyone (or nearly everyone) to agree? Here are some tips:

Reaching a Consensus

- Ask everyone in the group for ideas and suggestions. Listen carefully to each person's ideas.
- Discuss each idea and how it would (or wouldn't) work.
- Select the idea that most people agree will work well.
- If you select more than one idea, try to combine them into one plan—a plan everyone can agree on.

 Tip Remember that to reach a consensus, everyone must be agreeable. This doesn't mean everyone thinks the decision is the best decision; it means everyone agrees to accept the decision.

Evaluating Your Work

How did your group do? The proof that your group succeeded is a successful product. Before you hand in your project, judge the work your group accomplished. You can do this by having everyone answer and discuss these questions:

- Does our final product meet all the requirements of the assignment?
- Did all the group members do their jobs and contribute to the final product?
- Are we proud to say that this is our product?

 **Note** If you have to answer "no" to any of these questions, you may want to go back and revise your work. Then answer the questions again.

Sharing Books

One common group project is to talk about a story or novel you have all read. Below you will find some guidelines for discussing fiction.

Before You Begin

Group members should list the ideas they plan to share.

The Plot

- What is the most important or exciting event in the story?
- What parts of the story remind you of your own life? In what way?
- What other stories is this one like?

The Characters

- Who are your favorite characters? Why?
- How did the main character change during the story?

Overall Effect

- Do you think the book has a good ending? If you were the author, how would you have ended the book?
- Do you think the title fits the book?
- What is the author trying to tell the reader about life?
- Who else should read this book?

As You Share

In a small group (no more than six), sit facing each other.

- Look at the person who is speaking.
- Listen carefully to one another and write down your reactions and questions.
- Add to what the others say about the book.
- Make sure you share your personal thoughts about the book, too.
- Stay on track and enjoy the conversation!

Taking Tests

You're having a test? This happens all too often, doesn't it? Taking a test is a good way for you—and your teacher—to find out what you have learned. (And what you haven't learned.) But tests don't have to be a big deal. If you follow these two simple rules, you'll do just fine: **be prepared** and **pay attention**.

On the following pages, you'll find many strategies and tips for doing your best on tests. There are tips for taking objective tests and responding to writing prompts. There are also tips to help you remember things better.

To do well on tests, you will need to do well in class. Start with a self-examination to see how organized you are and how you approach your schoolwork. Then follow the tips in this chapter.

What's Ahead

- Preparing for the Test
- Taking the Test
- Responding to Writing Prompts
- The Objective Test
- Remembering for Tests

Preparing for the Test

Ask questions.

- What will be on the test? (Ask your teacher.)
- What kind of test will it be? (Multiple choice? Essay?)

Review your notes.

- Reread your class notes carefully. (Get any notes or materials you may have missed.)
- Rewrite your most important notes or put them on note cards.

Review your textbook.

- Skim your textbook. (Also review quizzes and worksheets.)
- Read difficult material out loud as you review.

Taking the Test

Listen attentively.

- Listen carefully to your teacher. How much time will you have? Can you use notes, a dictionary, or your handbook?

Read carefully.

- Take a quick look at the whole test, so you know which questions will take the most time.
- Then go back and read the directions carefully. Be on the lookout for words like *always, only, all,* and *never.*
- Don't spend too much time on any one question.

Check closely.

- Double-check to be sure you have answered all the questions. (Check each answer if you have time.)
- Ask your teacher about any questions that still confuse you.

Responding to Writing Prompts

Sometimes test questions are prompts that ask you to share what you know about a certain topic by writing about it. Here are two samples:

> In a paragraph, explain what happens in a volcanic eruption.
> In a paragraph, describe a volcanic eruption.

Each prompt asks you to write about the topic in a different way. The first asks you to *explain* a process, and the second asks you to *describe* an eruption.

1 Find the key word.

It is important to understand the key words used in test questions. Here are some common ones.

Compare/contrast ■ To compare, tell how two things are alike. To contrast, tell how things are different. A prompt may ask you to compare, contrast, or both. (*Compare and contrast the Arctic and the Antarctic.*)

Define ■ To define something, tell what it means, what it is, or what it does. (*Define ultraviolet light.*)

Describe ■ To describe something, tell how it looks, sounds, smells, tastes, and/or feels. (*Describe the book's main character.*)

Explain ■ To explain something, tell how it works, how it happens, or how to do it. (*Explain the effects of acid rain.*)

List ■ To list, give a number of facts, ideas, reasons, or other details about the topic. (*List five reasons the American Revolution began when it did.*)

Persuade ■ To persuade, give facts and reasons that would convince someone to agree with your opinion or position. (*Write a note that persuades your friend to help you clean the school grounds.*)

2 Make good use of your time.

Here's how to make the best use of your time:

- Carefully read or listen to all directions.
- Find out how much time you have for the test.
- Think about the prompt before you begin writing.
- Find the key word and think carefully about it.
- Make a simple plan or list for your writing.
- Once you begin, keep writing! (See pages 42 and 117.)

3 Focus on the key word.

The two answers below are completely different, even though they cover the same topic. The first answer *explains*; the second one *describes*.

- **Explain what happens in a volcanic eruption.** The answer tells how a volcanic eruption happens.

> The extreme heat at the center of the earth melts rock deep inside the earth. The melted rock is called magma. Magma gets mixed with gas and rises through cracks in the earth toward the surface. The hot, gas-filled magma is under great pressure. The pressure causes the gas and melted rock to blast out of the volcano.

- **Describe a volcanic eruption.** The answer tells how a volcanic eruption looks, sounds, and smells.

> A volcanic eruption is an amazing sight. Huge dark clouds rise over the volcano, and hot rivers of melted rock flow down its sides. Sometimes large chunks of hot rock are blasted into the air in ear-splitting, earth-shaking explosions. Hot ash and dust settle on everything around the volcano, and a burning smell fills the air for miles around.

The Objective Test

To do well on an objective test, keep the following hints in mind.

Multiple-Choice Test

■ Read all the choices carefully. Don't just mark the first correct choice, because there may be more than one correct answer. If there is, look for a choice such as "all of the above" or "both *a* and *b*."

Question: Mammals are animals that
   a. produce milk   **b.** grow hair   **c.** fly   **(d.)** both a and b

■ A question may ask you to find a mistake in one of the choices. Look to see if one of the choices is "no mistake."

Question: Mark the sentence that needs to be corrected.
   a. Cows and dogs are mammals.
   b. Mammals do not lay eggs.
   c. People are mammals.
   (d.) No mistake

■ Look for negative words like *not, never, except,* and *unless.* Also watch for numbers.

Question: The following two animals are not mammals.
   (a.) shark   **b.** kangaroo   **c.** horse   **(d.)** spider

■ A question may ask you to mark the choice that matches a sample sentence. Read all the choices carefully.

Question: Mark the sentence below in which control has the same meaning as in the following sentence:

Some mammals keep the insect population under control.
   a. She tried to control her temper.
   b. The pilot adjusted the right control.
   (c.) The Salk vaccine helps keep polio under control.

True/False Test

■ On a true/false test, read the entire question before answering. For a statement to be true, the entire statement must be true.

■ Watch for words like *all, every, always, never.* Statements with these words in them are often false.

Question: Mark each statement below with "True" or "False."

_____ **1.** Plastic can never be recycled.
_____ **2.** All plastic can be recycled.
_____ **3.** Vinyl is a kind of plastic used to make tires.

Answers: All are false. **1.** *Some* plastic can be recycled. **2.** Not *all* plastic can be recycled. **3.** The first half is true—vinyl is a kind of plastic—but it is not used to make tires.

Matching Test

■ Before you make any matches, read both lists quickly.
■ Check off each answer you use.

Question: Match the product (on the left) to the recycled material that it is made from (on the right).

_____ Asphalt   **a.** Motor oil
_____ Mulch for plants   **b.** Christmas trees
_____ Motor oil   **c.** Tires

Answers: **(c)** Asphalt, **(b)** Mulch for plants, **(a)** Motor oil

Fill in the Blanks

■ Read each sentence completely before filling in the blank.

Question: Fill in the blanks below with the correct answers.

1. Paper makes up about _____ of our trash.
2. _____ and _____ can be recycled.

Answers: **1.** one-third **2.** plastic, glass, etc.

Remembering for Tests

In addition to knowing how to take a test, you have to remember the material you're being tested on. Here are some tips for remembering what you have learned.

Use graphic organizers. ■ They help you organize information, and that makes the information easier to remember. (See pages 383–386.)

Use acronyms. ■ Acronyms are made up of the first letters of the words in a phrase or group of words. NATO, for example, is an acronym for North Atlantic Treaty Organization. To help you remember things, you can create your own acronyms.

> **HOMES** . . . **H**uron, **O**ntario, **M**ichigan, **E**rie, **S**uperior
> *(the Great Lakes)*
>
> **ROY G. BIV** . . . **R**ed, **O**range, **Y**ellow, **G**reen, **B**lue, **I**ndigo, **V**iolet
> *(the colors of the rainbow)*

Use poems. ■ Sometimes a simple (even silly) poem can help you remember things. Do you remember either of these?

> "i" before "e," except after "c," . . .
>
> In 1492, Columbus sailed the ocean blue.

Use songs. ■ Sometimes a familiar song can help you remember things. You can substitute something you want to remember for the words in the song.

A   B   C   D   E   F   G   H   I

Talk to others. ■ Here are some ways that talking to others will help you learn and remember information:

- ■ Form a study group. Ask each other questions.
- ■ Teach someone else what may be on the test.
- ■ Recite out loud the key points you need to remember.

Draw or visualize. ■ Drawing or picturing something in your mind can help you remember. Here's an example of a drawing used for remembering prepositions.

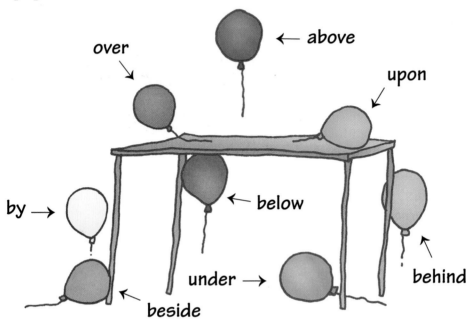

Rewrite it. ■ There are many ways to use writing to help you learn and remember. You can begin by writing in a journal or learning log. (See pages 115–120 and 121–124 for more suggestions.)

Write in a blog or electronic journal to reflect on what you learn.

Carry note cards around and use them like flash cards anytime during the day.

Taking Good Notes

If you were told to get bagels, orange juice, a dozen eggs, a gallon of milk, and a loaf of bread at the store, you *might* remember everything. If you had a list handed to you, remembering would be a lot easier. And if you wrote the list yourself, you might not even need to look at it once you got to the store. That's how powerful writing is as a learning tool!

Note taking is a very important writing tool, but it's not just writing down everything you hear. It's listening carefully and writing down the important ideas in your own words. This is what being a good note taker is all about. The next two pages can serve as your note-taking guide.

What's Ahead

- Guidelines for Improving Note-Taking Skills
- Sample Note Page

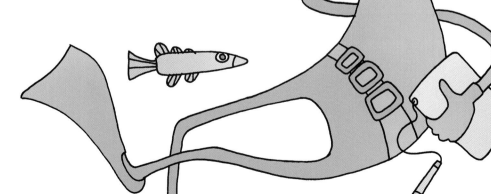

Guidelines for Improving Note-Taking Skills

The guidelines that follow will help you improve your note-taking skills. Read and follow each hint carefully.

Pay attention!

1. Listen carefully.

2. Put the date and subject at the top of each page.

3. Write neatly and quickly!

Be brief!

1. Write down just the important ideas— not every single word.

2. Summarize what is put on the board or overhead projector.

3. Draw pictures if they make the ideas clearer.

Be organized!

1. Use numbers or words to help organize your notes (1st, 2nd, before, after).

2. Read over your notes; recopy those that are hard to read.

3. Use a pen or marker to highlight the main points.

Sample Note Page

Below is a sample note page from a student in a social studies class. Notice all the different ways the student records information. Key ideas and points are written down, but not in full sentences or paragraphs.

Subject, date, and page number are listed.

Lists help organize notes.

A quick drawing shows the idea.

State names are abbreviated.

Key terms are circled.

Social Studies   Nov. 12   Page 6

5 Regions of the United States

1. Northeast
2. Southeast
3. Midwest
4. Southwest
5. West

West
• 9 states
• CO, WY, MT, UT, CA, NV, ID, OR, WA
• Climate varies
• Rocky Mountains
• Desert
• Pacific Ocean
• Biggest city: Los Angeles
• Earthquakes happen
• San Andreas fault
    – causes earthquakes
    – in California
    – huge geologic plates meet

Proofreader's Guide

Marking Punctuation

Period

A **period** is used to end a sentence. It is also used after initials, after abbreviations, and as a decimal point.

At the End of a Sentence	Use a period to end a sentence that makes a statement, a command, or a request. **Taro won the fishing contest.** (statement) **Take his picture.** (command) **Please pass the bait.** (request)
After an Initial	Place a period after an initial in a person's name. **Susan B. Anthony** **J. K. Rowling**
As a Decimal	Use a period as a decimal point and to separate dollars and cents. **Robert is 99.9 percent sure that the bus pass costs $2.50.**
After Abbreviations	Use a period after an abbreviation. **Mr.** **Mrs.** **Ms.** **Jr.** **Dr.** **p.m.**
After Final Abbreviations	Use only one period when an abbreviation is the last word in a sentence. **When Josie is nervous, she whistles, wiggles, winks, etc.**

Ellipsis

An **ellipsis** (three spaced periods) is used to show omitted words or sentences and to indicate a pause in dialogue.

Tip When writing an ellipsis, leave one space before, after, and between each period. On a computer, your software may automatically change three dots without spaces to an ellipsis. In that case, leave out the spaces.

To Show Omitted Words	Use an ellipsis to show that one or more words have been left out of a quotation.
	Complete Quotation:
	"All I know is that something long and shiny was on my line. It leaped out of the water a dozen times and finally got away."
	Shortened Quotation:
	"All I know is that something long and shiny . . . finally got away."
At the End of a Sentence	If the words left out are at the end of a sentence, use a period followed by an ellipsis
	"All I know is that something long and shiny was on my line. . . . It finally got away."
To Show a Pause	Use an ellipsis to indicate a pause in dialogue.
	"That's . . . incredible!" I cried.

Comma

Commas are used to keep words and ideas from running together. They tell your reader where to pause, which makes your writing easier to read.

Between Items in a Series	Place commas between words, phrases, or clauses in a series. (A *series* is three items or more in a row.) **I know someone who likes pepperoni, pineapple, and olives on her pizza.** (words) **During the summer I read mysteries, ride my bike, and play basketball.** (phrases)
In Dates and Addresses	Use commas to separate items in addresses and dates. **We had a huge family reunion on July 4, 2015, at Montrose Beach.** **Mia's new address is 3344 South First Street, Atlanta, GA 30200.** Tip Do not use a comma between the state and ZIP code.
To Keep Numbers Clear	Place commas between hundreds, thousands, millions, and so on. **Rodney's car has 200,000 miles on it. He's trying to sell it for $1,000.** Tip Commas are not used in years: 1776, 1999, 2010.
To Set Off Interruptions	Use commas to set off a word, phrase, or clause that interrupts the main thought of a sentence. **As it turned out, however, Rodney sold the car for $250.**
To Set Off Dialogue	Set off the exact words of the speaker from the rest of the sentence with a comma. **The stranded frog replied, "I'm just waiting for the toad truck."** No comma is needed when *reporting* rather than *repeating* what a speaker said. **Talia said she missed her bus yesterday.**

Comma (continued)

In Direct Address	Use commas to separate a noun of direct address (the person being spoken to) from the rest of the sentence. **Please, Carla, learn some new jokes.**
Between Two Independent Clauses	Use a comma between two independent clauses that are joined by coordinating conjunctions *and, but, or, nor, for, so,* and *yet.* **Aquarium workers love animals, so they regularly rescue injured ones.** **The team rehabilitated the injured sea lion pups, and then they released them.** Tip Do not connect two independent clauses with a comma only. (See page 468 for more information about independent clauses.)
In Letter Writing	Place a comma after the salutation, or greeting, in a friendly letter and after the closing in all letters. **Dear Uncle Jim,** (greeting) **Your niece,** (closing) **Sincerely,** (closing)
To Separate Adjectives	Use commas to separate two or more adjectives that equally modify a noun. **I like the feel of warm, salty water when I go wading.** Tip Use these tests to discover if adjectives modify equally: ■ Switch the order of the adjectives; if the sentence is still clear, the adjectives modify equally (use a comma). ■ Insert *and* between the adjectives; if the sentence reads well, use a comma when *and* is omitted.
To Set Off Interjections	Use a comma to separate an interjection or a weak exclamation from the rest of the sentence. **Wow, look at that sunrise!** **Hey, why are you up so early!**

To Set Off Appositives	Use commas to set off *appositives.* An appositive is a word or phrase that renames the noun or pronoun that comes before it. **My father, a great cook, makes the best egg rolls in town.** (an appositive phrase)
To Set Off Introductory Phrases and Clauses	Use a comma to separate a long phrase or clause that comes before the main part of the sentence. **After checking my knee pads, I skated off.** (phrase) **If you practice often, skating is easy.** (clause)

Semicolon

The **semicolon** is sometimes used in place of a period; other times, it works like a comma.

To Join Two Independent Clauses 	Use a semicolon to join two independent clauses when there is no coordinating conjunction between them. **My aunt has a new motorboat; I wish I were old enough to drive it.** **She takes me fishing in it; however, I still don't get to drive it.** Tip *Independent clauses* can stand alone as separate sentences. (See page 468 for more information about independent clauses; see page 489 for an explanation of coordinating conjunctions.)
To Separate Groups of Words That Contain Commas	Use a semicolon to separate a series of phrases if any of the phrases already contain commas. **We crossed the stream; unpacked our tents, fishing poles, and cooking gear; and finally took time to have lunch.** Tip The second phrase contains commas. Therefore, semicolons are used to separate the three main phrases.

Colon

A **colon** is used to introduce a list or to draw attention to the information that follows. Colons are also used in business letters and between the numbers expressing time.

To Introduce a List	Use a colon to introduce a list following a complete sentence.
	Snorkelers need the right equipment: fins, masks, and life belts.
	When introducing a list, the colon often comes after summary words like *the following* or *these things*.
	Scuba divers often see the following: barracuda, eels, turtles, and jellyfish.
	Tip It is incorrect to use a colon after a preposition or a verb.
	⊘ **I made a salad of: lettuce, tomatoes, cucumbers, and broccoli.** (The colon is incorrectly used after the preposition *of*.)
	⊘ **My favorite salad toppings include: bacon, raisins, sunflower seeds, and croûtons.** (The colon is incorrectly used after the verb *include*.)
After a Salutation	Place a colon after the salutation of a business letter.
	Dear Ms. Koplin: Dear Chairperson:
Between Numbers in Time	Place a colon between the parts of a number indicating time.
	The race begins at 1:30 p.m.
	I'll meet you at 12:00 noon.
As a Formal Introduction	Use a colon to introduce an important quotation in a serious report, essay, or news story.
	President Lincoln concluded the Gettysburg Address with these famous words: "that government of the people, by the people, for the people, shall not perish from the earth."

Hyphen

A hyphen is used to divide a word at the end of a line. Hyphens are also used to join or create new words. (Note: Your computer may place hyphens automatically at the end of lines.)

To Divide a Word	Use a hyphen to divide a word when you run out of room at the end of a line. Divide words only between syllables. (The word *en-vi-ron-ment* can be divided in three places.) **Gaylord Nelson showed concern for the envi-ronment by founding Earth Day.** **Tip** Here are some other guidelines for hyphenating words: ⊘ Never divide a one-syllable word: **showed**. ⊘ Never divide a one-letter syllable from the rest of the word: **i-dentity**. ⊘ Never divide contractions: **haven't, shouldn't**.
In Compound Words	Use a hyphen in certain compound words. **well-done all-star off-key**
Between Numbers in Fractions	Use a hyphen between the numbers in a fraction. **One-fourth of the group gobbled seven-eighths of the cake!**
To Form an Adjective	Use a hyphen to join two or more words that work together to form a single adjective *before* a noun. **blue-green sea sister-proof closet** **tooth-filled smile well-worn jeans**
To Create New Words	Use a hyphen to form new words beginning with the prefixes *self, ex, great, all,* and *half.* A hyphen is also used with suffixes such as *free* and *elect.* **self-made all-purpose fat-free** **great-aunt half-baked president-elect**
To Join Letters and Words	Use a hyphen to join a letter to a word. **T-shirt T-ball X-ray U-turn**

Dash

A **dash** is used to show a break in a sentence, to emphasize certain words, or to show that a speaker has been interrupted.

In a Sentence Break	Use a dash to show a sudden break in a sentence. **The skateboard—if you didn't notice—has a wheel missing.**
For Emphasis	Use a dash to emphasize a word, a series of words, a phrase, or a clause. **You can learn about many subjects—from customs to careers—on the Internet.**
In Interrupted Speech	Use a dash to show that one person's speech is being interrupted by another person. **Well, hello—yes, I—that's right—yes, I—sure, I'd love to—I'll be there!**

Apostrophe

An **apostrophe** is used to form plurals, to form contractions, to show that a letter or letters have been left out of a word, or to show possession.

In Contractions	Use an apostrophe to show that one or more letters have been left out to form a contraction. The list below shows some common contractions.

Common Contractions

couldn't (could not)	haven't (have not)	she's (she is)
didn't (did not)	I'll (I will)	they'll (they will)
doesn't (does not)	isn't (is not)	they're (they are)
don't (do not)	it's (it is; it has)	wouldn't (would not)
hasn't (has not)	I've (I have)	you'd (you would)

To Form Plurals	Use an apostrophe and *s* to form the plural of a letter or a sign.
	A's (letter) **+'s** (sign)
In Place of Omitted Numbers or Letters	Use an apostrophe to show that one or more letters or numbers have been left out.
	class of '99 (*19* is left out)
	fixin' to go (*g* is left out)
To Form Singular Possessives	Add an apostrophe and *s* to make the possessive form of most singular nouns.
	My sister's hobby is jazz dancing.
	Lucas's hobby is collecting pencil stubs.
	Gus's hobby is fishing.
To Form Plural Possessives	Add just an apostrophe to make the possessive form of plural nouns ending in *s*.
	the girls' logrolling team
	For plural nouns not ending in *s*, add an apostrophe and an *s*.
	children's book
To Form Shared Possessives	When possession is shared by more than one noun, add an apostrophe and an *s* to the last noun.
	Jim, Jeb, and Jerry's fish.

Quotation Marks

Quotation marks are used to enclose the exact words of the speaker, to show that words are used in a special way, and to punctuate titles.

To Set Off Direct Quotations	Place quotation marks before and after spoken words. **"Rosa Parks is one of our true American heroes," the teacher reminded her students.**
Placement of Punctuation	Put periods and commas that come at the end of quoted words *inside* quotation marks. **Trey said, "Let's make tuna sandwiches."** **"I like salami," replied Richard.** Place question marks or exclamation points *inside* the quotation marks when they punctuate the quotation; place them *outside* when they punctuate the main sentence. **"Will we have chips and pickles?" asked Trey.** **"Yes!" replied Rich.** **Did you hear Mom say, "We're out of pickles"?**
For Special Words	Quotation marks may be used to set apart a word that is being discussed. **The word "scrumptious" is hard to spell.**
To Punctuate Titles	Place quotation marks around titles of songs, poems, short stories, essays, and chapters of books. Also use quotation marks with articles found in magazines, newspapers, encyclopedias, or electronic sources. **"America the Beautiful"** (song) **"McBroom Tells the Truth"** (short story) **"Water, Water Everywhere"** (chapter) Tip When you write a title, capitalize the first word, the last word, and every word in between except for articles (*a, an, the*), short prepositions (*by, for, with*), and coordinating conjunctions (*and, or, but*).

Question Mark

A **question mark** is used after a direct question (an interrogative sentence) and to show doubt about the correctness of something.

After a Direct Question	Place a question mark at the end of a direct question. **Would you like to visit other galaxies?**
To Show Doubt	Place a question mark in parentheses to show that you aren't sure a fact is correct. **The ship arrived in Boston on July 23(?), 1652.**

Exclamation Point

An **exclamation point** is used to express strong feeling. It may be placed after a word, a phrase, or a sentence.

To Express Strong Feeling	**Surprise!** (word) **Happy birthday!** (phrase) **Wait for me!** (sentence)
	Tip Never use double exclamation points in school writing assignments or in business letters.

Parentheses

Parentheses are used around words included in a sentence to add information or to help make an idea clearer.

To Add Information	Use parentheses to add information. **The map (figure 2) will help you understand the explorer's route.**
To Make an Idea Clearer	Use parentheses to make an idea clearer. **Five of the students provided background music (humming very quietly) for the singer.**

Italics and Underlining

Italics is a printer's term for type that is slightly slanted. Italics are used for many types of titles and for special words. (Note: In handwritten material, each word or letter that should be in italics is underlined. If you use a computer, you should use italics.)

For Titles	Use italics (or underlining) for titles of plays, books, newspapers, magazines, television programs, movies (videos), music albums, and other complete works.
	The Wiz or **The Wiz** (play)
	Exploring an Ocean Tide Pool (book)
	Pinky and the Brain (television program)
	The Prince of Egypt (movie)
For Special Words	Use italics (or underlining) to indicate names of aircraft and ships.
	Columbia or **Columbia** (spacecraft)
	Merrimac (Civil War ship)
	Use italics (or underlining) to indicate foreign words.
	E pluribus unum, **meaning "out of many, one," is written on many US coins.**
	Use italics (or underlining) to indicate words discussed as words, rather than for their meaning.
	The word *freedom* means different things to different people.

Punctuation Marks

é	Accent	,	Comma	( )	Parentheses
'	Apostrophe	—	Dash	.	Period
*	Asterisk	/	Diagonal/Slash	?	Question Mark
[ ]	Brackets	...	Ellipsis	" "	Quotation Marks
^	Caret	!	Exclamation Point	;	Semicolon
:	Colon	-	Hyphen	__	Underscore

Editing for Mechanics

Capitalization

Proper Nouns and Proper Adjectives	Capitalize all proper nouns and proper adjectives. A proper noun names a specific person, place, thing, or idea. A proper adjective is formed from a proper noun. Proper Nouns: **Beverly Cleary** **Golden Gate Bridge** **Boston Celtics** **Thanksgiving** Proper Adjectives: **American citizen** **Chicago skyline** **New Jersey shore**
Names of People	Capitalize the names of people and also the initials or abbreviations that stand for those names. **C. S. Lewis** **Sacagawea** **George H. W. Bush** **Harriet Tubman**
Words Used as Names	Capitalize words such as *mother, father, aunt,* and *uncle* when these words are used as names. **Ask Mother what we're having for lunch.** (*Mother* is used as a name; you could use her first name in its place.) **Ask my mother what we're having for lunch.** (In this sentence, *mother* describes someone but is not used as a name.)

Capitalization (Continued)

Geographic Names	Capitalize geographic names that are either proper nouns or proper adjectives.

Planets and
heavenly bodies . . . . **Earth, Jupiter, Milky Way**

Continents . . . . **Europe, Asia, South America, Australia, Africa**

Countries. . . . . **Chad, Haiti, Greece, Chile, Jordan**

States . . . . **New Mexico, Michigan, West Virginia, Delaware, Iowa**

Provinces. . . . . **Alberta, British Columbia, Québec, Ontario**

Cities. . . . . **Montreal, Portland**

Counties . . . . **Wayne County, Dade County**

Bodies of water . . . . **Hudson Bay, North Sea, Lake Superior, Saskatchewan River, Indian Ocean, Gulf of Mexico**

Landforms . . . . **Appalachian Mountains, Bitterroot Range, Capitol Reef**

Public areas . . . . **Vietnam Memorial, Sequoia National Forest**

Roads and
highways. . . . **New Jersey Turnpike, Interstate 80, Central Avenue, Adam's Apple Road**

Buildings . . . . **Pentagon, Oriental Theater, Empire State Building**

Titles Used with Names	Capitalize titles used with names of persons.
	President Reagan
	Dr. Martin Luther King, Jr.
	Mayor Sharon Sayles-Belton
	Tip Do not capitalize titles when they are used alone: the president, the doctor, the mayor.
Historical Events	Capitalize the names of historical events, documents, and periods of time.
	Boston Tea Party **Stone Age**
	Emancipation Proclamation
Abbreviations	Capitalize abbreviations of titles and organizations.
	MD (doctor of medicine)
	ADA (American Dental Association)
Organizations	Capitalize the name of an organization, an association, or a team and its members.
	Chicago Bulls **the Democratic Party**
	Republicans **Doctors Without Borders**
Titles	Capitalize the first word of a title, the last word, and every word in between except articles (*a, an, the*), short prepositions, and coordinating conjunctions.
	National Geographic Kids [magazine]
	"The Star-Spangled Banner" [song]
	Aliens of the Deep [movie]
	In My Pocket [book]
	Tip Don't lowercase every short word in a title. Even though *my* is a short word, it is not an article, a preposition, or a coordinating conjunction.
First Words	Capitalize the first word of every sentence.
	Our first basketball game is on Saturday.
	Capitalize the first word of a direct quotation.
	Jamir shouted, "Keep that ball moving!"

Capitalization (continued)

Days and Months	Capitalize the names of days of the week, months of the year, and holidays. **Wednesday** **March** **Easter** **Arbor Day** **Passover** **Memorial Day** `Tip` Do not capitalize the seasons. **winter spring summer fall (or autumn)**
Names of Religions, Nationalities, Languages	Capitalize the names of religions, nationalities, and languages. **Christianity, Hinduism, Islam** [religions] **Australian, Somalian, Chinese** [nationalities] **English, Spanish, Hebrew** [languages]
Official Names	Capitalize the names of businesses and the official names of their products. (These are called *trade names*.) **Budget Mart** **Crispy Crunch cereal** **Choconut candy** **Smile toothpaste** `Tip` Do not, however capitalize a general descriptive word like *toothpaste* when it follows the product name.

Capitalize	*Do Not* Capitalize
January, March	winter, spring
Grandpa (as a name)	my grandpa (describing him)
Mayor Bewley	Ms. Bewley, the mayor
President Washington	George Washington, our first president
Ida B. Wells Elementary School	the local elementary school
Lake Ontario	the lake area
the South (section of the country)	south (a direction)
planet Earth	the earth we live on

Numbers

Numbers 1 to 9	Numbers from one to nine are usually written as words; all numbers 10 and over are usually written as numerals. one three 10 115 2,000 Except Numbers being compared should be kept in the same style. **Students from 8 to 11 years old are invited.** **Students from eight to eleven years old are invited.**
Very Large Numbers	You may use a combination of numbers and words for very large numbers. **15 million 1.2 billion** You may spell out large numbers that can be written as two words. **three million seven thousand** If you need more than two words to spell out a number, write it as a numeral. **3,275,100 7,418**
Sentence Beginnings	Use words, not numerals, to begin a sentence. **Fourteen new students joined the chess club.**
Numerals Only	Use numerals for numbers in the following forms: money . . . . **$3.97** decimals . . . . **25.5** percentages . . . . **6 percent** chapters . . . . **chapter 8** pages . . . . **pages 17–20** addresses . . . . **445 E. Acorn Dr.** dates . . . . **June 19** times . . . . **1:30 p.m.** statistics . . . . **a vote of 5 to 2** identification numbers . . . . **Highway 50**

Plurals

Nouns Ending in a Consonant	Form the plurals of most nouns by adding *s*. **balloon → balloons** **shoe → shoes** Form the plurals of nouns ending in *sh*, *ch*, *x*, *s*, and *z* by adding *es* to the singular. **brush → brushes** **bunch → bunches** **box → boxes** **dress → dresses** **buzz → buzzes**
Nouns Ending in *o*	Form the plurals of most words ending in *o* by adding *s*. **patio → patios** **rodeo → rodeos** Form the plurals of most nouns ending in *o* (if they have a consonant letter just before the *o*) by adding *es*. **echo → echoes** **hero → heroes** Except Musical terms and words of Spanish origin form plurals by adding *s*; check your dictionary for other words of this type. **piano → pianos** **solo → solos** **taco → tacos** **burrito → burritos**
Nouns Ending in *ful*	Form the plurals of nouns that end with *ful* by adding an *s* at the end of the word. **two spoonfuls** **three tankfuls** **four bowlfuls** **five cupfuls**
Nouns Ending in *f* or *fe*	Form the plurals of nouns that end in *f* or *fe* in one of two ways. **1.** If the final *f* is still heard in the plural form of the word, simply add *s*. **goof → goofs** **chief → chiefs** **safe → safes** **2.** If the final *f* has the sound of *v* in the plural form, change the *f* to *v* and add *es*. **life → lives** **loaf → loaves** **knife → knives**

Nouns Ending in y	Form the plurals of common nouns that end in *y* (if there is a consonant letter just before the *y*) by changing the *y* to *i* and adding *es*.

sky → skies   **diary → diaries**

story → stories   **musky → muskies**

Form the plurals of nouns that end in *y* (if there is a vowel before the *y*) by adding only *s*.

donkey → donkeys   **boy → boys**

key → keys   **day → days**

Form the plurals of proper nouns that end in *y* by adding only *s*.

There are two Judys in our class.

Compound Nouns	Form the plurals of most compound nouns by adding *s* or *es* to the important word in the compound.

sisters-in-law   **maids of honor**

secretaries of state   **life jackets**

Irregular Spelling	Some nouns form plurals by taking on an irregular spelling.

child → children   **goose → geese**

man → men   **woman → women**

foot → feet   **tooth → teeth**

ox → oxen   **crisis → crises**

cactus → cacti *or* **cactuses**

Adding an 's	The plurals of symbols, letters, and words discussed as words are formed by adding an apostrophe and *s*.

two ?'s and two !'s   **x's and o's**

a's and an's

Tip For more information on forming plurals and plural possessives, see page 439.

Abbreviations

An **abbreviation** is the shortened form of a word or phrase.

Common Abbreviations	Most abbreviations begin with a capital letter and end with a period, though some use no periods. Tip The following abbreviations are always acceptable in both formal and informal writing: Mr. Mrs. Ms. Dr. Jr. MD BCE CE a.m. p.m. (A.M., P.M.) In formal writing, do not abbreviate the names of states, countries, months, days, or units of measure. Also do not use signs or symbols (%, &) in place of words.
Acronyms	An acronym is a word formed from the first letter or letters of words in a phrase. Acronyms do not end with a period. **SADD** (**S**tudents **A**gainst **D**estructive **D**ecisions) **CARE** (**C**ooperative for **A**merican **R**elief **E**verywhere) **PIN** (**p**ersonal **i**dentification **n**umber) **radar** (**ra**dio **d**etecting **a**nd **r**anging)
Initialisms	An initialism is like an acronym except the letters that form the abbreviation are pronounced individually. **TV** (**t**ele**v**ision) **DVD** (**d**igital **v**ersatile **d**isc) **PSA** (**p**ublic **s**ervice **a**nnouncement) **CIA** (**C**entral **I**ntelligence **A**gency) **ASAP** (**a**s **s**oon **a**s **p**ossible)

State Abbreviations

Alabama	**AL**	Kentucky	**KY**	North Dakota	**ND**
Alaska	**AK**	Louisiana	**LA**	Ohio	**OH**
Arizona	**AZ**	Maine	**ME**	Oklahoma	**OK**
Arkansas	**AR**	Maryland	**MD**	Oregon	**OR**
California	**CA**	Massachusetts	**MA**	Pennsylvania	**PA**
Colorado	**CO**	Michigan	**MI**	Rhode Island	**RI**
Connecticut	**CT**	Minnesota	**MN**	South Carolina	**SC**
Delaware	**DE**	Mississippi	**MS**	South Dakota	**SD**
District of Columbia	**DC**	Missouri	**MO**	Tennessee	**TN**
Florida	**FL**	Montana	**MT**	Texas	**TX**
Georgia	**GA**	Nebraska	**NE**	Utah	**UT**
Hawaii	**HI**	Nevada	**NV**	Vermont	**VT**
Idaho	**ID**	New Hampshire	**NH**	Virginia	**VA**
Illinois	**IL**	New Jersey	**NJ**	Washington	**WA**
Indiana	**IN**	New Mexico	**NM**	West Virginia	**WV**
Iowa	**IA**	New York	**NY**	Wisconsin	**WI**
Kansas	**KS**	North Carolina	**NC**	Wyoming	**WY**

Address Abbreviations

Avenue	**AVE**	Lake	**LK**	Rural	**R**
Boulevard	**BLVD**	Lane	**LN**	South	**S**
Court	**CT**	North	**N**	Square	**SQ**
Drive	**DR**	Park	**PK**	Station	**STA**
East	**E**	Parkway	**PKY**	Street	**ST**
Expressway	**EXPY**	Place	**PL**	Terrace	**TER**
Heights	**HTS**	Plaza	**PLZ**	Turnpike	**TPKE**
Highway	**HWY**	Road	**RD**	West	**W**

Common Abbreviations

AC alternating current	**FM** frequency modulation	**oz.** ounce
a.m. ante meridiem	**kg** kilogram	**pd.** paid
BCE before the common era	**km** kilometer	**pg.** page (or p.)
CE the common era	**kw** kilowatt	**p.m.** post meridiem
COD cash on delivery	**lb.** pound	**qt.** quart
DA district attorney	**MD** doctor of medicine	**RSVP** please reply
DC direct current	**mpg** miles per gallon	**vs.** versus
etc. and so forth	**mph** miles per hour	**yd.** yard

Checking Your Spelling

- **Check your spelling** by using a dictionary or a list of commonly misspelled words (like the one that follows).
- **Check a dictionary for the correct pronunciation** of each word you are trying to spell. Knowing how to pronounce a word will help you remember how to spell it.
- **Look up the meaning of each word.** Knowing how to spell a word is of little use if you don't know what it means.
- **Practice seeing the word in your mind's eye.** Look away from the dictionary page and write the word on a piece of paper. Check the spelling in the dictionary. Repeat this process until you can spell the word correctly.
- **Make a spelling dictionary.** Include any words you misspell in a special notebook. (See page 360.)
- **Practice.** Learning to become a good speller takes time.

A

about	actual	alone	animal	argument
above	address	along	anniversary	arithmetic
absent	adventure	a lot	anonymous	around
accept	advertisement	already	another	arrival
accident	advise	although	answer	article
accompany	afraid	always	anybody	artificial
accurate	after	American	apartment	athlete
ache	against	among	apologize	athletic
achieve	agreement	amount	application	attention
across	allowance	ancient	appreciate	attitude
	all right	angel	April	attractive
	almost	angle	aren't	audience

August
aunt
author
automobile
autumn
avenue
awful
awhile

B

baggage
balloon
banana
bargain
basement
beautiful
because
become
been
before
beginning
behind
believe
belong
between
bicycle
birthday
biscuit
blanket
blizzard
bought
breakfast
brilliant
brother
brought
bruise
buckle
building
built
burglar
business

busy
button
buy

C

cafeteria
calendar
called
campaign
candidate
canoe
canyon
captain
careful
careless
casserole
caterpillar
caught
celebration
cemetery
century
certain
certificate
change
character
chief
children
chimney
chocolate
choir
choose
Christmas
church
city
civilization
classmates
classroom
climate
closet
cocoa
cocoon

color
come
coming
committee
community
company
complete
concert
congratulate
cooperate
cough
could
couldn't
country
courage
courteous
courtesy
cousin
criticize
cupboard
curious
customer

D

dairy
dangerous
daughter
day
dear
December
decorate
definition
delicious
describe
desert
dessert
developed
didn't
different
difficulty
disappear

disastrous
discover
discussion
distance
divide
division
doctor
does
done
doubt

E

early
earth
Easter
easy
edge
either
electricity
elephant
emergency
encourage
enormous
enough
entertain
environment
every
everybody
exactly
excellent
exercise
exhausted
expensive
experience
explain
expression
eyes

F

face
familiar

family
famous
fashion
faucet
favorite
February
fierce
fifty
finally
first
football
foreign
forty
forward
found
fountain
fourth
fragile
Friday
friend
from
front
fuel
full

G

gadget
generally
generous
genius
gentle
geography
getting
goes
gone
government
grade
graduation
grammar
grateful
great

grocery
group
guarantee
guard
guardian
guess
gymnasium

H

half
handkerchief
handsome
happened
happiness
haven't
having
hazardous
heard
heavy
height
history
holiday
honor
horrible
hospital
hour
humorous
hundreds

I

icicle
ideal
identical
imagine
immediately
immigrant
impatient
important
impossible
incredible
independent

individual
influence
innocent
instead
intelligent
interested
island

J

January
jewelry
journal
journey
judgment
juicy
July
June

K

kitchen
knew
knife
knives
know
knowledge

L

language
laughed
league
leave
length
lesson
letter
light
lightning
likely
listen
literature
little
loose

lovable

M

magazine
making
manufacture
many
March
marriage
material
mathematics
May
maybe
mayor
might
millions
minute
mirror
Monday
money
morning
mountain
music
musician
mysterious

N

natural
necessary
neighborhood
neither
never
nice
noisy
none
no one
nothing
November
nuclear
number

O

obey
occasion
o'clock
October
office
often
once
operate
opposite
other
outside

P

package
paragraph
parallel
party
pasture
patience
peace

people
picture
piece
played
pleasant
please
pleasure
point
poison
practice
prejudice
preparation
present
president
pretty
principal
privilege
problem
products
psychology
pumpkin

Q

quarter
quickly
quiet
quit
quite
quotient

R

raise
ready
really
reason
receive
recognize
remember
restaurant
right
rough
route

S

safety
said
salad
salary
sandwich
Santa Claus
Saturday
says
scared
scene
school
sentence
September

several
shoes
should
since
skiing
something
sometimes
soon
special
started
store
straight
studying
suddenly
Sunday
suppose
sure
surprise
surround
swimming
system

T

table
teacher
tear
temperature
terrible
Thanksgiving
their
there
they're
though
thought
thousands
through

Thursday
tired
together
tomorrow
tonight
traveling
trouble
truly
Tuesday
turn

U

unconscious
unfortunately
until
unusual
upon
use
usually

V

vacation
vacuum
vegetable
vehicle
very
violence
visitor
voice
volume

W

wasn't
weather
Wednesday
weight

weird
welcome
welfare
were
we're
when
where
whether
which
while
whole
whose
women
world
wouldn't
write
writing
wrote

Y

yesterday
young
your
you're
yourself

Using the Right Word

You need to use "the right words" in your writing and speaking, and this section will help you do that. First, look over the commonly misused words on the next 10 pages. Then, whenever you have a question about which word is the right word, come back to this section for help. (Remember to look for your word in a dictionary if you don't find it here.)

a, an	**I played a joke on my dad.** (Use *a* before words beginning with a consonant sound.) **I put an ugly rubber chicken under his pillow.** (Use *an* before words beginning with a vowel sound.)
accept, except	**Please accept my apology.** (*Accept* means "to receive.") **Everyone except me finished the test.** (*Except* means "other than.")
allowed, aloud	**We are allowed to read to partners in class.** (*Allowed* means "permitted.") **We may not read aloud, however.** (*Aloud* is an adverb meaning "clearly heard.")
a lot	**A lot of my friends like jeans with holes in them.** (*A lot* is always two words.)

already, all ready	I **already** finished my homework.
	(*Already* is an adverb telling when.)
	Now I'm **all ready** to play some buckets.
	(*All ready* is a phrase meaning "completely ready.")
ant, aunt	An **ant** is an insect.
	An **aunt** is a close relative.
ate, eight	I **ate** a bowl of popcorn.
	He had **eight** pieces of licorice.
bare, bear	She put her **bare** feet into the cool stream.
	She didn't see the **bear** fishing on the other side.
blew, blue	I **blew** on my cold hands.
	The tips of my fingers looked almost **blue**.
board, bored	A **board** is a piece of wood.
	You feel **bored** when there's nothing to do.
brake, break	Pump the **brake** to slow down.
	You don't want to **break** a bone.
bring, take	Please **bring** me my glasses.
	(*Bring* means "to move toward the speaker.")
	Take your dishes to the kitchen.
	(*Take* means "to carry away.")
by, buy	Did a hawk just fly **by** my window?
	I better **buy** some new glasses.
can, may	**Can** I go off the high dive?
	(I am asking if I have the "ability" to do it.)
	May I go off the high dive?
	(I am asking for "permission" to do something.)
capital, capitol	The **capital** city of Texas is Austin.
	Be sure to begin Austin with a **capital** letter.
	My uncle works in the **capitol** building.
	(*Capitol*, with an "ol," is used when writing about a government building.)

cent, scent, sent	Each rose costs 99 **cents.** **The scent** (smell) of the flowers is sweet. Dad **sent** Mom a dozen roses.
chose, choose	David **chose** to take drum lessons. His mom wants him to **choose** a different instrument. (*Chose [chōz]* is the past tense of the verb choose *[chüz].*)
close, clothes	**Close** the basement door. Then put the **clothes** in the dryer.
coarse, course	A cat's tongue feels **coarse,** like sandpaper. I took a **course** called "Caring for Cats."
creak, creek	Old houses **creak** when the wind blows hard. The water in the nearby **creek** is clear and cold.
dear, deer	Amber is my **dear** friend. The **deer** enjoyed the sweet corn in her garden.
desert, dessert	Cactuses grow in the **desert** near our house. My favorite **dessert** is strawberry pie.
dew, do, due	The **dew** on the grass got my new shoes wet. I **do** my homework right after school. The report is **due** on Wednesday.
die, dye	The plant will **die** if it isn't watered. The red **dye** in the sweatshirt turned everything in the wash pink.
doesn't, don't	She **doesn't** like green tomatoes. (*Doesn't = does not*) I **don't** either. (*Don't = do not*)
fewer, less	We had **fewer** snow days this winter. (*Fewer* refers to something you can count.) That meant **less** time for ice skating. (*Less* refers to something you cannot count.)

| find, fined | Did you **find** your book? |
| | Yes, but I was **fined** because it was overdue. |

| fir, fur | **Fir** trees are evergreen trees. |
| | Polar bears have thick **fur** coats. |

| for, four | You may eat the kiwis **for** a snack. |
| | The **four** of you may also share the crackers. |

good, well	Ling looks **good** in that outfit.
	(*Good* is an adjective modifying the noun "Ling.")
	It fits her **well**.
	(*Well* is an adverb modifying the verb "fits.")

| hare, hair | A **hare** looks like a large rabbit. |
| | My **hair** looks like a wet rabbit. |

| heal, heel | It takes a long time for a blister to **heal**. |
| | Gracie has a blister on her **heel**. |

| hear, here | I couldn't **hear** your directions. |
| | I was over **here**, and you were way over there. |

| heard, herd | We **heard** the noise, all right! |
| | It sounded like a **herd** of charging elephants. |

| heir, air | An **heir** is a person who inherits something. |
| | **Air** is what we breathe. |

| hi, high | Say **hi** to the pilot for me. |
| | How **high** is this plane flying? |

| hole, whole | A donut has a **hole** in the middle of it. |
| | Montel ate a **whole** donut. |

| hour, our | It takes one **hour** to ride to the beach. |
| | Let's pack **our** lunches and go. |

its, it's	This backpack is no good; **its** zipper is stuck.
	(*Its* shows possession.)
	It's also ripped.
	(*It's* is the contraction of "it is.")

knew, new	I **knew** it was going to rain. I should have not worn my **new** shoes.
knight, night	The **knight** stood guard by the iron gates. Torches were lit for the long **night**.
knot, not	I have a **knot** in my shoelaces. I am **not** able to untie the tangled mess.
know, no	Do you **know** all the dates for our history test? **No**, let's study them together.
knows, nose	Mr. Beck **knows** at least a billion historical facts. His **nose** is always in a book.
lay, lie	Just **lay** the sleeping bags on the floor. (*Lay* means "to place.") After the hike, we'll **lie** down and rest. (*Lie* means "to recline.")
lead, lead, led	Some old paint contains **lead**. [lĕd] I get to **lead** the ponies around the show ring. [lēd] Yesterday the drill team **led** the parade past the arena. [lĕd]
learn, teach	I need to **learn** these facts about the moon. (*Learn* means "to get information.") Tomorrow I have to **teach** the science lesson. (*Teach* means "to give information.")
loose, lose	Lee's pet tarantula is **loose**! (*Loose [lōōs]* means "free or untied.") No one but Lee could **lose** a big fat spider. (*Lose [lōōz]* means "to misplace or fail to win.")
made, maid	Yes, I have **made** a big mess. I need a **maid** to help me clean it up.
mail, male	Most men receive **mail** on their computers. Men are **male**; women are female.
meat, meet	I think **meat** can be a part of a healthful diet. We were so excited to finally **meet** the president.

metal, medal	Gold is a precious **metal**. Is the Olympic first-place **medal** actually made of gold?
miners, minors	Some coal **miners** suffer from black lung disease. **Minors** are young people who are not legally adults.
oar, or, ore	You use an **oar** to row a boat. Either Kim **or** Akisha will do the rowing. Iron **ore** is a mineral.
one, won	Markus bought **one** raffle ticket. He **won** the bike with that single ticket.
pain, pane	Cuts, bruises, and broken bones cause **pain**. I can finally see through the **pane** of clean glass.
pair, pare, pear	A **pair** (two) of pigeons roosted on our windowsill. To **pare** an apple means to peel it. A ripe **pear** is sweet and juicy.
passed, past	The school bus **passed** a stalled truck. In the **past**, most children walked to school.
peace, piece	Ms. Brown likes **peace** and quiet in her room. I like a **piece** of cake in my lunch.
plain, plain, plane	Toni wanted a **plain** (basic) white dress. The coyote ran across the flat **plain**. A stunt **plane** can fly upside down.

pore, pour, poor	A **pore** is a tiny opening in the skin. Please **pour** me another glass of juice. Rich is the opposite of **poor**.
principal, principle	Our **principal** is a strong leader. (The noun *principal* is a school administrator; the adjective *principal* means "most important.") She asks students to follow this **principle**: Respect each other, and I'll respect you. (*Principle* means "idea" or "belief.")
quiet, quit, quite	Libraries should be **quiet** places. **Quit** talking, please. I hear **quite** a bit of whispering going on.
raise, rays, raze	Please don't **raise** (lift) the shades. The sun's **rays** are very bright this afternoon. To **raze** means "to tear something down."
read, red	Have you **read** any books by Betsy Byars? [rĕd] I like to **read** adventure stories. [rēd] Why are most barns painted **red**? [rĕd]
right, write, rite	Is this the **right** (correct) place to turn **right**? I'll **write** the directions on a note card. The pastor performed the marriage **rite** (ceremony).
road, rode, rowed	My house is one block from the main **road**. I **rode** my bike to the pond. Then I **rowed** the boat to my favorite fishing spot.
scene, seen	The movie has a great chase **scene**. Have you **seen** it yet?
sea, see	A **sea** is a body of salty water. I **see** a tall ship on the horizon.
seam, seem	The **seam** in my jacket is ripped. I **seem** to always catch my sleeve on the door handle.

sew, so, sow	Shauna loves to **sew** her own clothes. She saves her allowance, **so** she can buy fabric. I'd rather **sow** seeds and watch my garden grow.
sit, set	May I **sit** on one of those folding chairs? Yes, if you help me **set** them up first.
some, sum	I have **some** math problems to do. What is the **sum** of 58 + 17?
son, sun	Joe Jackson is the **son** of Kate Jackson. The **sun** is the source of the earth's energy.
sore, soar	Our feet and legs were **sore** after the long hike. We watched hawks **soar** above us.
stationery, stationary	Wu designs his own **stationery** (paper) on the computer. A **stationary** bike stays in place while you pedal it.
steal, steel	You can **steal** third base, but don't take it home! Many knives are made of **steel**.
tail, tale	A snake uses its **tail** to move its body. "Sammy the Spotted Snake" is my favorite tall **tale**.
than, then	Jana's card collection is bigger **than** Erica's. (*Than* is used in a comparison.) When Jana is finished, **then** we can play. (*Then* tells when.)
their, there, they're	What should we do with **their** cards? (*Their* shows ownership.) Put them over **there** for now. **They're** going to pick them up later. (*They're = they are*)

threw, through	He **threw** the ball at the basket.
	It swished **through** the net.
to, **too,** **two**	Josie passed the ball **to** Shannon.
	Lea was **too** tired to guard her.
	(*Too* means "very.")
	The fans jumped and cheered, **too**.
	(*Too* means "also.")
	Shannon easily scored **two** points.
waist, **waste**	My little sister's **waist** is tiny.
	No part of the buffalo went to **waste**.
wait, **weights**	I can't **wait** to go to the gym.
	We lift **weights** and play basketball.
way, **weigh**	Show me the **way** to the gym.
	Birds **weigh** very little because of their hollow bones.
weak, **week**	The opposite of strong is **weak**.
	There are seven days in a **week**.
wear, **where**	The crossing guards **wear** yellow ponchos.
	Where do you think they got them?
weather, **whether**	I like rainy **weather**.
	I go jogging **whether** it's raining or not.
which, **witch**	**Which** book should I read?
	You'll like *The Lion, the Witch, and the Wardrobe*.
who, **which,** **that**	The man **who** answered the door was my dad.
	(*Who* refers to people.)
	The movie, **which** was very funny, ended too soon.
	(*Which* refers to nonliving objects or animals.)
	The puppy **that** I really wanted was sold already.
	(*That* may refer to animals, people, or nonliving objects.)

who, whom	**Who** ordered this pizza? The pizza was ordered by **whom**?
who's, whose	**Who's** that knocking at the door? (*Who's = who is*) **Whose** door are you talking about?
wood, would	Some baseball bats are made of **wood**. **Would** you like to play baseball after school?
you're, your	**You're** talking to the right person! (*You're = you are*) You can pick up **your** pizzas after the game.

Understanding Sentences

A sentence is made up of one or more words that express a complete thought. A sentence begins with a capital letter and ends with a period, a question mark, or an exclamation point.

 Tip Find more information about sentences in "Writing Basic Sentences," pages 75–80, and in "Combining Sentences," pages 81–84.

Parts of a Sentence

Subject

A subject is the part of a sentence that does something.

Marisha baked a chocolate cake.

A subject can also be the word that is talked about.

She is a marvelous cook.

Simple Subject	A simple subject is the subject without the words that describe or modify it. **Marisha's little sister likes to help.**
Complete Subject	The complete subject is the simple subject and all the words that describe it. **Marisha's little sister likes to help.** (*Marisha's little sister* is the complete subject.)
Compound Subject	A compound subject has two or more simple subjects. **Marisha and her sister frosted the cake.**

Predicate

A predicate (verb) is the part of the sentence that says something about the subject.

> **Marisha baked a cake for my birthday.**
> (*Baked* tells what the subject did.)

Simple Predicate	A simple predicate (verb) is the predicate without the words that modify or complete it. **Marisha baked the cake yesterday.**
Complete Predicate	The complete predicate is the simple predicate with all the words that modify or complete it. **Marisha baked the cake yesterday.** (The complete predicate is *baked the cake yesterday.*)
Compound Predicate	A compound predicate has two or more simple predicates, or verbs. **She decorated it and hid it in the cupboard.**

Modifier

A **modifier** is a word or a group of words that describes another word.

> **My family planned a surprise party.**
> (*My* modifies *family*; *a* and *surprise* modify *party*.)
> **They hid behind the door and waited quietly.**
> (*Behind the door* modifies *hid*; *quietly* modifies *waited*.)

Subject-Verb Agreement

The subject and verb of a sentence must "agree" with one another. If you use a singular subject, use a singular verb. If you use a plural subject, use a plural verb. (See page 79.)

> **Anthony helps Miss Park.**
> (The singular subject *Anthony* agrees with the singular verb *helps*.)
> **The boys help Miss Park.**
> (The plural subject *boys* agrees with the plural verb *help*.)

Clauses

A **clause** is a group of words that has a subject and a predicate. A clause can be independent or dependent.

Independent Clause	An independent clause expresses a complete thought and can stand alone as a sentence. **I ride my bike to school**
Dependent Clause	A dependent clause does not express a complete thought and cannot stand alone as a sentence. Dependent clauses usually begin with a subordinating conjunction like *when*. **when the weather is nice** **Tip** Some dependent clauses begin with a relative pronoun like *who* or *that*. An **independent clause** plus a **dependent clause** form a complex sentence. **I ride my bike to school when the weather is nice.**

Phrases

A **phrase** is a group of words that cannot stand alone as a sentence.

Noun Phrase	This is a noun phrase. It lacks a predicate. **the student**
Verb Phrase	This is a verb phrase. It lacks a subject. **wrote a report**
Prepositional Phrase	This is a prepositional phrase. (See page 488.) **about George Washington**
Appositive Phrase	This is an appositive phrase. **our first president**

Tip When you put these phrases together, they become a sentence.

The student wrote a report about George Washington, our first president.

Types of Sentences

Simple Sentences	A simple sentence has only one independent clause (and states only one complete thought). However, it may have a compound subject or a compound predicate and still be a simple sentence.

> **My knees ache.**
> (Simple subject, simple predicate)
>
> **Cory and I skated for two hours.**
> (Compound subject, simple predicate)
>
> **My face and neck look red and feel hot.**
> (Compound subject, compound predicate)

Compound Sentences	A compound sentence is made up of two or more simple sentences joined by a comma and a coordinating conjunction (*and, but, or*), or by a semicolon. (See page 489 for more about coordinating conjunctions.)

> **I've skated in Los Angeles, but I have never been to New York.**
> (The conjunction *but* connects two independent clauses.)
>
> **Los Angeles is 30 miles from my home; New York is 3,000 miles away.**
> (A semicolon connects two independent clauses.)

Complex Sentences	A complex sentence contains one independent clause (in black) and one or more dependent clauses (in red). Dependent clauses begin with a subordinating conjunction like *because* or a relative pronoun like *who* or *that*.

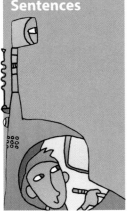

> **Because it was raining, the game was called off.**
>
> **The students, who were wet and cold, got back on the bus.**

Kinds of Sentences

Declarative Sentences	Declarative sentences make statements. They tell something about a person, a place, a thing, or an idea. **The capital of Florida is Tallahassee.** **Lisha swims in the ocean.**
Interrogative Sentences	Interrogative sentences ask questions. **Did you know that Florida's major industry is tourism?** **Have you ever gone snorkeling?**
Imperative Sentences	Imperative sentences give commands. **Wait for me.** Tip Imperative sentences use an understood subject (you). (You) **Never swim alone.** (You) **Stay here.**
Exclamatory Sentences	Exclamatory sentences communicate strong emotion or surprise. **I just saw a dolphin!** **Watch out for sharks!**

Sentence Sense

- A sentence is one or more words that express a complete thought.
- A sentence has two basic parts—a subject and a predicate (verb).
- A sentence makes a statement, asks a question, gives a command, or shows strong emotion.
- A sentence begins with a capital letter and ends with a period, a question mark, or an exclamation point.
- More information on sentences is included in "Writing Basic Sentences," pages 75–80, and in "Combining Sentences," pages 81–84.

Understanding Our Language

All the words in our language have been divided into eight groups. These word groups are called the *parts of speech*, and each group includes words that are used in the same way in a sentence.

Parts of Speech

Nouns   Words that name a person, a place, a thing, or an idea
(Bill, office, billboard, confusion)

Pronouns   Words used in place of nouns
(I, me, her, them, who, which, those, myself, some)

Verbs   Words that express action or state of being
(is, are, run, jump, swim)

Adjectives   Words that describe a noun or pronoun
(tall, quiet, three, neat)

Adverbs   Words that describe a verb, an adjective, or another adverb *(gently, easily, fast, very)*

Interjections   Words that show emotion or surprise and are set off by commas or exclamation points *(Wow, Oh, Yikes!)*

Prepositions   Words that show position or direction and introduce prepositional phrases *(on, near, over, on top of)*

Conjunctions   Words that connect words or groups of words
(and, or, because)

Nouns

A **noun** is a word that names a person, a place, a thing, or an idea.

Person: Nadia, friend, Josh, parent
Place: home, Miami, city, backyard
Thing: baseball, homework, secret
Idea: happiness, trouble, friendship

Kinds of Nouns

Common Nouns	A common noun is any noun that does not name a specific person, place, thing, or idea. Common nouns are not capitalized. **man park team holiday**
Proper Nouns	A proper noun names a specific person, place, thing, or idea. Proper nouns are capitalized. **Miguel Cabrera Chicago**
Concrete Nouns	A concrete noun names a thing that can be seen or touched. Concrete nouns are either common or proper. **magazine cactus Washington Monument**
Abstract Nouns	An abstract noun names something that cannot be seen or touched. Abstract nouns are either common or proper. **love democracy Christianity Buddhism**

Number of Nouns

Singular Nouns	A singular noun names one person, place, thing, or idea. **room paper pen pal hope**
Plural Nouns	A plural noun names more than one person, place, thing, or idea. **rooms papers pen pals hopes**

Special Types of Nouns

Compound Nouns	A compound noun is made up of two or more words. **backyard** (written as one word) **blue jeans** (written as two words) **two-wheeler** (written as a hyphenated word) **sister-in-law** (written as a hyphenated word)
Collective Nouns	A collective noun names a collection of persons, animals, or things. Persons: **class team clan group family** Animals: **herd flock litter pack colony** Things: **bunch batch collection**
Specific Nouns	Specific nouns are used to make your writing come to life. Tip See page 104 for more on specific nouns.

Gender of Nouns

The gender of a noun refers to its being feminine *(female)*, masculine *(male)*, neuter *(neither male nor female)*, or indefinite *(male or female)*.

Gender of Nouns	Feminine (female): **cow hen mother sister women** Masculine (male): **bull rooster father brother men** Neuter (neither male nor female) **tree closet cobweb** Indefinite (male or female): **child pilot parent dentist**

Uses of Nouns

Subject Nouns	A noun may be the subject of a sentence. The subject is the part of the sentence that does something or is being talked about. **Joe gave Nadia a note.** (The noun *Joe* did something, *gave Nadia a note.*)
Predicate Nouns	A predicate noun follows a form of the verb "be" (*is, are, was, were,* etc.) and renames the subject. **The book is a mystery.** (The noun *mystery* renames the subject *book*; it is another name for the subject.)
Possessive Nouns	A possessive noun shows ownership. To form a possessive noun, use an apostrophe and *s.* **The book's ending is a big surprise.** (The *'s* added to *book* shows that the *ending* is part of the book.)

Nouns as Objects

Direct Objects	A noun is a direct object when it receives the action of the verb. **Nadia read the book.** (*Book* is the direct object because it receives the action of the verb *read.*)
Indirect Objects	A noun is an indirect object when it names the person to whom or for whom something is done. **Joe gave Nadia the book.** (The book is given "to whom"? The book is given to *Nadia*, the indirect object.)
Objects of a Preposition	A noun is an object of a preposition when it is part of a prepositional phrase (*on the shelf*). **Nadia put the book on the shelf.** (The noun *shelf* is the object of the preposition *on.*)

Pronouns

A **pronoun** is a word used in place of a noun.

Carlotta rescued an injured sandpiper.

She took it to a veterinarian.

(*She* is a pronoun that replaces the proper noun *Carlotta*. *It* is a pronoun that replaces the noun *sandpiper*.)

Antecedents	An antecedent is the noun that a pronoun refers to or replaces. All pronouns have antecedents. **Anju's skateboard glides easily now that it is oiled.** (*Skateboard* is the antecedent of the pronoun *it*.)
Agreement of Pronouns	The pronouns in your sentences must agree with their antecedents in number and person. **Anju's skateboard works great now that it is oiled.** (The pronoun *it* and its antecedent *skateboard* are both singular, so they agree.) **The other kids' boards look like they could use some oil, too.** (The pronoun *they* and its antecedent *boards* are both plural, so they agree.)
Number of Pronouns	Pronouns can be either singular or plural. **I flipped my skateboard.** **We flipped our skateboards.**

Personal Pronouns

Singular: I, me, you, he, she, him, her, it

Plural: we, us, you, they, them

Person of Pronouns

First-Person Pronouns	A first-person pronoun is used in place of the name of the speaker. **I like blue-moon ice cream.** (*I* replaces the speaker's name.)
Second-Person Pronouns	A second-person pronoun is used to name the person or thing spoken to. **Su, have you decided on a flavor?** (*You* replaces the name *Su*, the person being spoken to.)
Third-Person Pronouns	A third-person pronoun is used to name the person or thing spoken about. **Jon said that he wants pumpkin ice cream.** (*He* replaces *Jon*, the person being spoken about.)

Singular Pronouns

	Subject Pronouns	Possessive Pronouns	Object Pronouns
First Person	I	my, mine	me
Second Person	you	your, yours	your
Third Person	he, she, it	his, her, hers, its	him, her, it

Plural Pronouns

	Subject Pronouns	Possessive Pronouns	Object Pronouns
First Person	we	our, ours	us
Second Person	you	your, yours	you
Third Person	they	their, theirs	them

Tip *My, your, our, its,* and *their* come before nouns and function as possessive adjectives. Other pronouns such as *his* or *her* may or may not come before nouns.

Uses of Pronouns

Subject Pronouns	A subject pronoun is used as the subject of a sentence. **I like to tell jokes.** **They really make people laugh.** **Singular:** I, you, he, she, it **Plural:** we, you, they
Object Pronouns	An object pronoun is used as a direct object, as an indirect object, or in a prepositional phrase. **Mr. Otto encourages me.** (*Me*, a direct object, receives the action of the verb *encourages*.) **Mr. Otto often gives us extra help with math.** (*Us*, an indirect object, names the people for whom something is done.) **My friends made a funny card for him.** (*Him* is the object in the prepositional phrase *for him*.) **Singular:** me, you, him, her, it **Plural:** us, you, them
Possessive Pronouns 	A possessive pronoun shows ownership. It can be used before a noun, or it can stand alone. **Gloria finished writing her story.** (*Her* comes before the noun *story*.) **The idea for the plot was mine.** (*Mine* can stand alone.) **Before a noun:** my, your, his, her, its, our, their **Stand alone:** mine, yours, his, hers, its, ours, theirs

Other Types of Pronouns

Relative Pronouns	A relative pronoun connects one part of a sentence with a word in another part of the sentence. **Any fifth grader who wants to join our music group should see Carlos.**
Interrogative Pronouns	An interrogative pronoun asks a question. **Who is going to play the keyboard?**
Demonstrative Pronouns	A demonstrative pronoun points out or identifies a noun without naming it. **That sounds like a great idea!**
Intensive and Reflexive Pronouns	An intensive pronoun stresses the word it refers to. A reflexive pronoun refers back to the subject. **Carlos himself teaches each student.** (intensive) **Carlos taught himself.** (reflexive)
Indefinite Pronouns	An indefinite pronoun refers to people or things that are not named or known. **Nobody is here to record the concert.**

Types of Pronouns

Relative
who, whom, whose, which, what, that, whoever, whatever, whichever

Interrogative
who, whose, whom, which, what

Demonstrative
this, that, these, those

Intensive and Reflexive
myself, himself, herself, itself, yourself, themselves, ourselves

Indefinite

all	both	everything	nobody	several
another	each	few	none	some
any	each one	many	no one	somebody
anybody	either	most	nothing	someone
anyone	everybody	much	one	something
anything	everyone	neither	other	such

Verbs

A **verb** shows action or links the subject to another word in the sentence. The verb is the main word in the predicate part of the sentence.

The boys hike along the river.
(The verb *hike* shows action.)

I am happy about that.
(The verb *am* links the subject *I* to the word *happy*.)

Action Verbs

An action verb tells what the subject is doing.

I watched most of the game.

I left after the third quarter.

Transitive Verbs	An action verb is called a transitive verb if it is followed by an object (*noun* or *pronoun*). The object makes the meaning of the verb complete. **Ann Cameron writes books about Julian.** (The meaning of the verb *writes* is completed by the noun *books*.)
Verbs Followed by a Direct Object	A direct object receives the action of a transitive verb. The direct object answers the question *what?* or *whom?* after the verb. **Raffi composes songs for little children.** (The noun *songs* is a direct object. *Composes* is a transitive verb.)
Verbs Followed by an Indirect Object	An indirect object receives the action of a transitive verb, indirectly. An indirect object names the person *to whom* or *for whom* something is done. **Books bring children joy.** (*Children* is an indirect object. *Bring* is a transitive verb, and *joy* is a direct object.)

Linking and Helping Verbs

Linking Verbs	A linking verb links a subject to a noun or an adjective in the predicate part of the sentence. **That car is a convertible.** (The verb *is* links the subject *car* to the noun *convertible*.) **Mom's new car looks incredible.** (The verb *looks* links the subject *car* to the adjective *incredible*.)
Helping Verbs	Helping verbs (also called auxiliary verbs) include *has*, *had*, and *have*; *do* and *did*; and forms of the verb "be" (*is, are, was, were*, etc.). **Lee will write in his journal later.** (The verb *will* helps state a future action, *will write*.) **Lee has been writing in his journal every day.** (The verbs *has* and *been* help state a continuing action, *has been writing*.)

Linking Verbs

The most common linking verbs are forms of the verb *be*:

is, are, was, were, am, being, been

Other linking verbs include the following:

smell, look, taste, remain, feel, appear, sound, seem, become, grow, stand, turn

Helping Verbs

The most common helping verbs are listed below:

shall, will, should, would, could, must, can, may, have, had, has, do, did

The forms of the verb *be* are also helping verbs:

is, are, was, were, am, being, been

Tenses of Verbs

The time of a verb is called its *tense.* Tense is shown by endings (talk*ed*), by helping verbs (*did* talk), or by both (*have* talk*ed*).

Present Tense Verbs	The present tense of a verb states an action that is *happening now* or that *happens regularly.* I **play** soccer. We **practice** every day.
Past Tense Verbs	The past tense of a verb states an action or state of being that *happened at a specific time in the past.* Anne **kicked** the soccer ball. She **was** the goalie for our last game.
Future Tense Verbs	The future tense of a verb states an action that *will take place.* It is formed by using *will* or *shall* before the main verb. I **will play** soccer this summer. We **shall practice** every day.

Perfect Tenses

Present Perfect Tense Verbs	The present perfect tense states an action that *is still going on.* Add *has* or *have* before the past participle form of the main verb. Alexis **has slept** for two hours.
Past Perfect Tense Verbs	The past perfect tense states an action that *began and was completed in the past.* Add *had* before the past participle form of the main verb. Jondra **had slept** for eight hours.
Future Perfect Tense Verbs	The future perfect tense states an action that *will begin in the future and end at a specific time.* Add *will have* before the past participle form of the main verb. Riley **will have slept** for ten hours.

Forms of Verbs

Singular and Plural Verbs	A singular verb is used when the subject in a sentence is singular.
	Ben likes cream cheese and olive sandwiches. (The subject *Ben* and the verb *likes* are both singular.)
	A plural verb is used when the subject is plural.
	Black olives taste like wax. (The subject *olives* and the verb *taste* are both plural.)
	Tip When a subject and verb are both singular or plural, they agree in number. (See page 467.)
Active and Passive Verbs	A verb is active if the subject is doing the action.
	Kara threw a fastball. (*Threw* is active because the subject *Kara* is doing the action.)
	A verb is passive if the subject does not do the action.
	A fastball was thrown by Kara. (*Was thrown* is passive because the subject *fastball* is not doing the action.)
Regular Verbs	Most verbs in the English language are regular. Add *ed* to regular verbs to state a past action; use *has, have,* or *had* with the *ed* form to make perfect tenses.
	I play. / He calls. Yesterday I played. / Yesterday he called. I have played. / He has called.
Irregular Verbs	Some verbs in the English language are irregular. Instead of adding *ed*, the word changes to state a past action. (See the chart on page 483.)
	I speak. / She runs. Yesterday I spoke. / Yesterday she ran. I have spoken. / She has run.

Common Irregular Verbs

The principal parts of some common irregular verbs are listed below. The part used with the helping verbs *has, have,* or *had* is called the *past participle.*

Present Tense:	I hide.	She hides
Past Tense:	Yesterday I hid.	Yesterday she hid.
Past Participle:	I have hidden.	She has hidden.

Present Tense	Past Tense	Past Participle	Present Tense	Past Tense	Past Participle
am, are	was, were	been	lie (recline)	lay	lain
begin	began	begun	make	made	made
bite	bit	bitten	ride	rode	ridden
blow	blew	blown	ring	rang	rung
break	broke	broken	rise	rose	risen
bring	brought	brought	run	ran	run
burst	burst	burst	see	saw	seen
catch	caught	caught	set	set	set
come	came	come	shake	shook	shaken
dive	dove, dived	dived	shine (light)	shone	shone
do	did	done	shrink	shrank	shrunk
draw	drew	drawn	sing	sang, sung	sung
drink	drank	drunk	sink	sank, sunk	sunk
drive	drove	driven	sit	sat	sat
eat	ate	eaten	speak	spoke	spoken
fall	fell	fallen	spring	sprang, sprung	sprung
fight	fought	fought	steal	stole	stolen
fly	flew	flown	swear	swore	sworn
freeze	froze	frozen	swim	swam	swum
give	gave	given	swing	swung	swung
go	went	gone	take	took	taken
grow	grew	grown	tear	tore	torn
hang	hung	hung	throw	threw	thrown
hide	hid	hidden, hid	wake	woke	woken
know	knew	known	wear	wore	worn
lay (place)	laid	laid	weave	wove	woven
lead	led	led	write	wrote	written

Adjectives

Adjectives are words that modify (describe) nouns or pronouns. Adjectives tell *what kind, how many,* or *which one.*

> **Male** peacocks have **beautiful** feathers.
>
> The feathers are **colorful**.
>
> (An adjective after a linking verb is called a *predicate adjective*.)

Articles	The words *a, an,* and *the* are adjectives called *articles.* **Owlet is the name for a baby owl.**
Proper and Common Adjectives	Proper adjectives (in **red**) are formed from proper nouns. They are capitalized. Common adjectives (in **purple**) are any adjectives that are not proper. **On a cold Wisconsin day, a Hawaiian vacation sounds wonderful.**

Forms of Adjectives

Positive Adjectives	The positive (base) form of an adjective describes a noun without comparing it to another noun. **A hummingbird is small.**
Comparative Adjectives	The comparative form of an adjective compares two people, places, things, or ideas. **A hummingbird is smaller than a sparrow.** (The ending *er* is added to one-syllable adjectives.) **Hummingbirds are more colorful than sparrows.** (*More* is added before most adjectives with two or more syllables.)
Superlative Adjectives	The superlative form of an adjective compares three or more people, places, things, or ideas. **The hummingbird is the smallest bird I've seen.** (The ending *est* is added to one-syllable adjectives.) **The parrot is the most colorful bird in the zoo.** (*Most* is added before most adjectives with two or more syllables.)

Irregular Forms of Adjectives

Positive	Comparative	Superlative
good	better	best
bad	worse	worst
many	more	most
little	less	least

Special Kinds of Adjectives

Compound Adjectives	Compound adjectives are made up of more than one word. Some compound adjectives are spelled as one word; others are hyphenated. **Many white-throated sparrows live in our evergreen bushes.**
Demonstrative Adjectives	Demonstrative adjectives point out specific nouns. *This* and *these* point out nouns that are nearby, and *that* and *those* point out nouns that are distant. **This nest has four eggs and that nest has two.** **These eggs will hatch before those eggs will.**
Indefinite Adjectives	Indefinite adjectives tell approximately (not exactly) *how many* or *how much.* **Most students love summer.** **Some days are rainy, but few days are boring.**
Predicate Adjectives	Predicate adjectives follow linking verbs and describe subjects. **The apples are juicy. They taste sweet.**
Two-Syllable Adjectives	Some two-syllable adjectives show comparisons either by their *er/est* endings or by modifiers like *more* and *most.* friendly friendlier friendliest friendly more friendly most friendly

Adverbs

Adverbs are words that modify (describe) verbs, adjectives, or other adverbs. Adverbs tell *how, when, where, how often,* and *how much.*

> **The softball team practices regularly.**
> (*regularly* modifies the verb *practices.*)

> **Yesterday's practice was extra long.**
> (*Extra* modifies the adjective *long.*)

> **Last night the players slept quite soundly.**
> (*Quite* modifies the adverb *soundly.*)

Types of Adverbs

Adverbs of Time	Adverbs of time tell *when, how often,* or *how long.* **Max batted first.** (when) **Katie's team played weekly.** (how often) **Her team was in first place briefly.** (how long)
Adverbs of Place	Adverbs of place tell *where.* **The first pitch curved inside.** (where) **The batter leaned forward.** (where)
Adverbs of Manner	Adverbs of manner tell *how* something is done. **Max waited eagerly for the next pitch.** (how)
Adverbs of Degree	Adverbs of degree tell *how much* or *how little.* **The catcher was totally surprised.** (how much) **He scarcely saw the fastball coming.** (how little) Tip Adverbs often end in *ly,* but not always. Words like *not, never, very,* and *always* are common adverbs.

Forms of Adverbs

Positive Adverbs	The positive (base) form of an adverb does not make a comparison. Max plays **hard** from the first pitch to the last out.
Comparative Adverbs	The comparative form of an adverb is formed by adding *er* to one-syllable adverbs or the word *more* or *less* before longer adverbs. He plays **harder** than his cousin plays. He plays **more often** than his cousin does.
Superlative Adverbs	The superlative form of an adverb is formed by adding *est* to one-syllable adverbs or the word *most* or *least* before longer adverbs. Max plays **hardest** in close games. Max plays **most often** in center field.

Special Forms of Adverbs

Positive	Comparative	Superlative
well	better	best
badly	worse	worst
quickly	more quickly	most quickly
fairly	less fairly	least fairly

Tip Do not confuse *well* and *good*. *Good* is an adjective and *well* is usually an adverb. (See page 485.)

Interjections

Interjections are words or phrases that express strong emotion. Commas or exclamation points are used to separate interjections from the rest of the sentence.

Wow, look at those mountains!

Hey! Keep your eyes on the road!

Prepositions

Prepositions are words that show position or direction and introduce prepositional phrases.

Our cats do what they please in our house.

Object of a Preposition	The object of the preposition is the noun or pronoun that comes after the preposition. **Smacker watches from the desk drawer.** (The noun *drawer* is the object of the preposition *from.*) **Then Smacker ducks inside it.** (The pronoun *it* is the object of the preposition *inside*. The antecedent of the pronoun *it* is the noun *drawer* in the previous sentence.)
Prepositional Phrases	Prepositional phrases include a preposition, the object of the preposition (a noun or a pronoun), and any words that modify the object. **Jo-Jo sneaks toward the gerbil cage.** (*Toward* is a preposition, *cage* is the object of the preposition, and *the* and *gerbil* modify *cage.*)

Common Prepositions

aboard	below	in	through
about	beneath	inside	throughout
above	beside	into	till
across	besides	like	to
across from	between	near	toward
after	beyond	of	under
against	but	off	underneath
along	by	on	until
along with	down	onto	up
among	during	out	up to
around	except	outside	upon
at	except for	over	with
before	for	past	within
behind	from	since	without

Conjunctions

Conjunctions connect individual words or groups of words.

> The river is wide **and** deep.

> We can fish in the morning **or** in the evening.

Coordinating Conjunctions	A coordinating conjunction connects equal parts: two or more words, phrases, or clauses. **The river rushes down the valley, and then it winds through the prairie.** (The conjunction *and* connects two independent clauses to make a compound sentence.)
Correlative Conjunctions	A correlative conjunction is used in pairs. **Either snow or wind can make the trip dangerous.** (*Either* and *or* work as a pair in this sentence to connect two words.)
Subordinating Conjunctions	A subordinating conjunction often introduces the dependent clause in a complex sentence. **Our trip was delayed when the snowstorm hit.** **We stayed in town until the snow stopped.**

Common Conjunctions

Coordinating
and, but, or, nor, for, so, yet

Correlative
either/or, neither/nor, not only/but also,
both/and, whether/or, as/so

Subordinating
after, although, as, as if, as long as, as though, because, before, if,
in order that, since, so, so that, that, though, unless, until, when, where,
whereas, while

Tip Relative pronouns can also connect clauses. (See page 478.)

Your Handbook Index

The index is your guide to using the *Writers Express* handbook. It will help you find specific information. For example, if you want to find a list of state abbreviations so you can address a letter, you can look under "abbreviations" or under "state." Both entries will tell you where to turn in your handbook to find the information.

D

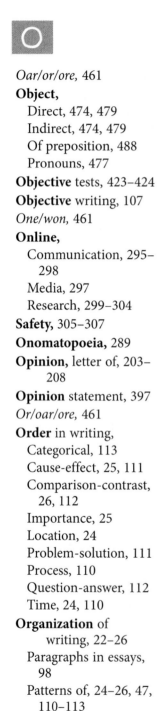